America ASLEEP kNOw MORE

Giving Aid and Comfort
To The Enemy

Eleventh Hour Wake Up Call to
Sleeping Pastors, Leaders,
Families and Nation

For More Information Contact
America ASLEEP kNOw MORE
P.O. Box 130
Humansville, MO 65674
www.asleepknowmore.com

Dr. Gregory Thompson

Giving Aid and Comfort to the Enemy

Copyright © 2009 by Dr. Gregory Thompson
Published by 21st Century Press
Springfield, Missouri U.S.A.
Printed in U.S.A.

21st Century Press is an evangelical Christian publisher dedicated to serving the local church with purpose books. We believe God's vision for 21st Century Press is to provide church leaders with biblical, user-friendly materials that will help them evangelize, disciple and minister to children, youth and families.

It is our prayer that this book will help you discover biblical truth for your own life and help you meet the needs of others. May God richly bless you.

21st Century Press
2131 W. Republic Rd.
PMB 41
Springfield, MO 65807
www.21stcenturypress.com
800-658-0284

Cover Design: Keith Locke

ISBN 978-0-9817769-8-9

21stCENTURY
P R E S S
READING YOU LOUD AND CLEAR.

Table of Contents Chapter

~~~~Special Heartfelt Thanks~~~~

"Since my youth I have been blessed by the people that our Lord and Savior Jesus Christ put into my path, yet my appreciation for these men and women was not as great as it should have been. While I have been influenced by some great men, I want to take a moment to thank some special ladies that have been instrumental in this book coming into your hands.

First, I wish to thank my mother Mary Thompson who prayed for me daily and knew that my need for prayer was great. My Second Grade teacher once told my mom how sweet a child I was, and my Mother thought that she should pull out a picture to see if they were talking about the same boy. My mother always encouraged us to be good Christians in all the decisions we made, and though I failed often in this, she loved me anyway and kept on praying. One day I got it, because of her prayers the Holy Spirit came to me and guided me to a relationship with Jesus.

My sister Paula South also felt it was her duty to keep me on a positive path, so she would pray and advise her younger brother. Most of all, she always gave me a great and powerful example to follow in her love for Jesus.

Then along came my beautiful wife Cindy. The Lord put this Christian Lady into my path because she was so centered on the Father, Son, and Holy Spirit and He gave me an opportunity to equally yoke with someone that would help strengthen me in my walk with Jesus, for eternity.

Then the Lord gave me another special friend Jan Novak-Voeltzke. She has been in the battles caused by the powers and principalities much longer than I have been, and encourages me in this Ministry that has been given me. She has spent many hours in editing this book so that you could enjoy it.

(Please note: The following *Foreword* of this book is the foundation of the book and it is important that you not skip over it in order to get right to the reading of the book. Please be sure to read the *Foreword*! It contains very important information.)

Foreword and Additional Acknowledgements

"And be not conformed to this world; but be you transformed by the renewing of your mind, that you may demonstrate what is that good, and acceptable, and perfect, will of God." (Romans 12:2)

Would you be wise? Then listen to the words of Jesus: *"Repent, for the Kingdom of Heaven is at hand." (Matthew 4:17)*

Some of my statements made in this book, having made them as a result of my obedience to and love for Jesus and His children, may cause some to be *offended*. One is not a Christian for long when one realizes that the Word can cause *discomfort* to those sitting on the fence of indecision—which happens to all of us from time-to-time. Please do not mistake being *offended* with being *convicted by the Holy Spirit*. Like Patrick Henry stated: *"If I should hold back my opinions at such a time for fear of giving offense, I should consider myself as guilty of treason to my country, and of an act of disloyalty to the Majesty of Heaven, Whom I revere above all kings."*

Would you knowingly give aid and comfort to any enemy determined to hurt, kill, and enslave you and everyone that you love and know? Or, worse yet, would you sit back in

silence and let anyone put the children at risk of going to hell for eternity?

Know this: Most of you have been programmed to think that you know everything, or at least all that is necessary to make you happy, and have a comfortable quiet lifestyle with your family. You are told in different ways that it is not necessary to fight for the truth that you will hear and read about in this book, or you may be afraid to do so because shining light on the evil will start the collapse of those who have been giving aid and comfort to the enemy of God, family, and country. Those enemies of you and your family will win the revolution now being waged if you remain comfortable on your pillow, compromise God's word to be accepted, or feel it is inconvenient to know the truth. Or there may be someone who has stood for truth very well at one time or another, and therefore excuse yourself from the raging battle occurring now as you reason: *"I've done my share."* Further, perhaps you are home schooling your children or they are in a private Christian school and you mistakenly believe that they are untouchable to the enemy. The result is you become indifferent and apathetic or even lazy and do nothing. Or, perhaps you are one who wants to become involved in the battle but do not know what to do or who to contact.

The overwhelming majority of Americans, which probably includes you and me, have been disobedient to God in this regard, and thus have given aid and comfort to the enemies of God, family, and country, as they silently work to destroy our freedoms and our families and our nation. Yes, in many ways we have been *traitors out of ignorance or laziness or fear*, and we must do some things to rectify our culpability that caused the moral decay and loss of children's moral and eternal lives, leaving them so sadly helpless, in this country. *Traitor* is a harsh word to use to identify those who live seemingly quiet church-going and peaceful lives, but uninvolved lifestyles, as our nation falls into decay is an accurate description of one staying out of a battle that is so raging in our land of the free. The leadership of both the Republican and Democratic parties have been *traitors,* can now be identified as *traitors,* to God, family, and country. The gates of hell will prevail against the Republican and Democratic parties and every other entity because of these treasonous acts.

If you have the courage to read this book, you will see how you have been or are now disobedient to God, and a traitor to God, family, and country. Most are traitors out of blind ignorance, but there are some that are traitors out of *choice.* No matter where you stand in the past or now, you can turn to God, and listen to the words of Jesus, "Repent….Go and sin no more." Stand for the young children and for the future and help in some way to return our nation to its former greatness.

My Prayer:
"My Lord Jesus Christ, Your love has been so great for me, and many times I have ungratefully abandoned You. When I abandon You, I abandon my family and my nation, not only becoming a traitor to You, but a traitor to my family and nation. I love You with all my heart, and because of that love, I am sincerely sorry for ever having offended You. Christ, I do adore You, and I do praise You, and I do love You so much, because by Your Blood You freely shed upon Your cross, You have redeemed the world. I wish to live and die always united to You. Help me to carry my cross with Your perfect peace and resignation, and deliver me from evil, that I may never again give aid and comfort to the enemy. Use me, by Your grace, to open the eyes of the blind to see, to open their ears to help them hear Your Word, and to be used as Your servant to bring souls to You. Lord Jesus, grant that I may love You always, and then do with me as You will."

Will you run? Some of you may now *run* because you would rather not know the truth; some may *run* as cowards or give some other excuse not to go on. But if you are courageous enough to go forward, know that you will hear from some of the top experts in the world imparting information to you that can protect you and those you love. I give all honor and glory to God, who has given me the knowledge, wisdom, and understanding of the times, and I use that knowledge for you and your flock and your family. I am also grateful to God for putting me in the path of other warriors that, with love, have not compromised when it comes to the Word of God.

There are many people in government, education and its unions, media, and even pastors in some pulpits that do not want you to know the truth in this book, so that they can keep you in the dark. When this happens, and you allow it to, you will continue to give them aid in their plan for America's decline into Socialism, or aid their deceit and ignorance, and comfort them in their deception or in their lack of courage or laziness. If we should hold back this truth for fear of giving offense, then we must consider ourselves guilty of treason to our families and country, and disloyalty and rebellion to God, Who is above all earthly leaders and kings. *Remember this*, (I will be asking you to *remember* certain things as we go along) that if one continues to close ones eyes and ears to what is happening in our Nation, and refuses to act after learning the truth, *all of us* will suffer greatly at the expense of one's inaction. As the boat sinks, we will all be on it together.

In addition to the previously mentioned people, I want to acknowledge and thank the following true men and women who have been fighting the enemy with no fear, because they stand firmly in God's absolute truth:

Minutemen United, Dr. (Coach) Dave Daubenmire, Pastor Mark Kiser, Dr. Alan Keyes, Pastor Rusty Thomas, James Hartline, Joey Davis, Pastor Joseph R. Larson, Judge Roy Moore, Janice (Jan) Novak-Voeltzke, Bill and Patsy Hewitt, Dr. David Noebel, Bud Williams, Pastor Ernie Sanders, Judy Leach, Jim Day, Flip Benham, Dr. Scott Lively, Dr. D. James Kennedy, Dee Wampler,

Dr. Phyllis Schlafly, John A. Stormer, Dr. Robert Dreyfus, E. Ray Moore, Jim Harrison, Dr. Bruce Shortt, Pastor Charles Jennings, Pastor Bill Dunfee, Rich Kendal, Pastor Garrett Lear, R.L. Beasley, Dr. Wes Scroggins, Jim Carroll, Jerry Blevins, Carl Crawford, Kevin Thompson, John Chalfant, William (Bill) Federer, Pastor Mark Holick, Pastor Steve Highlander, Dr. Z. Nichols, Mark Cahill, Gary DeMar, John Diamond, Tom Munds, Todd Bridgeman, Pastor Larry Bogie, Pastor Harry Pischura, Pastor Jason Tatterson, Danny Fish, David Meier, Shannon Watterson, Glen Eidson, Keith Newcomb, Pastor Danny Douglas, Pastor Rick Scarborough, Michael Chapman, Jim Cabaniss and The Christian Veterans, Exodus Mandate State Directors and members, all their families, and many in the Constitution Party putting Christ first, that are a part of the remnant standing against the enemies of God, family, and country.

Without the aid of the Holy Spirit, and the contributions of the mentioned patriots above staying in the Word of God, and some I have failed to mention, with their allegiance to the ***One* true God and His Son Jesus Christ, filling all of us with His Holy Spirit**, this work would not be possible.

Please join in this prayer from me and hopefully from you who are willing to enlist in the army of God:

> *"Dear Lord, in Your awesome Being, to think that You would give me/us a thought allows me/us to feel Your love so deeply in my/our life/lives. We know You see into our hearts. May I/we never cause You another tear and teach me/us to love You more and more each day. You know when I/we stand or lay down at night. When You ask me/us, because of my/our love for You, to feed Your sheep, may I/we always let You speak to them through our yielding hearts to you. So many of Your children are at risk; so many of Your children parish for a lack of knowledge. Use me/us, Your servant(s), to*

9

*warn Your children, so that they may protect the souls of
Your/their children. You are my/our Rock. Prepare
my/our hands for war and my/our minds for battle. The
enemy is warring against and amongst us while the
people are blind or lazy, asleep, disobedient, hard-
hearted or rebellious, and are therefore, defenseless.
May I/we be used by You to help to restore Your
children, and may I/we be granted Your wisdom to win
souls for You. I/we love You and seek to touch Your
Face. All honor and glory to You, God, in the Holy
name of Jesus our Lord, I am Gregory, your servant
child, and by Your grace, I/we are ready to work for
you. Amen"*

Whether you fit the definition of a *'useful idiot'* as spoken of
their workers by the Atheistic Socialist/Communist leadership, or
you fit the opposite end of the spectrum as a seven-day-a-week
Christian, or you fit somewhere in-between, this book will have
some insights for you that can change your life now, and the
future of your children and nation, and could possibly affect your
eternity, if you will allow it.

You can run--you can hide--but nothing can keep you from the
real possibility that you could be called home by God by
morning. If it is possible that you could be dead by morning, and
you are intelligent enough to know that it is possible, **what then?**

Could being a *'traitor'* affect yourself and those around you? Do
you know if you are a *traitor*? Some are *traitors* because of their
own personal selfish agenda, knowingly or unknowingly in
rebellion to God. Some have been *traitors* in the past or are
traitors now because of blind ignorance. Some don't even know
that they are *traitors*. Knowing the truth that is revealed in this
book will help you to know and to act to set free those, that
through ignorance, may be *silent traitors* to God, family, and
country.

This book will focus on the a *wakeup call* and provide actions God can use as He speaks to you, through you, to save our country—the Christian church allied with the Christian organizations and Christian families working within it together in unity—and to reestablish Jesus as the foundation of this once great Nation, because **any other solution will fail**, as it always has.

This book will also expose, in helpful but not in great detail, the aims and goals and intentions of the enemy within our nation's borders, so that the reader will not be left unaware of what has happened to our country morally, is happening, and will continue to happen, until our nation loses its sovereignty completely, and Christianity as we know it will no longer be allowed. (See Chapter 1 and note Joe Larson's essay.)

Carnally, you may think that it would be good to imprison or execute as *traitors* many people in the government and academia because of their willingness to go against God, family, and country and in doing so have caused extreme harm to our children. Know there are those in power that will just set another dog in their place. Unknowingly, people believe electing a new person will save them, due to the propaganda that the powerful produce and control. Subversively and cunningly, appealingly, with this propaganda, they convince the people—many being compassionate and "socially" minded Christians—that they should be happy to be a slave to the nanny-State. Of course, most people do not even know how deeply they have been deceived and lied to by the propaganda machines as they are led into the "nanny state" lifestyles and all that this lifestyle actually entails.

The corruption has been and is so great in the Democratic Party, and increasingly in the Republican Party, that we would be better off to tar and feather most of them and start all over.

Wolves in sheep clothing, *Republicans in Name Only (RINOs)* President Bush, and Presidential candidates (Giuliani, Romney), and McCain, are just part of a growing number in their party, who now give some allegiance to the Atheistic Socialist/ Communist agenda, and work to further the One-World government (Globalism a.k.a. One-World Government system under Socialism/Communism dictatorship).

Under Democratic leadership, and now some Republican leadership as well, there has been a greater increase in shameful funding for abortion, the slaughter (murder) of the innocent, than any time in history. Coming soon, under the guise of *Medicated Termination of Life*, and taking 'sedation' to an extreme, whereby food and fluids are removed from a person who is terminally ill, under sedation, at their request, we will soon use this form of *assisted suicide*. Recently, a woman who had signed forms to donate her organs (which, remember, must be removed while the patient is alive!) had "brain died" and was supposedly in a vegetative non-able-to-think status, for 17 minutes. While discussing the organ donations, she suddenly awakened and began totally clear and lucid conversation with her relatives. Mercy killing or assisted suicide is exactly that—killing and suicide.

These elected officials have ruled to grant an increase in the number of positions, in particular within the teaching profession, to openly homosexual people who are living in sin, against the wishes of the majority of the American citizens, are role models for innocent children.

Further, our representatives, against the will of the people, are supporting the religion of Islam which, in its extreme, is radical and that endorses and commands murderous terrorist-jihadist war activities against mainly Christians and Jews in the name of Allah. By keeping the citizens mislead and misinformed, they are contributing to our downfall. They are leaving open the borders to Illegal Aliens while they force us, the tax payers, to pay billions of dollars to support them. These open borders also encourage and allow more foreign terrorists to enter our country illegally, as they plan subversively to overtake our country, along with an enormous amount of illegal drug activities and the resultant gang warfare and overcrowding of our prisons and jails, along with their subsequent health and welfare abuse.

What is called Liberalism/Socialism/Communism *seems* to be such an *appealing* and *compassionate* way and that is how the dictators "sell" it to a gullible unknowing, often well-meaning and compassionate people. It is really, quite simply, tolerance for sin and corruption resulting from disobedience of our laws and the laws of God. Needless to say, as well as is observed, the Justice Department is allowed to call Christians that preach the Word of God "*haters*," (as in the case of speaking out against homosexuality or Islamic jihad), by the laws and decisions the Judges hand down that *intolerantly* rule against law-abiding truly compassionate but discerning Christians. Christians may hate the sin but they do love the sinner very much with Christ-like love. Most liberal politicians and Judges support the **hate crimes legislation** that has language *that will be used against the right to free speech of Christians—unknowingly assisting the illegals and terrorists to use our own Constitution for their illegal activities while using it against our own legal citizens and nation.* In reality, this same hate crimes legislation could be used against Christians as they are restrained from exercising their free speech and being hatefully and erroneously labeled as "homophobes" or xenophobes.

Over the past several decades, the Liberal Democratic Party has been fully infiltrated and is currently led by the Liberal Humanist/Socialists/Communists/Progressivists/Environmentalists/Collectivists/Populists and Global Warming gods. The Party is almost completely filled with the Communist Party's *useful idiots* that are bigoted against Christianity's God, family, and our sovereign Nation. The evidence to support this truth is overwhelming. *Carnally,* we might think about protecting our families and nation by excising this ugly cancer by any means, as it is rotting us internally. Ultimately, by the Grace of God, after we show the Christian church and Christian family how they have been duped, most subtly and subversively, into being traitors against God, family, and country, by remaining silent, we have the possibility that this once great Nation can survive *if* we care enough to work and act toward that end. We can, once again, *be salt and a beacon of light to the world,* if we immediately act on the truth with our voices, actions, and prayerful and financial support of the workers for Truth.

We can no longer vote for the lesser of two evils. If they support evil or have blood on their hands in any way, we cannot vote for those that are disobedient to God, or give aid and comfort to the enemy in any way.

The Liberal Democratic Party and their allies (one being the National Education Association Teachers Union) is full of evil, and their platforms continue to be a cancer, rotting America from the inside, with their false Social(ist) Justice programs and Liberation Theology mixed with their other false Religions of Secular Humanism.

The Republican Party has been infiltrated by evil, too, and abusive news-propaganda-media is destroying the Party, progressively. They believe the American people are stupid enough to believe their rhetoric, and sadly many do, and that the people can be convinced to vote for the least of two evils. In the following pages, we will expose just how the Liberal Left Democratic Party gains and retains their Liberal brainwashed voters who now have become the majority in our Nation (through the NEA's public school dictatorship of Socialist curriculum and Socialist psychological behavioral modification programs.)

Christians, must remain faithful and obedient to God's truths, remain praying, and remain repentant of every sin. And if we do,

He promises to take care of the results. Christians must never again vote for the least of two evils, but must take on the mantle of a true Christian, and a true patriot. God will reward our actions if we work in concert with His laws and desires and as He directs it.

I pray that living waters will flow from your belly with every word that you speak in HIS truth and with the love and forgiveness of Jesus, no matter the cost.

WARNING!!! The author seeks this book to be used as a tool to keep God's children from losing all their freedoms. Hopefully, Christians will see and hear the truth; hopefully, some unbelievers will be able to see and benefit, too, and take action. It will offend some, because the Truth will offend and divide those not standing solidly submitted to God, making some uncomfortable. They will have to make a decision to stand with God, or rationalize why it is alright for them to stand with man. Freedom or Slavery—Life or Death—Heaven or Hell—for yourself and those you serve, is your choice. I pray that there are Christian pastors, Christian teachers, and Christian parents that are strong enough to read these words and that they respond to the Holy Spirit as He gives them the strength to be Christians of conviction, rather than in name only. **Proverbs 9:8 tells us:** *Reprove not a scorner lest he hate thee; rebuke a wise man (woman) and he (she) will love thee*. Lovingly I ask, "Which are you?"

Know this truth: The only answer for keeping this once great country from decaying further and becoming a by-gone word, is for the people to repent for the evil we have allowed to happen, give honor and glory to Jesus for His forgiveness, submit to His beckoning call to service, and wisely restore Him as the foundation of our Nation, once again. Any other action that man will perform is doomed to failure and the children will suffer greatly while here on earth, and be at risk of going to hell for eternity as a result of an atheistic, rotting culture.

As a word to unbelievers who may be reading this book, I would like to say that through the Grace of God I am writing this book with contributions from His devoted remnant. We know the absolute Truth that God is the Alpha and the Omega. He is the same yesterday, today, and forever. He is the Creator of the universe and all honor and glory is to be given to our God, His Son Jesus, the King of Kings and Lord of Lords. God is offering you His Grace through the power of the Holy Spirit to know Jesus Christ, His Son, so that by listening to His Word, you may be saved from eternal damnation in Hell, and then, with His indwelling you will recognize the real Truth about what is happening in our nation—and perhaps what has happened to you if you have been educated in the government public schools. Without Him, one cannot recognize real truth. You get to choose, the same as each of us have done, and that choice in your heart will take you to heaven or hell for eternity, and **that choice may, in *fact*, start your eternity, *beginning today*.** Once you choose to follow Jesus, nothing compares to the peace and adventure that is in store for you. It has been for us and for all those who have gone before us, as attested to in God's Holy Word—the Bible. I promise you, you will have a great adventure in your new life.

I ask that God's Holy Spirit will guide each person that reads this book, and that the Holy Spirit will actively guide my hand and mind as I write, because if the Holy Spirit is not with the reader and with me you will not see or hear or understand His Truth. Many are confused by what they read in the Scriptures, if they have not invited the Holy Spirit to be with them. He must also be with me as I write, for this book to be a useful tool in the hands of the reader. God loves each of you so much and wishes to touch each one. My prayer is that He will use this vessel, and the contributions of other vessels He has put in my path, to serve Him together and to warn His children.

The times are urgent, the WAR is raging, and all parts of our society in this once great Nation that was established by and for God, have been infiltrated *by traitors* against God, family, and country.

I will primarily focus on two rebellious entities that are giving "aid and comfort" to the enemy. While all parts of the government and the news and entertainment media have been infiltrated by Atheistic, Communist groups with agendas that are controlled by those that direct their steps—the international bankers and other wealthy elite—we will deal with the individual culpability of pastors, teachers, and parents in our government public schools and churches.

We all MUST ask ourselves: *"Is it possible that you or your neighbor or your pastor is a traitor to God, family, and country?"* The question can be insulting and shocking—it was to me when I drew the courage and asked it of myself—but when you know that giving aid and comfort to the enemy is *treason*, you must be the judge of your own actions, and then decide if you will have the courage to stand with God to save the families and the nation. Look at the *evidence* of the state of our decadent culture, and then decide who you will stand with: Jesus or man. Pray before you start. Keep His Word, the Bible, close by. Your soul and the soul of those you touch will be affected for eternity, when you sign-on to be used. There will be many that are now blind, or ignorant, that are *traitors to some degree* and will realize this because of the frankness in this book. You will come to understand why most of the former prophets were killed when they told the truth to people of a Nation that had gone astray from God.

"Beloved, beware lest you also, being led away with the error of the wicked, fall from steadfastness. But grow in grace, and in the knowledge of our Lord and Savior Jesus Christ. To Him be the glory both now and forever. Amen." **(2 Peter 3:17)**

"Blessed are the pure in heart; for they shall see God."
(Matthew 5:8)

(Reminder: If you have not done so—before continuing on— please go back and read the Foreword, as it is a very important foundation/introduction to the book.)

Chapter 1

<u>Treason Against God, Family, and Country</u>
Protecting the Sacred Cow and Sacrificing the Children on the Altar of Belial

"But while men slept, his enemy came and sowed tares among the wheat, and went his way." (Matthew 13:25)

WAR!!! There is no neutral ground as the battle rages in this country, dividing families and taking away our religious freedoms that are given by God and not man. There are overt traitors that walk amongst us acting with arrogance in the government, media, church, and the public education system.

First off, I want to salute and give a great *thank you* to Joseph R. Larson Chairman of *Restoring America* for the great article that follows, giving all of us a dramatic and most insightful and clear picture of a *concise* but *precise* history of American Education. It explains a great deal about *how we got where we are* and *where we are going as a people and nation,* if we all carefully connect the dots he has painstakingly provided for us. Thanks to Joe we do not have to read a thick volume to acquire this head knowledge regarding American Education, how it started and how it, *through Socialist Progressivism, the Federal Education Department Programs and the National Education Association Teachers Union, got us where we are today as a nation.* Joe has done it for us. There are volumes on this subject, but space allows only for this brief but well-put-together work. A wise and thoughtful reader will do the dot-connecting and hopefully be aroused into action, as Joe has, to combat the evil that is bound to be inflicted upon us, if we don't!

"(--)ism's and Education or How We Got into This Mess!

Joseph R. Larson

Because I (Joe Larson) believe in full truth and disclosure I must inform you that I am a God fearing, Bible believing, flag waving, gun owning, Constitution loving, capitalistic, disabled American Veteran. You now know where I stand.

I call my presentation; **"(--)ism's and Education."** America's children and our future as a nation are in serious danger. I will not only prove this statement to be true, but I will also show you who our Enemies are; and how they have and do work to deceive and control us. Some of you will become angry, some of you sickened, and some of you even frightened.

Recent News Items:

1. A high school in Ohio denied the right of the senior class to include the American flag in their class photo. It was too controversial.
2. Cupertino, CA forbids the study and reading of the *Declaration of Independence* and other historical documents—because the name of God appears in the document and we have a *"wall of separation of church and state"* and cannot promote religion.

3. Carrier Mills, IL students in grade school are ordered to cross-dress for one day, much to the humiliation of some.

4. About two years ago, [top] ranking seniors in America's top 55 liberal arts colleges and universities were given an old-fashioned high-school history exam, 81% received a grade of D or F. Thirty-five percent, of our nations best and brightest, thought that the phrase: *"From each according to his ability, to each according to his needs"* was found in OUR Constitution! **[This my friends is the Marxist slogan]** Over fifty-percent believed that the phrase: *"wall of separation of church and state"* is also found in OUR Constitution. **It is not there, but it can be found in the old "Soviet Constitution."**

About the same time the *National Center for Education Statistics* issued a lengthy report entitled, ***"What Democracy Means to Ninth-Graders: U.S. Results from the International IEA Civic Education Study.*** Results Show:

- "that 84% of American 9th graders believe it is government's responsibility to control prices;
- that 65% believe it's the government's responsibility to guarantee everyone a job;
- that 64% believe government should reduce differences in income and wealth among our citizens; [redistribution of wealth?]
- that 66% believed government should support and control industry;
- that 88% believed government should provide basic health care for everyone."

Friends, this stuff is right out of the *10 Planks of the Communist Manifesto*. Still unconvinced?

1. According to the *George Barna Research Group* only 10% of American's actually possess a biblical worldview.
2. Numerous studies reveal the *majority of Christians* [adult and teen] think and act virtually no different than non-believers.
3. Studies by **Doctors Gary Railsback and Norm Geisler** showed that **"....in 1981,** 50% of students from Christian homes were denying their faith before they graduated from college. Today the figure is over 75%."
4. *The Nehemiah Institute,* using years of research, study and polling, sadly claims that *the typical Christian student in a* **Christian high school** *is scoring [in testing] as a Secular Humanist. The typical student in a* **Public School** *scores as having a Socialist Worldview.*

The Fifth Federal Circuit Court has previously ruled that speeches and pronouncements from Presidents like George Washington, John Quincy Adams, Abe Lincoln and Dwight David Eisenhower *"cannot be taught in the public schools in their district because the content is unconstitutional."*

In 1962 *The U.S. Supreme Court "prohibited the saying of prayer in public schools."* In 1963 *the same court "banned Bible teachings in the public schools .* **In 1980** they *"ordered schools to remove the Ten Commandments from student view."* Allow me to paraphrase their ruling: *If students see the Commandments, they might read them. If they read them, they might study them. If they study them, they might follow them...and that would be unconstitutional.*

Since 1962: teen suicide is up 500%...child abuse is up 2,300%...illegal drug use among teenagers up 6,000%...

criminal arrests of teens up 1505%... births to unwed teenager girls up 500% ... and SAT Test scores, *dumbed-down twice*, are 10% lower. [These figures all come from the federal government.]

I should tell you about a report issued **in late 2003** by the *American Psychiatric Association* that stated a new syndrome has appeared. It is called *Celebrity Worship Syndrome*, in which roughly one-third of the people in Western societies vicariously devote and attach their self identity, values, income and passion to the "Famous." "Devote and attach their self identity, values, income and passion"......this is how we, as Christians, should be emulating Jesus.

In the European Union, which touts itself as being Secular, only about two (2) percent of the people claim to be fundamental Christian. In England, as well as France, more Muslims attend Mosques than Christians attend church and Muslims are a minority. Christianity in Secular nations is dying (—these Secular nations used to be Christian!).

Some information to ponder:

If you survey people at pro-life meetings or events you will find they average having four children per family. People who attend Church on Sunday and pray regularly average three children per family. Most Americans, 86% of them claim to be Christian, average 2.1 children per family. People, who are pro- abortion, feminists, homosexual or lesbian activists, or belong to other liberal far-left groups, average one-half of one child per (their descriptions of) family. Demographically speaking Conservatives should be winning by a large margin, as the ranks of the liberals will in time be decimated by a form of self-imposed collective suicide.

(Ah! But that doesn't happen!) Their response is to use our educational system to reproduce their selves intellectually, since obviously they are not going to reproduce themselves biologically. In other words...they fill their lost ranks by taking OUR Children! (They are stealing and indoctrinating them in the public school classrooms across America.)

Abe Lincoln wisely told us that: *"The philosophy of the schoolroom in one generation will be the philosophy of the government in the next."*

We, the American people were warned. Their have been many *watchers* shouting their warnings, but their warnings fell on mostly deaf ears. After all, **the** *steps of the enemies were so small, so insignificant,* **and** *the decline so imperceptible to most*, that people *gradually* got accustomed to the changes and sensed no immediate threat.

(Author's note: "Small, slow, insignificant, imperceptible, gradually progressively"—*remember these words*, they are buzz-words for the route to Socialism and that is how Socialism/Communism takes over a country and turns it into a third-world dictatorship! We are nearly there.)

A famous poet once explained this phenomenon when he wrote:

> *Vice is a monster of so frightful mien*
>
> *As to be hated—needs but to be seen;*
>
> *Yet seen too oft! familiar with her face,*
>
> *We first endure, then pity, and then embrace.*

(Author's note: Think! First Health/Sex Education, Drug Education, pre-marital sex [not love and devotion after marriage], thence abortion, thence homosexuality and lesbianism, Socialism—all taught under the false guise of *public school American education—all while being dummied down in their academics, at the same time.* **See that poem come to light**: *"oft familiar"* and especially the last line: *"....endure, pity, then embrace."* For our poor children it is *gradual seduction into depraved lifestyles and ruined lives. For all of us living in our nation it is a gradual decline into Communism!* Now back to Joe.)

GRADUALISM: one of the means Satan uses to deceive us.

I find it interesting that one of the first laws in America was **"The Old Deluder Satan Law"** which began with the words: ***"Whereas Satan's greatest weapon is the ignorance of men, we hereby......."***

(Author's note: Please excuse me, Joe, one more time. Making and keeping the people ignorant is another spoke in the wheel of Socialism. Wonder why our children have been intentionally dummied down in the public schools through the National Education Association's (NEA) *Teachers' Union* curriculum? Wonder why a Teacher's Union should be in charge of and *dictate* our children's curriculum and textbooks? If this had been and should be now scrutinized and questioned by all of us—the way it should have been and must be—we would have known it's because of their Socialist hidden agendas. By now, all U.S. citizens should be aware of our standing in the world academically—close to the bottom! NEA cares not a whit about academics and our children. They are single-minded, end-result,-one-goal oriented—Socialism! for our nation. This is why they are working feverishly right now to either eliminate or completely regulate and control all Private Schools and Home Schools. Forward, march! Joe. The following is so important.)

Ignorance is bliss, right?

What does the Bible say? **(Psalm 111)** *"Wisdom begins with the fear of GOD."*

Throughout history, rulers and court intellectuals have aspired to use the educational system to shape their nations. The model for this was set by Plato in *"The Republic."* Plato's model was ancient Sparta, *where children were taken from their parents early in life* and *molded into soldiers for the militaristic Spartan society.* Plato's blueprint *came to specify that parents were not to know their children, nor children to know their parents;* and *the society was to be based upon community of property and community of family.* Both children and property were controlled by the State.

(Keep in mind, the author states, the NEA's convention agenda of June 2007 spoke determinedly of needing to control the children from birth to Kindergarten, through *government regulated and controlled* NEA pre-school day-care. [Radical feminism, another spoke of Socialism, was used to remove the mothers from the home initially—you know: *It takes a [Socialist] village to raise a child.* mantra. NEA is aggressively planning for this and how it will be accomplished. They consider children who are raised in Christian homes with Christian morals and Christian faith, prior to attending public schools, as mentally/psychologically ill. Socialism *is an atheist religion—it cannot exist in, or take over, a Christian nation. It must eliminate Christianity first in order to gain total control because Christians believe in a One True God and individualism, and not the State as god or that we exist for the common good/group. In Socialism (as in Caesar) the State must reign as god and the citizens must bow to the State.* Onward, Joe.)

This model was used by Prussia, Soviet Russia, Fascist Italy, and later Nazi Germany. **In 1717** Prussia, under

King William I, set up Europe's first National system of education adopting much of Plato's totalitarian model. The King of Prussia claimed it the duty of the government [himself] to see, think and act for the whole community. **By 1806** Prussia had mandatory school attendance, government certification of teachers, and had abolished semi-religious private schools. Parents could be fined or their children taken away by the state for any form of non-compliance.

When a unified German Nation was finally created it was the Prussian school model that prevailed. **The German education as stated, must fashion the person, and fashion him in such a way, that he cannot be otherwise than that which the state wills him to be. "The prime fundamental of German education is that it is based on a national principle...it is education *to the state*, education *for the state*, education *by the state*. The State is the supreme end in view."** Later the Soviet Union modeled its school system off the Prussian/German model.

(This is sounding just too familiar, too scary, if one knows anything at all about our American public school educational system—no individualism, no God-given talent/gifts to be used as God wishes them to be used—only the State's dictatorship. This is *also known as slavery!*)

Why Am I telling you all of this? I want too Introduce you to American Education and our Enemies.

The problem with America's educational system began early in our history.

In 1805, Unitarians took control of Harvard University. [A Unitarian is a member of a faith that rejects the Trinity of God, stresses the free use of reason (man's), believes in a united world community (One World Order—Globalism) and advocates Liberal Social action.] During this period the Harvard lead Unitarians began the push for public education. Why?

Unitarians believed man was essentially good. And that evil in this world was the direct result of *poverty* and *ignorance.* (This is a major Socialist *doctrine.)* **Robert Owen, a well-known and out-spoken Unitarian**, [known to us today as the **Father of Modern Socialism**] told the world that a person's character is determined by *education and upbringing, not by a sinful nature.* Secular public schools would transform students into agents of unlimited benevolence. Thus the crusade for public education began.

Guess what? The socialists became eager allies of the Unitarians in the push for public education. You can surely see the results of our student's unlimited benevolence—Right? Wrong!

(Take a look at our suffering, dummied down and undisciplined, promiscuous, depressed, hopeless drop-out drugged children walking around in their meaningless lifestyles, *educated* under the influence of the Secular Humanist Public Schools, leading confused lives, unable to hold decent jobs after 12-16 years of public schooling. God is concerned about all children—not just those attending private or home schools. Indeed it begs the question: *How in the world have we allowed it to get this bad for our children and our nation without recognizing and defeating this absurd institution called public schooling?—the Author's comments.)*

2 Timothy 4 states*: "The time will come when men will not put up with sound doctrine. Instead, to suit their own desires, they will gather around them a great* *number of teachers to say what their itching ears want to hear. They will turn their ears away from Truth and turn aside to Myths."*

From the beginning of America's colonies until **nearly 1837**, education in America was purchased through private schools of choice. The churches provided free schools to all who would come. **Horace Mann, a Harvard elite man**, believed his mission was to remove educational *control from the communities and the people*—delivering control to the state.

By 1857, The National Education Association [The NEA] Teachers Union was founded and even then it was calling for nationalized education. *(We must remember this: This is supposed to be a TEACHER'S Union to protect the benefits of the teachers only—not a dictator of school curriculum and procedures and political machine, both of which it has become almost exclusively.)* One of **NEA's founders, Zalman Richards**, at the Union's **1858 convention**, condemned private education with scorn. He asserted that private schools were degrading to the teaching profession. Private schools soon became the object of scorn and ridicule among NEA Union members, and **by 1885** some outspoken representatives were even going so far as to claim both children and property belonged, not to the people, but to the State. (We are hearing the same story now.) Remember "Sparta?" Remember: the *Tenth plank of the Communist Manifesto*: "Free education for all children in public schools [and] combination of education with industrial production" [school - to-work]. (This is a huge portion of the U.S. Federal Education Department's goals now that are actually being enacted.) **By 1905** the American government was spending nearly 22% of all public funds on public education.

The **Socialist "Fabian Society" formed in the late 1800's**, the forerunner of most Socialists groups in America had as their motto *"Make Haste Slowly."* [In other words...Gradualism] *"Democratic Socialism"* became the battle cry to socialize the United States of America. Their goal was to "permeate and penetrate," then control from *deep within*. Their **first** target in America was education, the **second** was religion and **third** the government. Their attack plan was simple: a few highly educated elite believers would work themselves into positions of power and influence not only in higher education but organizations that distributed money. [Example: Many worked their way into large foundations like Pew, Ford, Rockefeller and Carnegie where they would help control and direct to whom vast sums of money would go.]

(Author's note: Currently these same foundations support the *brainwashing facilitators,* who have been thoroughly indoctrinated by their Masters in the Socialist movement in public universities, to indoctrinate teachers via their teachers' seminars and so-called retreats.)

In the U.S. their followers would use language as their first line of *attack and deceit*. They would wear no badge, nor socialist label, but were to call themselves "Liberal," "Progressive" and even "Moderate".. *Words* were the weapon of choice for this new (revolutionary silent) war. By changing and shifting word meanings they would cover their true purpose, by lying and deceit. Everything would be done under the banners of *"Reform"* and *"Social Justice,"* suggesting all was for the *public "common" good*, for *humanitarian reasons*, for *true democracy* and finally *for the children*. The buzzwords of Socialism, were, and are today, "Social" and "Democracy."

[Remember hearing the *WORDS:* Social Engineer, Social Justice, Social Welfare, Social Reform, Social Science, Social Studies and Socialization of the Child— and let them ring loud and clear and never forget them, and think of them with utter skepticism and distrust every time you hear them. These words are selling out your children and your nation.]

Robert Conquest, the historian of the Stalin era, writes in *"The New Criterion"*

"A Communist once told me his method. First you explain to a Christian sympathizer that Communism is compatible with Christianity. That accomplished, you explain that Christianity is not compatible with Communism. A Communist never does anything under his own name that he can do under someone else." This is the height of conspiracy and deceit.

First we are told that Christian morality requires that we adopt the Liberal program. Then, when the Liberal regime is entrenched, we are told that it excludes Christian morality.

QUOTES Your school never taught you in history:

Democracy is indispensable to Socialism. **V. I. Lenin**

Democracy is the road to Socialism. **Karl Marx**

The goal of Socialism is Communism. **V. I. Lenin**

Communism is Socialism in a hurry. **V. I. Lenin**

(How *gradually [there's that word again]* we were led out of our founded *Republic* into a *Democracy.)*

Norman Thomas, Socialist and member of the Civil Liberties Union, boldly told the world: *"The American people will never knowingly adopt Socialism, but under the name of Liberalism, they will adopt every fragment of the Socialist program until one day America will be a Socialist nation without ever knowing how it happened."*

(Joe has reminded the author, who would like to add a comment here, that the Communists predicted in **1917** that, *without firing a bullet, America will drop like an over ripened fruit into the hands of Communism.* Are we as a people going to help that come true by our negligence, our ignorance, or our fear?)

In the **early 1900s**, because of unrest in Europe, thousands of Socialists flocked to America for safety. Large numbers held degrees in the fields of psychology, sociology and psychiatry, (behavioral sciences, dealing with behavior and [social] change). Many went on to become college and university professors. It was during this period that an Italian communist **Antonio Gramsci** came up with a way to accomplish his political objectives. Communism/Socialism would become a *long term struggle* for the *hearts and minds* of the people. **Gramsci advocated a long march through the cultural institutions: education, entertainment, the press and yes, even the Church. Cultural Marxism was born.**

Unlike the elite "Fabians," this was a cause all like-minded Socialists could involve themselves in—heart and soul—and they have!

In 1932, George S. Counts, a Fabian Socialist who taught at Columbia University *Teachers College* and worked under grants from the Rockefeller Foundation, [Remember them] contended that *"America had entered a new age where ignorance* *must be replaced by knowledge, competition by cooperation, trust in Providence by careful planning , and private capitalism by some form of Socialized economy."* How about that: *A Fabian Socialist elite teaching in one of America's biggest and best teacher colleges---teaching the teachers who would teach America's children.* And some of you wonder how America has moved so far left!

In 1936, the *National Education Association Teachers Union (NEA)* stated their position, from which they have never wavered: *"We stand for Socializing the individual" (They indeed have—and made "Socialization of the Child" household words across America)* The NEA in its *"Policy For American Education"* stated: *"The major problem of education in our times arises out of the fact that we live in a period of fundamental Social change. In the new democracy [we were a Republic] education must share in the responsibility of giving purpose and direction to Social change."* **The major function of the school is the Social orientation of the individual.** *"Education must operate according to a well-formulated social policy."*

(Author's comment: However, *in its deception*, the NEA had never come out and said that by *Socializing* they meant stealing the children and indoctrinating them and using them as pawns to create Socialism in America. They truly are *Master of Deceit*!)

William Carr, NEA Administrator's article in *NEA Journal,* **October 1947**: *"As you teach about the United Nations, lay the ground for a stronger United Nations by developing in your students a sense of world community—Teach those attitudes which will result ultimately in the creation of world citizenship and world government."* [Silly us—we thought they intended to teach our children pure, learnable academics!]

Paul Haubner, Specialist for the NEA, told us: *"The schools cannot allow parents to influence the kind of values-education their children receive in school—that is what is wrong with those who say there is a universal system of values. [Christians?] Our (Humanistic) goals are incompatible with theirs. <u>We must change their values</u>."*

Now we meet **John Dewey**, who is called *"the father of modern education,"* who was an avowed Socialist and Humanist. He is the co-author of the *"Humanist Manifesto"* **and was cited as belonging to fifteen Marxist-front organizations by the Committee on Un-American Activities.** Do the words "the father of modern education" now take on new meaning? Remember, Dewey taught the professors who would train America's teachers.

Dewey was obsessed with **"the group."** In his own words: *"You can't make Socialists out of individualists. Children who know how to think for themselves spoil the harmony of the Collective Society which is coming, where everyone is interdependent— the child,"* said Dewey, *"must always be made to feel part of a group. He must indulge in group thinking and group activity."*

[In the 1990's, American public schools adopted the practice of *cooperative learning.* **The *"Group-think"* learning format exists in nearly every subject today in the public school classrooms. The children are trained and guided to all come up with the same preset conclusions or be coerced by humiliation to do so. Isn't that amazing?]**

John Dewey, was also a follower of the teachings of **German Psychologist Wilhelm Wundt.** *Both men viewed children as animals requiring guidance, control and molding.*

After visiting the Soviet Union, **Dewey** wrote six articles on the *"Wonders of Soviet Education."* Soviet students were judged on their abilities:

1)   To adapt to change;
2)   For their collective spirit;
3)   On their reactions to groups and individuals designated "enemies of the state;"
4)   To subordinate morality "to the interests of the class struggle."

Note: The Soviet family was declared a "basic form of slavery."

School to Work, in America, is based on the *Soviet School System*.

Today, there are over 800 federally mandated education programs, and *Outcomes Based Education,* **and** *School to Work* are major part of **Goals 2000** and **No Child Left Behind**. (In short, folks, we've been 'had" by our Federal Government and NEA's Teachers Union schools, for many decades.)

Rosalie Gordon, writing on **Dewey's** Progressive (Socialist) education in her book *"What's Happened to Our Schools,"* stated: *"The Progressive system has reached all the way down to the lowest grades to prepare the children of America for their role as the Collectivists of the future. "The group"—not the individual child—is the quintessence of Progressivism."*

(Please note author's comment: Progressivism and Collectivism are buzz-words that Socialism hides behind—"for the *common good*." Every couple of years, Socialism falls under a new "title"—a.k.a. Environmentalism, Globalism, Liberalism, ad nausea—simply to deceive the we the people and to keep we the people deceived. **Constantly remember:** We are talking about an Atheistic ungodly Religion so lying and cheating is permitted for *"the cause." However, they can NEVER lie to each other as that would threaten "the cause!" They are Masters of Deceit!* Back to Joe.)

> *"Our major concern that the school should provide a purified environment for the child—this means stacking the cards in favor of the particular systems of value we [the Humanists] possess. We must move to make certain every Progressive School will use whatever power it may possess in opposing and checking the forces of social Conservatism."* **John Dewey**

> *"There has grown up some consciousness of the extent to which a future new society of changed purposes and desires may be created by a deliberate humane treatment of the impulses of youth. This is the meaning of education."* **Stated by John Dewey in "Human Nature and Conduct," 1922. P.94**

> **(1 John 4:5-6)** *They are from the world and therefore speak from the viewpoint of the world, and the world listens to them. We are from God, and whoever knows God listens to us. This is how we recognize the **Spirit of Truth and the spirit of falsehood**.*

What else did **Dewey** believe? He was co-author of the *Humanist Manifesto.*

Abbreviated version of the *Humanist Manifesto*:

1. Man gradually emerged by chance from lower forms of life over millions of years.
2. Man creates god out of his own experiences.
3. Man is his own authority and is not accountable to any higher power.
4. There are no absolute rules to live by.
5. All men should be exposed to ***diverse** "realistic" viewpoints, including profanity, immorality, and perversions as acceptable modes of self-expression.* (**NOTE: This is what Liberal Socialists mean when they push to teach "diversity"— acknowledging promiscuity, homosexuality, abortion, illegal drugs, as normal.**)
6. All forms of sexual expression are acceptable/ (To date, under the homosexual list of activities—there are over 30, including bestiality and so much more.)
7. Government ownership or control of the economy should replace private ownership of property and the free market economy.
8. "Global Citizenship" should replace National self-determination (National Sovereignty).
9. There is no hope of existence beyond the grave—no heaven or hell.

Today there are over 10,000 openly Marxist professors and thousands of Humanist professors controlling the State Universities and Colleges that produce America's teachers and other professionals. Varying forms of Marxist-Humanism are the predominant philosophies of the educational establishment; yet we repeatedly send our most precious gift (our children) off to THEM for "education" (indoctrination/brainwashing in Socialism/Communism). Basically, WE are letting the Devil educate our children.

For proof of that statement I refer you to **Luke 6:40 (NASB)**: *A pupil is not above his teacher; but everyone, after he has been fully trained, **will be like his teacher**."*

God speaks this same verse to us today! Do we want our children to have a Godless Humanist religion instilled in them, a cultural, socialist Marxist worldview, in which they believe there are no absolutes, [Is not God and His Word an Absolute], and that morality is defined by *group consensus* which evolves with a changing society?

(Colossians 2:8) *Beware lest any man spoil you through philosophy and vain deceit, after the traditions of men, after the rudiments of the world, and not after Christ.*

This is exactly what WE are doing to our children; they are being spoiled by man's philosophies and deceits after the traditions of men.

(II Corinthians 6:14) *Be ye not unequally yoked together with unbelievers: for what fellowship hath righteousness? And what communion hath light with darkness?*

Isn't this exactly what we do when we send our children to government schools?

The **United Nations Education Program** was approved in **1946** at the first *United Nations Educational, Scientific and Cultural Organization (UNESCO) General Conference.* One of the first items on its agenda was the creation of *"A Study of Education for International Understanding in the Primary and Secondary Schools and in Institutions of Higher Learning of Member States,"* to be conducted by the

Member States with the Assistance of the UNESCO Secretariat." Each nation was required to conduct a study of how textbooks treated the subject *of International Agencies and World Government*. **The National Education Association in 1954 published a book [in compliance with UNESCO] to instruct educators in the proper methods of teaching children about the benefits of World Government**. It had specific chapters dealing with each benefit and *one chapter on how to develop world-minded teachers. The issue of altering world history through educational textbooks was so important that two chapters were dedicated entirely to that subject.*

(This is now known as "revised false History and Geography" *with great emphasis on a "hate America" philosophy sowing discontent and dissatisfaction on almost every level of our society—into our children's minds—America is the cause of all the world's problems.* Author's comment.)

The *"Soviet Education Programs; Foundations, Curriculums, Teacher Preparation"* was *published in 1960 by the U.S Department of Health, Education and Welfare.* This document was the blueprint for the *School-To-Work* restructuring that would take place in America. **In 1961, Rep. John M. Ashbrook** tried to alert Congress as to the U.S. adoption of a soviet approach to education by citing a HEW document called *"A Federal Educational Agency for the Future."* **Ashbrook** called the new education program: *"A Blueprint for Complete Domination and Direction of our Schools from Washington."*

Two major federal initiatives were developed **in 1965** with funding from the *"Elementary and Secondary Education Act"* which was passed in that same year. One was the *"Behavioral Science Teacher Educational*

Program;" the other was a government publication *"Pacesetters in Innovation"*—a *584-page catalogue of behavior modification programs to be used by America's schools.* No, not 584 pages of *educational programs,* but *584 pages filled with behavior modification programs.* **In summary, the intent was to create future Americans who would accept the United Nations and the concept of a global nation and one world government.**

If schools really taught American History and Government, people would know that **in 1970** Congress recognized that the Federal Government had limited authority in education. In an *Amended "General Education Provisions Act"* Congress clearly stated a *"Prohibition against Federal Control of Education"* forbidding the Federal Government from exercising any *"direction, supervision, or control over the curriculum, program of instruction, administration or personnel of any education institution, school, or school system, or over the selection of library resources, textbooks, or other printed or published instructional materials by any educational institution or school system."* In case you are wondering, this law is still valid! The government and educational elite get around this law by a loophole, which allows federal funding of *"research and development."* All 800-plus federally mandated programs are using America's children as *Research Projects.* Does the term "guinea pig" come to anyone's mind? (Shame on us!)

Catherine Barrett, President of the National Education Association in 1976, gave a speech in which she said: *"First, we will help all of our people understand that school is a concept and not a place. We will not confuse "schooling" with education. The school will be the community, the community the* *school.* [This reflects the Communist view of education and lifetime control of the masses.] **Barrett** continued: *"We will need to recognize that so-called "basic skills" which currently represent nearly the total effort in elementary schools, will be taught in one-quarter of the present school day. The remaining time will be devoted to what is truly fundamental and basic—time for academic inquiry, time for students to develop their own interests, time for a dialogue between students and teachers—more than a dispenser of information, the teacher will be a conveyor of values, a philosopher [in secular humanism] (emphasis mine). Students will learn to write love letters and lab notes."*

(Author's note: The above is an accurate description of what classroom "activities and teaching" have become over the past few decades, in our nation)

1976, during America's bi-centennial, the NEA announced its new plan for education for the new world entitled **Global 2000**: *"We believe that teachers are the major resource through which to affect a world community based on the principles of peace and justice. We seek to make history rather than recall it ☐it is with this sobering awareness that we set about to change the course of American education for the twenty-first century by embracing the ideals of Global community, the equality and interdependence of all peoples and nations, and education as a tool to bring about world peace."*

In1978 J. Catherine Conrad, one of John Dewey's disciples, told the world exactly what was going on: *"We must,"* she said, *"help the God-indoctrinated person to realize that morals and ethics are manmade. We must teach him that he must update and discard* *his outdated, immoral, evil values, replacing them with rational ones."*

In the 1980's, the **DOE (Department of Education)** changed the character of public schools from *"teaching"* to *"workforce training,"* the *Soviet poly-technical system*. [You know, to work in factories to compete with third-world slavery factories—where the Government tells you where you are needed is where you will work.] This was done through a **DOE** work called **"Course Goals Collection."** *fourteen volumes of 15,000 goals covering every major subject taught in public schools.* Seventy thousand (70,000) copies were distributed to approximately 16,000 school districts then in existence. This is how *Outcome Based Education* made its way into the schools of America. **OBE's purpose is to change attitudes, values and beliefs.**

During the 1990's, we were given **Goals 2000** and **School-to-Work** programs that hopefully would transform our schools, which would eventually transform America. **School-To-Work** was put in place *not by legislation*, but *by Executive Orders of State Governors.* **Charlotte Iserbyt** in her book, *The Deliberate Dumbing Down Of America,* describes this transformation as: *"....the internationalization of education with the exchanges of data systems, curricula, methods, etc., all essential for the implementation of the International Socialist management and control system being put into place right now."*

In his last term, **President Clinton** issued an *Executive Order calling for all American schools to adopt "international education."* International education is defined in detail in the **U.N. World Declaration on Education for All 1990**. It is **"School-To-Work"** for the *world.* In the **March-April 2000 issue of Foreign Affairs, written by officials in the Clinton administration,** it states *that the new Federal system of education is based on standards developed by "international agreements."* The **U.N. World Conference on Education for All**, states that *"the ultimate goal of education is to work for international peace and solidarity in an interdependent world."* That, folks, is the beginning of the *New One World Order a.k.a. Globalism a.k.a Socialism/Communism.*

A 1996 poll revealed the surprising news that over 50% of Americans feared their government; perhaps this is the fulfillment of a warning by Thomas Jefferson:

"When all government, domestic and foreign, in little as in great things, shall be drawn to Washington as the center of all power, it will render powerless the checks provided of one government on another and will become as venal and oppressive as the government from which we have separated."

To be fair and balanced in this presentation, let us hear a few words from the opposing side.

Professor Chester M. Pierce, M.D., Professor of Education and Psychiatry at Harvard, has this to say: *"Every child in America entering school at the age of five is mentally ill because he comes to school with certain allegiances to our Founding Fathers, toward our elected officials, toward his parents, toward a belief in a supernatural being, and toward the sovereignty of this nation as a separate entity. It's up to you as teachers to make all these sick children well— by creating the international child of the future."*

"Every child in America comes to school 'insane' at the age of six because of the American family structure," as stated by **Humanist Philosopher, Ashley Montague,** told to 6000 California school board members

"We no longer see the teaching of facts and information as the primary function of education....building a new kind of people must be a part of education." **Dr. Shirley McCune** was speaking at a **Governor's Education Summit**. She went on to say: *"What is happening in America today—what we are facing is a total restructuring of our society."*

Question: Just whose society is she helping restructure, and by whose authority?

The **American Humanist Association** understands the importance of capturing the children, for they have written*: "In order to capture this nation, one has to totally remove moral and spiritual values and absolutes from the thinking of the child. The child has to think that there is no standard of right and wrong, that truth is relative, and that diversity is the only absolute to be gained."*

(Author's note: You know, *diversity*—all the sins mentioned in the Bible—*plus* Multi-Culturalism—everyone living and speaking the languages according to the countries they emigrated from—it sounds like the aftermath of God's judgment upon discovering the prideful building of the Tower of Babel when one goes to the grocery stores these days. What babble we hear in every aisle! The Globalism and One/New World Order thinkers have subversively and deceitfully pushed both of these systems on the sleeping unsuspecting trusting citizens of the United States of America for one reason only—Socialism/Communism—a newly formed USA-nation under dictatorship of the elitists.)

From **"Humanism: A New Religion,"** *"Education is thus a most powerful ally of Humanism. What can a theistic Sunday School's meeting for an hour once a week and teaching only a fraction of the children do to stem the tide of the five-day (school) program of Humanistic (Religion) teaching?"*

P. Blanchard, in "The Humanist" 1983, continues: *"I think that the most important factor moving us toward a Secular (Humanist) society has been the educational factor. <u>Our schools may not teach Johnny how to read properly, but the fact that Johnny is in school until he is sixteen tends toward the elimination of religious superstition.</u> The average American child now acquires a high school education, and this militates against Adam and Eve and all other myths of alleged history."*

The **feminist, lesbian author and spokesperson, Patricia Warren**, boldly told today's gay and lesbian community: *"It is the first fact of civilization that whoever captures the kids 'owns the future.'"* She went on to explain how: *"They must work to establish gay/lesbian clubs in all of America's major schools."*

Goals and Use of Psychiatry

"The poisonous certainties fed to us by our parents, our Sunday and Day school teachers, our politicians [and] our Priests help create neurosis." **G. Brock Chisholm Co-founder of World Federation for Mental Health**

"We can therefore <u>justifiably stress our particular point of view with regard to the proper development of the human psyche, even though our knowledge be incomplete. We must aim to make it permeate every</u>

educational activity in our national life," **John Rees-- once Deputy Director of the Tavistock Clinic— Britain's Psychological Warfare body.**

"The family is now one of the major obstacles to improved mental health, and hence should be weakened, if possible, so as to free individuals and especially children from the coercion of family life," **Chisholm and Rees** (both).

John J. Dunphy, writing in "**The Humanist Magazine,**" **1983,** said it all! *"The battle for mankind's future must be waged and won in the public school classroom—the classroom must and will become the arena of conflict between the old and the new—the rotting corpse of Christianity and the new Faith of Humanism.*

From the book, **"Brave New Schools"**—and quoted from a speech to the **National Advisory Council on Education, 1995—***"Critical thinking means not only learning how to think for oneself, but it also means learning how to subvert the traditional values in your society. You're not thinking 'critically' if you're accepting the values that mommy and daddy taught you. That's not 'critical.'"*

Some politicians agree. Listen to former **Senator Paul Hoagland of Nebraska**: *"The fundamentalist parents have no right to indoctrinate their children in their beliefs. We are preparing their children for the year 2000 and life in a Global One-World Society and those children will not fit in."*

Hillary Clinton, when speaking to the Richmond Virginia's Times Dispatch on reforming the nation's schools, made this remark: *"We need a remaking of the American way of politics, government, and life, indeed."*

She was a member of the **National Center on Education and the Economy**.

"Give me your four year olds, and in a generation I will build a Socialist State." *Vladimir Lenin*

"Our enemy is not those with guns, but Missionaries with Bibles." **Jiang Zhernin—Head of the Communist Party, People's Republic of China**

The official title of the Nazi party was "**The National Socialist Workers Party of Germany." The Nazi's called their selves "The Children of the New Age of World Order."** *Those who challenged the government's power were branded "Conservative Reactionaries" or worse yet, Christians were condemned as "right wing fanatics."* History teaches us that if we do not learn the lessons of the past we are doomed to repeat those mistakes. It seems it is happening quickly here in our country.

Our bureaucrats, politicians and educators are constantly blaming either parents, or lack of funds for our school's dilemmas. [They create the problem, can't solve it, so they play the *blame game!*] The answer is always more money and more government control. For well over fifty years the American voter has believed this line of (sorry but it best describes it) *crap.*

Victor Gollancz, a famous Socialist Publisher tells us why he believed that Socialism would take over America*:* *"Christians are not exactly bright, so it will be easy for Socialism to lead them down the garden path through their ideals of brotherly love and 'social justice'"*

Maybe it's (past) time the Christian men and women stand up for their families…. and their faith ….and put

God back in charge of this nation and schools, where He belongs. It's that simple. What do Christians do?

(Daniel 11:32) *"But the people who know their God shall stand firm and take action."*

(Exodus 23:24-25) tells us what must be done*: "You shall not worship their God's, nor serve them, nor do according to their deeds; but you shall utterly overthrow them, and break their sacred pillars in pieces."* God's solution, I wish I could say it had been mine. (end)

Joseph R. Larson, thank you for your care and concern and dedication to our Christian cause of *Restoring America.*

Our supposedly *"do-good and mislead falsely-compassionate Liberal Social Justice people" and "Multi-Culturalists"—elitists--*here in the USA—do not realize they have been called *"useful idiots"* by their Socialist Masters. For most of these people, who are educators throughout the elementary and secondary public schools and universities—this is not a very complimentary title, but it suits them perfectly. They don't understand what is going to happen to them at the hands of their Masters after they are "used" to successfully change our nation, perish that thought. They also are on the sinking boat—but their fate will be worse than the average Joe-citizen—they will have lived for as long as their Masters considered them *useful* to the revolution. For, you see, they are supposedly the *thinkers* (though they are really just puppets for their Masters) and *thinkers* are dangerous to a dictatorship—they lead revolutions. They must be pitied for having been so gullibly deceived and, prayerfully, it is hoped that they still will see the error of their ways—and leave the Socialist Party, as **ex-Communist Whittaker Chambers** did and as related in his book **"Witness,"** written after he fled for his life, testified in court, and remained in hiding for a long time—*before it is too late for them.*

Then there are the *silent traitors* that give aid and comfort to the enemy. And this is who this book is being written to. Do all of us have some culpability in the act of treason against God, family, and country? I will ask you the question that I asked myself, and wrestled with, before I answered to call of God to become involved. To what degree are you a *traitor* and what can you do once you know that you are one? To refuse to answer the questions or to stay ignorant of those things which affect our souls and lives, and the souls and lives around us, is disloyal to the King of Kings and puts our families and country at great risk.

Purposeful indifference and/or ignorance take on a level of foolish stupidity, and to know what to do and not do it is a sin. What will you say when the day arrives when you stand in judgment before the Son of God? (Know this: Truth is Absolute, and does not depend on your feelings or opinion; you will indeed some day kneel in front of Jesus for judgment.) *Will you say that you were too busy? Will you say that you were too old? Will you say that you were uncomfortable with the controversy? Will you say that you thought you had more time and it's just not fair?* Any excuse will be utter foolishness when standing in the presence of Jesus, because He will see your heart. Say a prayer that Jesus will take your hand and lead you through this writing into His truth. As you trust Him, you don't have to understand everything on your own and He will direct your thoughts and path.

It is rare indeed to find a Christian today who hasn't fulfilled the definition of a *traitor* against God, family, and country. Yet we also must recognize that it is sometimes through ignorance that a Christian has been a traitor against God, family, and country in the past. But to continue to be one today, when the affects of the liberal decay is so visible, is inexcusable. But there is hope, because knowing the truth will set you free and give you the desire to help effect change in our culture of immorality that exists in our nation today. It is your choice to allow God to give you insight and then to act. Your freedom, life, and eternity and the freedom, life, and eternity of those you touch, especially the children, will be impacted by how you choose.

> *"Do not pray for easy lives. Pray to be stronger men. Do not pray for tasks commensurate with your strength, but for strength commensurate to your tasks! Don't go barefoot! Many Christian are truthful, have their hearts free from sin, are sure of their salvation and they stay in the Word of God...but they are shoeless...they are not taking ground for the kingdom of God. We must thrust the sword of the Spirit into the hearts of men." Charles Spurgeon*

TREASON:
Violation of allegiance toward one's sovereign or country; the betrayal of one's own country by waging war against it, or by consciously and purposely acting to aid its enemies; Betrayal of trust or confidence; treachery.

The U.S. Constitution states:
Levying war against the United States or in adhering to their enemies, giving them aid and comfort; highest crime of a civil nature of which a man can be guilty.

SOVEREIGN:

Supreme in power, God is the Sovereign of the universe.
Superior to all others, as supreme lord or ruler;
One who possesses the highest authority without control;
A supreme magistrate;
Absolute sovereignty belongs to God alone.
Self-governing; independent. (as in a sovereign independent nation).

Where are the real Christian Church leaders, true shepherds that lead with conviction and not personal preference? May each of you hear the rebuke and reproof of the Holy Spirit's conviction in the following pages and repent of your apathy, laziness and false priorities. In so doing, the Truth will be able to seep into your souls and minds. Without the repentance, the light of Truth will be diminished. Know that Jesus gives His love and forgiveness as He tells each of you to go and sin no more, trust in Him, and come out onto the water, and into the valley of decision. If you look with pride at this testing/rebuke as a shameful insult because you refuse to see the guilt of your apathy, allow the love of your Father's forgiveness to work in you, stop and cry out in prayer for God to help you. This soul-searching is a must, if you are to come out of the valley of indecision and allow God to use you, as He wills to do. If you truly feel like it does not apply to you, and that you have allowed God to use you now and in the past, then what a joy to know that you are part of a working remnant. You will find that you will be in the company of many men and women who are working tirelessly in this endeavor. After learning what the Holy Spirit would have you know by the light of this writing, give it to another brother in love, to encourage him/her to also become a working saint. We are becoming a strong army of spiritual warriors contending for the faith.

Because of the sleeping and disobedient leadership in the church, we fail to act at His direction, to possess the land for Christ. In this regard, we allow the unrighteous to rule and put children at risk now, and their souls at risk for eternity. The church leaders stay comfortable and fat and their flocks are left to live in a world that hates Judeo-Christianity and seeks to destroy Jews and Christians.

The Church leaders have known for centuries that *abortion* is murder as babies' brains are sucked out of their skull and their bodies dismembered, shedding innocent blood that litterally "runs through our streets" from back alley ways by hospitals/clinics. This is rarely, if ever, spoken about from the pulpit as church leaders wish to remain non-controversial and try to let their congregations go in time to be the first at the restaurant table.

The Church leaders have known for centuries that *Sodomy* is an abominable sin, without speaking out about it, while allowing *homosexuals* to recruit the young in the public schools, while the clergy continue to base their success on how many members they have sitting in the pews, while being overly concerned about their monetary status—and who can build the largest and most extravagantly-entertaining church, or who can "argue" the Word of God more eloquently as did the Pharisees and Scribes.

The Church leaders embrace religions like Islam and the New Age Contemplative Religion, which propagate lies, while their congregants are sitting back as milk-drinking Christians, lacking their leaders' discipleship through neglect, and leave their faith, because the Church—its people, through the actions of its leaders, has lost the flavor of its salt. When Jesus referred to that He was talking about how, after salt lost its flavor and was ineffective, it was chopped up and used for roadways. The people do not realize they have been cheated—that their faith has not been properly discipled—and that that is the reason why they leave the Church and head by the millions to the false hedonistic New Age cults.

The Church leaders have known for centuries that *children seek the lures of evil and allow evil to rule in the land if they are not taught the Scriptures* in their educational system. Yet they and their sheep allowed it to be removed from the schools, and sit back in fear while the children are indoctrinated with the *theory* that they came from green algae pond-scum, and are teacher-engineered to kneel to a global Atheistic Humanist community instead of to God. They seem to be surprised and perplexed at our continuing degradation of our population. It truly appears that the *Church leaders do not care that the citizens, (as well as the Church members, and their children), are becoming more and more aware of this neglect.* They look for leadership and desire their Church to take an active stand against the evil that is permeating our society and provide some leadership in curtailing the further progression of these ills. And so they drop-out of their Church membership and go from-church-to-church in search of Truth and help for their families.

These areas of neglect will continue until the Church makes them stop, because the gates of Hell can prevail against every other entity but the Christian Church. Hitler stated he knew that he could destroy the Church at will, because of greed, pride, and fear. Jesus would look at much of the Church leadership with a *"woe to you hypocrites"* comment, whitewashed tombs full of dead men's bones. It is obvious in the Christian Churches that leadership speak with their mouth for the sheep to follow Christ, yet many leaders do not follow Christ themselves, because they know where He is going and the Cross is not comfortable for those with a foot in the world.

QUESTIONS: *Would, then, many in church leadership be considered as traitors and sinners by their actions or inactions?* Judgment indeed must begin in the House of God. Jesus expects all Christians to hear and obey. *Are not the church leaders expected to heed the words of God?*

> ***"Take no part in unfruitful works of darkness, but instead expose them."*** (Ephesians 5:11)

We can continue to sit back and be ashamed because we have done nothing as the children are being devoured by an immoral society and their souls are at risk for eternity because of our apathy, or we can listen to real men like Patrick Henry when he said:

> "In vain sir can we extenuate the matter, gentlemen may cry peace, peace, but there is no peace, the war has actually begun. The next gale we hear from the North will bring to our ears the clash of resounding arms. Our brethren are already in the field, why stand we here idle, what is it that gentlemen wish, what would they have?

Is life so dear and peace so sweet as to be purchased at the price of chains and slavery? Forbid it Almighty God, I know not what course others may take, but as for me, give me liberty or give me death."

He was indeed a Firebrand of the Revolution, and we are at a point of revolution again in this country, and need new firebrands for a new revolution like many of the men in this book, and the valiant man Scott Lively, who expresses well what is needed in church leaders, if they are to disciple men of valor that fight for God, family, and country.

MASCULINE CHRISTIANITY
Scott Lively, J.D., Th.D.

Scripture teaches in Genesis that when God created man in His image, He created us male and female. The implication is that God's character spans the full spectrum of masculine and feminine qualities. This attribute is also revealed in the person of Jesus, born as a male, but manifesting both masculinity and femininity in His actions. When exhibiting feminine qualities, Jesus was more nurturing and relationship oriented than any woman. When exhibiting masculinity, Jesus was more forceful and results-oriented than any man.

Unfortunately, the modern American church, along with the majority of its leaders, has rejected masculinity in favor of an effeminate Christianity. Too many (though by no means all) of today's pastors, priests, deacons and elders shrink timidly from the challenge of the world, more interested in decorating the interior of their church buildings than in doing cultural and political battle with the enemies of God. Ravening lions rage unchecked throughout the land, while Church leaders hold potlucks and retreats.

Where is the *masculine Jesus of the Bible* in the life of today's church?—the Jesus who threw down the tables of the moneychangers and drove them out of the temple with a whip? The Jesus who faced down and tamed the Gerasene demoniac? The Jesus who, to their faces, excoriated the cultural and political leaders of the day as a *"brood of vipers," and "whitewashed sepulchers full of dead men's bones"*? This masculine Jesus has been ejected from the American church. In His place is a false and emasculated Christ, as submissive and fearful of controversy as the men who now lead His flock.

Brethren, this is not an attack on femininity. If anything, the church should be commended for its appreciation for and fulfillment of the feminine aspects of its role. Such vital relationship-centered ministries as feeding the hungry, clothing the naked and soothing the broken-hearted are prospering today. These ministries are very much a reflection of the feminine side of Christ's complete personality.

Instead, this is vigorous rebuke to both women and men within the church who reject the masculine side of Christianity and have thus *abandoned those outside our "church families"* to fend for themselves against the forces of evil in the world. This is a rebuke to male church leaders, who channel their masculine competitiveness into sporting contests in church gymnasiums instead of contending for influence over the *community outside the church walls*. This is a rebuke to those pastors' wives who keep their shepherd husbands safely close to the flock *when they should be sometimes out hunting the bears and wolves.*

Masculine Christianity fights to champion what is right and to defeat evil. It is the applied force for good against which the gates of hell cannot prevail. It is an embodiment of the spirit of conquest in which the Great Commission was given. It is the unyielding determination to prevail against all odds and at any cost to achieve a righteous goal—even unto death on a cross. Masculine Christianity is the engine of revival: *prophetic, expansionist, uncompromising.*

In Biblical history, the greatest heroes of the faith exemplified masculine Christianity. Abraham did not sit idly by when his brother Lot was captured by the four kings. He armed his servants and went out to rescue him by force. Moses faced down Pharaoh in a series of aggressive confrontations. David fearlessly challenged and defeated Goliath and then cut off his head as a trophy of battle. God blessed these righteous men and *backed their righteous deeds with His power*. Josiah is honored in scripture as one of the most righteous of all the kings for banishing the *"perverted persons"* from the land and destroying the foreign idols. Joshua and Caleb were the only men of their generation allowed to enter the promised land because, of all the Israelite spies sent into Canaan, they alone called for immediate invasion of Canaan when the others backed away out of fear. John the Baptist, who boldly and publicly rebuked Herod for his sexual immorality, was praised by Jesus Himself. Jesus stated that among men there was none greater than John.

Extra-Biblical history is also replete with examples of masculine Christianity. The period of the American Revolution is one in which deeply religious men took up the sword to overthrow an unrighteous oppressor. The great missionary and reform movements are additional examples of masculine Christianity at work.

The defining characteristic of each of these examples is the conquest of evil by God's people—mostly men. Masculinity is by no means the exclusive domain of men, but it naturally has greater appeal to men in the same way that feminine ministries of the church appeal more to women. Indeed, this explains why the majority of church members today are women or married couples in which the husband attends church at the request of the wife. Where are the men of this generation? Though some are in church, they are significantly outnumbered by women, and they tend to be the least active members of the congregation. Is it any wonder in the light of the de-emphasis of masculinity by the church?

The church and this nation cry out for a revival of masculine Christianity, which is to say that we church leaders need to stop being such, for lack of a better word, *sissies,* when it comes to social and political issues. *We need to spend as much time confronting perpetrators as we do comforting victims*. We need to do less fretting, and more fighting for righteousness. For every motherly, feminine ministry of the church such as a Crisis Pregnancy Center or ex-gay support group, *we need a battle-hardened, take-it-to-the-enemy masculine ministry like Operation Rescue* (questions of civil disobedience aside). For every God-hating radical in government, academia and media *we need a bold, no-nonsense, truth-telling Christian counterpart: trained, equipped and endorsed by the local church.*

These are not easy words to hear for those in authority in the church today, but I offer no apology for saying them, because this is the hard truth that all of us must confront.

We are on the brink of utter defeat by our cultural adversaries and the church is only now beginning to wake up to the consequences of our past passivity. We are rapidly nearing a point in time when even a strong call to action, were it to be heard from every one of America's pulpits, would be insufficient to resolve our nation's moral crisis. There comes a point of no return in every declining culture.

I imagine we Christians as reclusive householders in an Old Testament walled city. A few of us have stepped out onto the street, confused and dazed, to find our city overrun by enemy soldiers with more coming over the walls. Buildings are burning, the watchmen are falling back under an incredible onslaught, *and most of our warriors are still sleeping soundly.* We have reached that split-second of decision in which we must choose whether to rush forward into battle on the chance that we can defeat the invaders, *or to surrender and look on in resignation as our children are marched off into slavery in a foreign land."* (end)

Thank you again Scott for your willingness to be scorned and ridiculed as you point out the truth of Scripture and are used by our Lord and Savior Jesus Christ to open the eyes and ears of His children.

The acknowledgment, reverence, and worship of the Lord are the very beginning, the foundation, of wisdom and knowledge. (Proverbs 1:7 and 9:10)

THE DEATH OF SHAME
Dr. (Coach) Dave Daubenmire
27 March 2008
NewsWithViews.com

Shame: *Painful feeling arising from the consciousness of something dishonorable, improper, ridiculous, etc., done by oneself or with another.*

I'm not really sure when it began, as it has been a gradual thing, I'm sure. But like the slow removal of a grass stain from a teenager's hack-around T-shirt, the impression has slowly been extracted from the conscience of America.

Whatever happened to shame?

I suppose some of it could be traced to Dr. Spock as he is responsible for so much of what is wrong with child-rearing these days, or to Benjamin Bloom or John Dewey, two acolytes-of-Atheism, men who promoted the Humanistic ideals that have replaced Christianity as the bedrock of our educational system. *"If it feels good, do it"* has replaced *"Thou shall not."*

But the bare-boned-bottom-line is that the goal of "building self-esteem" in our young children required the elimination of any type of negative reinforcement and led to the development of the value system we now see permeating the American culture.

Let me ask you again, "Whatever happened to shame?"

I'm sure I was a handful in elementary school. I was small in stature but big on the inside. Always striving to be the center of attention (big families teach you to fight to be noticed), I spent my early school daze with my nose stuck to a dot written on the chalkboard, standing face-first in the back corner of the classroom, or in isolation in the hallway where I couldn't distract the rest of the class.

In small town America in the fifties we still believed that *shame* was a good thing. My parents didn't call the principal, we didn't hire a lawyer, child psychologists were as common as cordless phones, and "mood altering medications" were something the hippies hadn't even thought of. In the 1950's they would have thrown you in jail for giving drugs to a young child.

Yep, I would have been the poster child for Ritalin. But instead of medicated, I was disciplined. Despite what the child experts want to tell us, applied lovingly, *shame* is a great teacher. I know it is a matter of opinion but I think I turned out all right.

It was 1989. I was over a decade into my "public-fool system" career when I first noticed it. I was teaching "special education" (in many cases this is nothing more than a made-up disability where schools warehouse students who won't behave:(read this on ADD) www.newswithviews.com when a 15 year-old thug named John came waltzing in late to class, basking in the glory of having been in the principal's office, and proudly strutting in to tell his fellow future-felons about *"the discipline"* he had just survived.

"F--- Him Man." John announced to his captive audience as his chain-linked ear-ring dangled under his long, scraggly, pot-perfumed hair. *"I ain't serving no f----in detention. I told that m-f---er that he ain't my old man so he could shove the detention up his a--. Who does that m-f---er think he is telling me that sh-t? I should have kicked his f---in a--."*

You may think I am making it up. Ask your child. This type of language is common-place in our "public" schools today. In 1989, John was a bit ahead of his time.

With all of the class waiting on my reaction, I uttered a phrase that I used often with troubled kids.

"You know the problem with most of you in here?" I declared to the room full of cultural-misfits. **"You are ashamed of what you should be proud of and proud of what you should be ashamed of."** (By the way, it took four years but I eventually tamed John—amazing what a little love and strong discipline will do for a malcontent.)

I thought of John as I looked around America this week. The results of this *false self-esteem* are all over the television. It has even crept into the church.

Hillary "misspoke" http://www.breitbart.com/article.php? about her dodging of the sniper bullets. Where I come from we call that lying. But if anyone were to accuse her of *"lying"* the outrage over such blatant *"judgmentalism"* of her actions would raise a hue and cry that would turn her into a sympathetic figure. In my hometown elementary school, Hillary's behavior would have earned her some time on a stool with a dunce-cap on. Today we laugh it off as *"fatigue,"* or *"mixed-memory."* (Let's see, can you remember confusing the specifics of the last time you had to dodge bullets?) Such blatant dishonesty should doom her career. She's running for leader of the free world for heaven's sake! But we'll brush it off as "Clintonesque." We've come to expect it from our leaders.

Eliot Spitzer is caught with his hand in the "cookie jar" and he doesn't have the decency to immediately exit "stage right." His too-proud-to-be-ashamed wife stands beside him as Spitzer tries to figure out a way to keep his job. The "cookie" into whose jar http://www.celebrityrumors.com his hand was caught is offered millions for her story. A "high-priced hooker" (as opposed to a low-priced hooker) becomes a hero. *No shame*. Like Monica, she will ride (sorry) Spitzer all the way to the bank. *You see, they are all proud of what they should be ashamed of.* Once again, America glorifies degeneracy.

Now the new governor of NY is self-identifying as a <u>former drug-using adulterer</u>. Former NJ governor James McGreevey is a "<u>gay American</u>." The <u>Mayor of Detroit</u> is oblivious to **shame.**

Britney, Paris, Lindsay, all have gotten rich off of despicable behavior. The <u>glorification of sluts</u> is featured even on mainstream news shows.

Look at what our culture has become. We have lost the ability to blush. Even those in our pulpits make excuses for sin. Families watch together on TV what my parents didn't speak of even in private.

Have you turned on the TV lately? Have you spent any time watching what our children are watching? Are you familiar with the MTV show <u>Jackass</u>, (WARNING: Should cause one to blush) where people become stars by doing things for which most folks would be embarrassed? How about "<u>The Real World</u>" which features the promotion of debauchery and adulterous behavior?

My Mom would have warned us to *"Stop encouraging such behavior."* She could wield a mean yardstick. She wasn't worried about her kids' self-esteem. She was worried about our self-respect.

"Everyone lies. We're all sinners, Coach!" Well, I guess you're right, but there was a time in America when you were taught to be ashamed of your sin. Sadly, those days have gone the way of sin-hating Christians.

I don't mean to pick on Hillary but has there ever been a more narcissistic couple than she and her husband? I mean, come on, has there ever been a pair that has been so natural at lying? Her recent "misstatement" is merely the latest in a long line of serial-perjury. *(He: I did not have sex with that woman; She: I don't know how those records got in my office, ad infinitum, ad nausea.)* It is a way of life with them; sadly, it is a way of life with most politicians…with most Americans, actually. They are a reflection of us.

But here is the tragic part. We know that they lie, yet we still consider them qualified for public service. Pastors endorse them, pundits justify their behavior, and Christians vote for the "lesser of the evils." "It's only politics" *(Is that John Dewey I hear?)* as they try to convince us that lying is no longer a big deal. Let me ask you something. In your personal life, do you trust liars?

My wife came home from substitute teaching in our local elementary the other day and she was distraught. *"The kids are out of control,"* She lamented. *"Discipline is non-existent. Everyone is afraid to do anything. The principals all look the other way. No-one will control the kids' behavior."* What is that popular term we hear today…."the chickens have come home to roost"….we no longer honor character. We glorify the character-less. (Author's note once again: The NEA schools caused the behaviors over the last few decades that they are now dealing with and do not know how to control what they have created in their own classrooms—so it *blame game time for them again.*)

America needs to feel more *shame*. We need to make it clear that some behaviors are not acceptable. We must teach our children that behaviors have consequences, that one's actions affect others. That the world doesn't revolve around them.

The Clinton supporters said everyone lies about sex. I don't. I don't have to. There was a day when one was ashamed of both lies and sex.

Shame on us, America. Shame on us for what we are not teaching our children. Shame on us for winking at sin. We reap

what we sow. Look at our current crop of shameless leaders.
Why should we expect anything different?

Whatever happened to shame?   (end)

Are many Pastors just dupes for Satan?
Repent and do what He calls you to do!

Satan is having his way: lying, killing, stealing, destroying, and
dividing. He has accelerated his work in the United States as
Humanistic Atheistic Socialism gains more and more control of
the minds, through our schools. Millions of Christians and their
children are at risk of going to hell for eternity, and that is his job.
Satan has many dupes: the Atheists, Pagans, Secular Humanists,
Communists, International Bankers, National Education
Association Teachers Union (NEA), American Association of
University Professors Union (AAUP)., American Civil Liberties
Union (ACLU), Planned Parenthood Federation of American
(PPFA) abortion mills, homosexuals, and others that take up his
cause to lie, kill, steal, destroy, and divide, and those are their
jobs that they perform superbly well. The deceit and destruction
is running rampant in the education system, media, government,
and entertainment, and many pulpits. So what are Christian
Pastors and their flocks to do? Their job is as Christ outlines for
them, not what they outline for themselves for comfort. These
types of pastors allow evil to dictate and prevail because of their
cowardice and laziness and lack of involvement. Repent and do
what is right in God's eyes.

We are to do everything with the love and forgiveness of Christ
as we stand firmly in His truth and in obedience to His
commands. God's wrath, as cited in the Old Testament, was
meted out every time there was disobedience and rebellion to His
Laws and Precepts. We need to loudly proclaim **Romans 1:16:**
*"For I am not ashamed of the gospel of Christ: for it is the
power of God unto salvation to every one that believeth."* While

loving God with all our heart, mind, soul and strength, and our neighbor as ourselves, we are *to abide in Christ, for without Him we can do nothing. Christ is Truth.* Truth will offend and divide people. You have to choose whether you stand on God's side or man's side. Truth evidently has offended many pastors. Defending truth separates the men from the boys. Many are afraid to take a chance and risk offending their flocks. When this happens, they show that they do not love their flocks and, moreover, their flocks know this, as our times grow shorter and shorter. Love your pastors and pray for them to have the manly courage to be obedient to their call.

Joseph Goebbels, the Nazi Propaganda Minister, stated: *"Not every item of news should be published. Rather, must those who control news policies endeavor to make every item of news serve a certain purpose."* Since the Pastors control the news that gets to their flock, I am sure that their policy is to endeavor to make every item of news serve a certain purpose, but who's purpose? If most of your message is cotton candy, the children will run to have their share. But a steady diet of cotton candy can poison and rot the system. Pray for your pastor to stand like a man of God, one like Peter that says to those in civil government, "It is better that we obey God, rather than man." Then there are the ones that talk strongly from the Word of God, but will not lead their flocks into the battles that determine where souls will be for eternity. Their walk does not match their talk, which is a great problem with true Christianity today. Most true men of God, true Christians who are involved in this battle for the hearts and souls of the children, are working through Christian organization and NOT through the Church. We could win the battle if the Church became involved. Pray again for such pastors, because they live in fear of actually taking a stand. The worldly system, controlled by evil, has now embraced them as they weaken their stand and are willing to compromise with those that are putting Christians at risk of going to hell for eternity, via the public school classrooms.

California has just signed into law, *a law put forth by a lesbian activist in the legislature*, that makes it necessary to teach all children, K-12, in the government public schools including some attacks on the Christian schools, that transgender sexuality, bisexuality, and homosexuality must be portrayed in a positive and accepting way. This is aggressively forced upon and against the morals and virtues of the majority of the people by the NEA. Where are the pastors regarding this horrendous insult to God and the children? Pastors that should have been the first ones on the front lines defending the children against this attack, to warn us of danger, are more concerned with maintaining their comfort and status quo, than in fulfilling their responsibilities to God, our Nation and families. They have been cowards because they have not trusted in the Word of God. They must remember that all power was given to Jesus and that He will be with them always, imparting His power to them, as He has done over the centuries, during all battles of good versus evil. They have allowed traitors and barbarians inside of the gates to destroy souls. Is the name tag that Arnold Schwarzenegger gave to the Democrats at a national convention when he called them "girly boys" going to be a name that sticks to the leadership/legacy of most pastors today? It appears to be true at this time—but the pastors must begin to show their manhood and shake off the shameful negativity that that name implies. As I prompt you to consider these very important questions, you must ultimately, honestly, be the judge of your own actions and, perhaps, after doing so, you will join the battle and encourage your congregants to take a stand.

Congregants, pray for your pastors, because they are commanded to Biblically resist all actions that are against God. Help them to become MEN instead of man-children that make all kinds of excuses not to engage. Jesus gave the command to "Go Ye" and another one to "Occupy until my return," and further, "Faith without works is dead." He did not say, "Come inside of a building and sit in a pew and that's all you have to do." He was angry with the people who sat in the Temple and did nothing but argue about Scripture. Silence is also a sin, and it is the banner of many pastors, who need your prayers.

If a law is put in place that is against God's laws, then we are obligated to obey God and not man, and this should be shouted unashamedly from the pulpits from coast-to-coast. I pray that God opens your eyes and ears, that the Holy Spirit strengthens you so that you run as David did, to meet Goliath, instead of shaking in your armor like the armies of the God of Israel. You must open your windows to pray to God like Daniel did even though the king said no. You must never bow your knee to anyone but God, as Shadrach, Meshach, Abednego, refused to do even though the king said to bow to me. If you resist and risk threats or disfavor, Jesus will one day say to you "well done my good and faithful servant." No one wishes to hear Him say, "I never knew you." Particularly pastors should never risk this hearing that declaration.

Pastors, understand this. If you (yes, you) are not willing to take a stand, you set your followers up to be led to the slaughter. The flock needs you to talk HIS Truth and then walk it in resistance to evil wherever it manifests itself in government, education, media, and the Church. Maybe an example for those of you in California, would be to take the recent laws supporting homosexuality, go to your capitol and pray, then burn the laws on the capitol steps to let the Governor and others that are traitors to God, family, and country know that these laws do not apply to you or your families, because they are against God's laws. This type of action needs to be taken.

Every legislator, judge, and governor or president that tries to put any law into affect that is against God's laws, and thus the family and the nation, should be met with resistance in a Biblical way. We are called to do good and to avoid evil; we are to obey God always, which translated means that you will disobey any law that is evil, that goes against His laws. As Christians we know that abortion and homosexuality are against His laws. "Render to

Caesar the things that are Caesar's….and to God the things that are God's." We cannot sit idly by as man's laws that are against God's laws, are adopted and held in higher regard than God's laws. While Jesus walked on this earth, His main function was teaching us God's ways and laws so that we would know how He expected us to live, for Him and for our own welfare. He expects us to uphold those teachings and not allow anyone to demand that we go against them. Not in the United States of America.

I pray that this message will be taken by the Holy Spirit into the hearts of pastors across this nation for God's glory and for the sake of our posterity. The moral decay continues to worsen in America daily and like Patrick Henry said: "It is in vain, sir, to extenuate the matter; gentlemen may cry peace, peace—but there is not peace. The war is actually begun! The next gale that sweeps from the North will bring to our ears the clash of resounding arms! Our brethren are already in the field! Why stand we here idle? What is it that gentlemen want? What would they have? Is life so dear and peace so sweet as to be purchased at the price of chains and slavery? Forbid it, Almighty God! I know not what course others may take: but as for me, give me liberty or give me death!"

Pastors do you know what you have to do so that some in your congregation and many across this nation will go to hell for eternity? NOTHING! Just continue to be silent.

REPENT! THEN GIVE ALL LOVE, HONOR AND GLORY TO GOD, for the Kingdom of Heaven is at hand.

Pray for your pastors and ministry leaders, because Satan is after them to kill, divide, distort, and destroy. Many times this is done by convincing them to be cowards and hide behind rhetoric, or redesigning Jesus to be sugar instead of salt. Gary DeMar does a wonderful work in his book, *Myths, Lies & Half Truths, How Misreading the Bible Neutralizes Christians.*

Gary states: *"How many times have you been left speechless when you heard the following objections to Christians getting involved in the issues of the day?*

* "Jesus didn't get mixed up in politics."

* "You can't impose your morality on other people." (the enemy does all the time, however.)

* "There is a separation between church and state."

* "It's never right to resist authority."

* "We're living in the last days—God will take care of it all"—thank God our forefathers did not have this attitude" Where *would* we be today?

* "Christians should remain neutral."

* "It's not right to judge what people do."

* `"Politics is dirty." (Perhaps because Christians are not involved in the process.)

* "Religion and politics do not mix."(Tell that one to our founding fathers!—author's note.)

* "Our citizenship is in heaven."
* "God's kingdom is not of this world."

These and many more objections are studied, evaluated, and answered in *Myths, Lies, and Half Truths*. Understanding what God's Word says about these often-recited but rarely examined challenges to Christian activism will determine the future of Christianity in America and around the world. In truth and in reality, the Bible states just the opposite of the above objections so *conveniently* used by lazy pastors/Christians. Our precious

Bible has many *inconvenient* truths that should be sought out and obeyed—if they had been, we would not have snowballed into the predicament of being the decadent and illiterate Nation we have shamefully allowed the USA to become.

With crisp insight, historical perspective, and clear scriptural scrutiny, Gary DeMar sets forth a comprehensive argument for Christian involvement in the world that God created for His people to prosper and enjoy." Pray for Gary's ministry and God's will in his life, as well as for all people involved in this field of intense, hard work.

Being able to rationalize that it is permissible to hide behind the above stated objections, or a few mercy-works, many church leaders are content to sit back, untouched by the burden that others are carrying for them. We know there are many Pastors who have people in their churches who wish to use the umbrella of their church to become active and form groups, but are not allowed to because these Pastors will not permit them to. I say to these people, "Find a church and Pastor who will allow you to be used within their Church." A church leader sitting under the influence of one of these objections, or causing inaction of the congregation by speaking sweetness and sugar instead of salt, will see little or no fruit. Further, the congregation listens to their Pastors as they use the above excuses, and this eases their consciences as they willingly follow their Pastor's example. We have to ask ourselves if such Church leaders are just males, or real MEN. Does he (the man-child) look to hide behind a reason not to lead, or behind a mercy ministry or program, spouting out a little pretend salt that many times comes from the world? Or does he (the MAN) confront and engage in the dark issues in the world acting as salt and light with a "Go Ye" leadership like Jesus commanded and like Jesus did? Paraphrased, **Jesus said:** *"Follow Me—you will do greater things because I go to the Father—I will send you the Comforter, Counselor to guide you in truth in all matters."* We must also remember that if the Apostles/Disciples had not "engaged and confronted" their times, and the early Bible translators, where would we be now? The pastor must stay wisely, with no fear, in the Word of God as he seeks to serve God by walking the walk and standing fearlessly in harms way for Jesus' children. The pastor that is a MAN is a rare thing today, and if you are blessed to have one where you attend church, or in your community, keep him daily in your prayers for continued courage and strength, and that he will be protected and delivered from all evil. *Scripture has it:* <u>*Work*</u> *out your faith in fear and trembling." Could that have been for our times? Because, indeed, when one becomes involved in this current battle, one does "fear and tremble" at times. Jesus even did! His apostles did to preserve the faith. Can we do less?*

Church leaders note this: Inaction plays into the hands of the evil in this world. As you are called and lead into action, do not fear as you stand on His word and remember this:

"For the word of God is quick, and powerful, and sharper than any two-edged sword, piercing even to the dividing asunder of soul and spirit, and of the joints and marrow, and is a discerner of the thoughts and intents of the heart." **Hebrews 4:12**

Bottom line: Are you willing to die for Jesus and sacrifice all that you have for the children in your care, so that Christ may live in them? Are you willing to be used as a vessel, to pick up your cross daily and do all that Jesus commands to help see that their souls will be in the presence of Jesus for eternity? In many cases, as the shepherd chooses, likewise the flock chooses. As you choose, with the knowledge that He has given you the command to engage, know that Jesus is looking into your heart as you do.

Another must-read on the subject of spiritual leadership, to help pastors and other ministry leaders, is John Chalfant's: *"Abandonment Theology: The Clergy and the Decline of American Christianity."* I will let one of the remnant servants, who was uncompromising in the word of God and is now with our Lord and Savior, speak on this book.

In the words of D. James Kennedy, *"John W. Chalfant's important book on "Abandonment Theology" is going to produce bountiful blessings upon the Christian ministries of this troubled land. He has captured the essence of militant Christianity as it relates to love of country and devotion to democratic principles which it is every citizen's opportunity and obligation to uphold. I believe that serious readers everywhere will find the imprint of the hand of God on this marvelous contribution to Christian and patriotic literature."*

What higher compliment could anyone give a book than to say that it had the imprint of the hand of God upon it? That was my prayer for my first book, and it is my prayer for this one, that the Holy Spirit will speak to you through this work. I have to follow that with the words of Don McAlvany of the *McAlvany Intelligence Advice,* (see the import of having this book on your reading list, no matter what your walk of life). Don says, *"In a mere 238 pages, John Chalfant encapsulates the cause-and-effect relationship between epochal spiritual and political struggles of our times. He offers foolproof, attainable, action-based solutions for the restoration of America's vanishing freedoms.*
"Abandonment Theology" is powerful, hard-hitting, and holds no punches. Fully documented, it is filled with Bible-based political realities, hope and inspiration. Chalfant contends: 'The most exhaustive book, ever written on politics, is the Bible.'
"Abandonment Theology" should be MUST reading for every American, including politicians, clergymen, businessmen, high school and college students, home schoolers and citizens from every rank and religious persuasion. This book contains some of the keys to the restoration of our country." Remember that the number one issue that must be addressed is to put Jesus back as the foundation of the nation.

You know, the enemy works relentlessly with total self-sacrificing abandonment for their cause and that is exactly why we are in the midst of a quiet revolution in our country—now raging full scale war against our future way of life and threatening our very freedoms. Can we people of God work any less hard? No, we must do more! I have to ask the questions: Are many pastors across the United States ashamed of the Gospel? Are they caught up in all of the objections that were mentioned earlier? Or are they so fearful they can't be a true *man* of God? Before I give you the reasons as to why the inactions of the Christian Pastors, Christian Teachers, and Christian Parents is so deadly, let me give you HOPE, so that you can read what is happening and know that God gives us the strength to overcome the evil.

As John Chalfant says, ***"We must obey God and engage in the fight as He commands us to do."*** (Might this author add: Surrender your will to God and repent of your sins so that you can take the speck out of the eye of those you will touch, after first removing the beam in your own.) *"Victory can be ours! That's God's promise to the faithful."*

But listen to the definition of *"Abandonment Theology"* and to some of the ugliness that has occurred since the Christian leadership has abandoned theology. John defines *"Abandonment Theology"*: ***"(It) is a term devised to describe a faith which deceptively pawns itself off as Christianity by operating in the name of Christ but which produces fruits destructive to America's God-given freedoms. It comprises what is left today of the militant, power-filled, full-dimensional Christian faith of America's Founders***—(Author's note: All the way back to writings of Columbus and the Mayflower Compact and through the Revolutionary War,) **after decades of erosion, watering down and trivializing God's action mandates by America's Abandonment Clergy. It is a "feel good" theology that patronizes Jesus Christ and thereby gains legitimacy while at the same time produces disobedience to the commands of God and the desertion of Christian duty."**

I want to stop here and ask His remnant to reread the above, if necessary, to encourage you to know that we are not alone in the battle, that there are more sons of Ischar out there that understand the times we live in, and are speaking up and standing up for the King of Kings. Take heart if you are one of those that was duped into being a part of the Abandonment Theology Clergy, and know that Jesus forgives and forgets. It is necessary to repent of your ignorance, pride, or whatever reason that kept you from obeying His commands—He will actually smile when you do so

Continuing to quote Chalfant, *"Abandonment Theology is so deadly that we are losing our liberties, and evil is triumphing in nearly every aspect of life. A terrible spiritual blindness has come over millions of unsuspecting, victimized Christians, who in turn have even allowed God, the Author of our liberties, to be, in effect, outlawed in our nation's public schools and institutions."*

Can you see now the connection between the Christian leadership, Abandonment Theology Clergy in the church, and the result of the rotting cancer that has been allowed to happen in the 'Sacred Cow' of government education? Can you see now the connection between the Christian leadership, Abandonment Theology Clergy, and sacrificing our children's souls on the Altar of Belial?

As John continues, *"Through decades of erosion, the Abandonment Clergy have succeeded in extracting from the Christian faith the teeth of vigilance, of action, of obedience to God. If the clergy taught their flocks to 'Fear God, and keep his commandments: for this is the whole duty of man' (Eccl. 12:13), America would not be plunging into the dark abyss as she is doing today. If you were America's enemy, wouldn't you try to get rid of God, too, starting with the schools? How have the Abandonment Clergy managed to triumph over such a nearly invincible heritage given to every American?"* John deals with this subject in his book. Please read it, and I want to personally thank you John for your work.

Another Christian Warrior who many times will be accurate on different issues that affect the souls of Americans and the future of our posterity is Chuck Baldwin. He tries to honor God first in his writings, and that should be a telling point for any information that people try to get you to buy into, as truth. Does it honor God first, and does it lead back to Scripture? May the Holy Spirit guide all of Chuck's steps, and may Chuck have a quiet spirit and let the Lord do the talking through His Spirit, as the Lord would do for all of those that are wise in seeking His Spirit. Otherwise, it would be better that they were silent.

Is the Handwriting on the Wall for America?
Chuck Baldwin

"In the same hour came forth fingers of a man's hand, and wrote over against the candlestick upon the plaster of the wall of the king's palace: and the king saw the part of the hand that wrote." Daniel 5:5 (KJV)

"And this is the writing that was written, MENE, MENE, TEKEL, UPHARSIN. This is the interpretation of the thing: MENE: God hath numbered thy kingdom, and finished it. TEKEL: Thou art weighed in the balances, and art found wanting. PERES: Thy kingdom is divided." Daniel 5:26-28 (KJV)

Secularists will not admit it, but nations rise and fall at the pleasure of Almighty God. America's founders certainly understood this fact. Even Benjamin Franklin, who was one of the least spiritual of America's Founding Fathers, told the delegates at the Constitutional Convention: *"We have been assured, Sir, in the sacred writings, that 'Except the Lord build the house, they labor in vain that build it.' I firmly believe this; and I also believe that without His concurring aid, we shall succeed in this political building no better than the Builders of Babel."*

Our first and greatest President, George Washington, agreed with Franklin. He said: *"No People can be bound to acknowledge and adore the invisible hand which conducts the Affairs of men more than the People of the United States."*

Thomas Jefferson, too, believed that nations rose and fell before God. He said: *"And can the liberties of a nation be thought secure when we have removed their only firm basis, a conviction in the minds of the people that these liberties are of the Gift of God? That they are not to be violated but with his wrath?"*

The sentiments expressed by Franklin, Washington, and Jefferson were expressed almost universally by America's founders. From the founding of these United States and throughout most of our history, people (even our leaders) understood that "God governs in the affairs of men" (Franklin). We understood that it was not so much our military might, industrial strength, or financial stability, but divine blessing that secured our liberty. We believed that scriptural injunction: ***"The horse is prepared against the day of battle: but safety is of the LORD." (Proverbs 21:31) (KJV)*** However, it appears obvious that most Americans (including Christians), and especially most of our political leaders, have forgotten this principle. As a result, many of us are asking the question: *"Is the handwriting on the wall for America? Have our days been numbered by God? Is our republic finished? Will God divide and conquer our country?"* Many are suggesting that the signs indicate the answer is *yes.*

For one thing, we have a Federal Government that is totally out of control. The checks and balances that were built into our Constitution have been all but eviscerated. For the most part, the people have no real input into their governance anymore. Between Big Media, Big Business, and vote fraud, even honest and fair elections may be a thing of the past.

The American people cannot trust their government spokesmen—or the media that is entrusted with the task of keeping them honest—to tell them the truth. The dishonesty and duplicity of our political and business leaders have produced an almost universal distrust among the American people. We have been lied to so often that it is hard to remember when we were last told the truth by almost anyone in Washington, D.C., especially at the Executive level.

Willful ignorance has destroyed the Church in America today.

Of course, America's pastors and churches are in the unique position of being able to lead our people to a revival of honesty and integrity. Yes, they have the power to restore Biblical principles and Constitutional government to America's public life. However, it would first require that they step away from their own infatuation and preoccupation with money and power long enough to see the handwriting themselves. That they refuse to do so is another sign that the handwriting is already on the wall. One does not have to possess the gift of prophecy to read the signs. The handwriting is there as plain as day in letters large enough that even a blind man can read them.

Christians should not bury their heads in their theology books, however. *Instead of wringing their hands and simply waiting for Jesus to return, we need to get in the fight to restore our constitutional republic.* The foundation is still there and millions of people—churched and un-churched—are ready and willing to fight with us. Plus, who can tell what God will do *if we act in obedience to Him with serious effort?* He will restore liberty and independence in this land [—for He promised: If the people who are called by My name will humble themselves, and pray, and return to Me, then I will hear from heaven and restore their land.] (paraphrased).

As Patrick Henry said during our initial struggle for independence, "[W]e shall not fight our battles alone. There is a just God who presides over the destinies of Nations, and who will raise up friends to fight our battles for us. The battle, Sir, is not to the strong alone. It is to the vigilant, the active, and the brave."

Is the handwriting on the wall for America? Yes, it is. But that does not mean there is nothing we can do. We can do everything we should do, knowing that there is a God in Heaven who "presides over the destinies of Nations."

It would be a good thing to reread this chapter, and then kneel down and pray, because we indeed have enemies within the gates, and God is judging the way Christians respond. Listen to the wisdom of someone in 42 B.C. that gave a warning, Marcus Tullius Cicero stated something appropriate for all times: *"A nation can survive its fools and even the ambitious. But it cannot survive treason from within. An enemy at the gates is less formidable, for he is known and carries his banner openly. But the traitor moves amongst those within the gate freely, his sly whispers rustling through all the alleys, heard in the very halls of government itself. For the traitor appears not a traitor...he speaks in accents familiar to his victims, and he wears their face and their arguments, he appeals to the baseness that lies deep in the hearts of all men. He rots the soul of a nation, he works secretly and unknown in the night to undermine the pillars of the city, he infects the body politic so that it can no longer resist. A murderer is less to fear."*
"JESUS said, "For what is a man profited if he shall gain the whole world, and lose his own soul? Or what shall a man give in exchange for his soul?" (Matthew 16:26)

Chapter 2

Biblical Obedience

Listen carefully and ask the Holy Spirit for understanding as I quote God's Word:

"Fear God, and keep his commandments, for this is the whole duty of man." (Ecclesiastes 12:13

The way that we say something can be perceived differently than what was intended, in the minds of those that hear it. I was talking to my good friend Rusty Thomas recently. As we talked about the moral decay against God's laws, and the tyranny in our government that was supporting this decay, I brought up the phrase *"civil disobedience."* This has been used many times in History when those in control of government have been against God, family, and country. Rusty made a profound statement that hit on the truth of it. Though in the eyes of those in control, it may look like *"civil disobedience,"* when in reality, we must question what *"civil obedience"* has come to mean in our current secular Godless society. Perhaps now, *civil disobedience* can in reality be more truly *civil obedience,* lining up with the Word.

We are called to have *"Biblical Obedience."* We are always called to obey God and do good. So when man's laws go against God's laws, we are to obey God and do good which, in the eyes of those in control of government or the media, may be called *civil disobedience* or uglier things. *Biblical obedience* calls us to engage outside the four walls of the church, with love and forgiveness, but a manly firmness in the Word of God, with no compromise. In reality, this demonstrates the greatest love, because it will be used by God to keep souls from going to Hell for eternity.

Warning: The following knowledge could keep a soul out of Hell, and it would be a good time to pray that the Holy Spirit open your eyes and ears.

This leads us into an article by David Wilkerson, Pastor of Times Square Church in New York, sent to me by a great friend in Christ, R.L. Beasley, the editor of *"The Beacon,"* a newspaper that will bless you.

Pillow Prophets
David Wilkerson

"Ezekiel stood alone against all the false prophets of Israel. These prophets would have nothing to do with the message of righteousness and impending judgment. Instead, they prophesied an era of peace, ease, and prosperity.

Ezekiel 13 is the very word of Jehovah against preachers and prophets who accommodate people with flesh pleasing words they said were from the Lord. Their words were designed to make God's people comfortable in the face of impending judgment.

In fact, they were satisfied to prophesy good times ahead from their great houses and ivory beds of ease—they sought to provide a pillow for every elbow. *"Woe to those who apply pillows unto all elbows..." (Ezekiel 13:20)*

Ezekiel was horrified at the sight of prophets who had developed an art of making God's people comfortable. The Lord had said, "My people have set up idols in their hearts; they are brazenly setting up stumbling blocks in iniquity; they are all estranged from Me because of their idols" Ezekiel 14:1-5. The true word of the Lord was, *"Jehovah says—eat your bread with trembling, and drink thy water with grieving and fainting—and say unto the people, her land shall be emptied of its fullness, because of the violence—cities will be laid waste, the land made desolate—there shall be no more vain visions or flattering prophecies" (Ezekiel 12:17-24)*

While Ezekiel went about calling the people to humility and repentance, trying to prepare God's people for the soon coming judgments, these pillow prophets went about prophesying the dreams and imaginations of their own hearts. God had not spoken to them, even though they prefaced their predictions with, "Hear the Word of the Lord." **God said, "I did not send them: they do not speak for Me."**

They carried with them fancy pillows to place under every elbow for all who flocked to their false prophesies. They placed handkerchiefs on the heads of every one of their disciples, a statement to others that meant, "Nothing but good times ahead. I see nothing ahead but peace and luxury." They walked among the poor and sick, with a lace kerchief on the head, as a sign of their confidence in the message of the prophets of self indulgence and comfort. Ezekiel thundered the Word of God at them, as the masses congregated to hear their pleasant words. *"You see for God's people a vision of prosperity, when there is no prosperity, saith the Lord Jehovah" (Ezekiel 13:16)*

"You follow after your own imagination—when actually you have seen nothing." Ezekiel 13:3. The pillow prophets are still with us! They talk about the Word of God, about prophecy, and they salt their soothing messages with a lot of Scripture. But there is falseness in what they preach. They are not preaching the Cross or holiness and separation. They make no demands on their followers. They seldom speak of sin and

judgment. They abhor the very mention of suffering and pain. To them, the heroes of Hebrews were faithless cowards and penniless losers who were afraid to claim their rights

Like the pillow prophets of Israel, their one supreme desire is to promote luxurious lifestyles and make people comfortable in their pursuit of the good life. They are not speaking for God. All they are doing is passing out pillows—one for every elbow to every follower.

No wonder the crowds flock to sit under their message—it's painless. There is not the call of Christ to deny self and take up a cross.

What is the difference between pillow prophets and Jehovah's true prophets? The preacher or parishioner who doesn't know the difference is on dangerous ground. With so many going about gathering huge followings, it is imperative to have Holy Ghost discernment. The confused prophets must be exposed by truth. Most of them sound like sincere, Bible loving men of God. But the Lord has given His people infallible tests to prove what is true and what is false. We are to test every man and every message—by the whole Word of God.

Let me bring to your attention three characteristics of a true prophet of God:

1) *A true man of God is consumed with a vision of the Lord Jesus Christ. He has been so overwhelmed, so mastered by that glorious vision, he can speak of nothing else. He* preaches the whole counsel of God— as it relates to Christ.

God said of the false prophets: ***"Woe unto the deceiving prophets who follow after their own imaginations...they have seen nothing."*** (Ezekiel 13:3)

Yet of Moses, it was said: ***"By faith he forsook Egypt, not fearing the wrath of the king; for he endured, as seeing Him Who is invisible."*** (Hebrews 11:27)

Jesus said of Abraham: ***"Abraham rejoiced to see my day: and he saw it, and was glad."*** (John 8:5,6)

Stephen had a glorious vision of Him. And he said: ***"Behold, I see the heavens opened, and the Son of Man standing on the right hand of God."*** (Acts 7:5,6)

Ananias said to Paul: ***"The God of our fathers hath chosen thee, that thou shouldest know His will, and see that Just One, and shouldest hear the voice of His mouth."*** (Acts 22:14)

To His own disciples, Jesus said: "In a little while the world will see Me no more, but you will see Me." (John 14:17)

The one thing every one of these men of God had in common was their life-controlling vision of Christ the Lord. Christ was the great and only cause in their life. They saw Him through the eye of faith.

Moses willingly forsook the ease and prosperity of Egypt to suffer privation in a wilderness because he had been mastered by a vision of Christ. Nothing else mattered now, not even his dream of becoming a great deliverer. He saw beyond all human ambition. He was weaned from all that was earthly because he had seen

Christ. He could endure anything, for nothing on earth could compare with what his spiritual eyes beheld.

Abraham became totally detached from this world and willingly became a foreigner on earth, for his eyes were fixed on a city whose builder and maker was God. But best of all, he had seen a vision of Christ on His throne in that holy city. Never again would he settle for things temporal or earthly. His faith was built upon his continual vision of Christ. He rejoiced and was glad, for he had eyes for the invisible, the eternal, Christ!

The moment Paul saw Him everything else on earth became dung to him. The very moment Christ was revealed in him, he determined to know nothing else among men but his Lord. He gladly endured hardships, shipwreck, stoning, beatings, privations, imprisonment. None of these things moved him because he gloried in his vision of the Lord.

Any man of God who is tied to this earth or the things of earth has seen nothing. If he had a vision of Christ, if he was in constant union with Christ, he could preach of nothing else. He would stand before the crowds, proclaiming: *"I count it all loss—it's all dung! It is Christ and Him alone. He is all; He fills all things; He is my very life."*

Like Isaiah, the true man of God who sees the Lord, high and lifted up, will fall on his face and weep over his sins and the sins of God's people. Then he will be purged and go forth in the power of his awesome vision to preach Christ.

God warned Israel: *"The prophets are like foxes..."* In other words, some have no single eye focused on Christ alone, but they have eyes filled with covetousness. They spoil the vine, taking the best for themselves. They go their own way, feeding their own egos!

These self-seeking prophets claimed to have heard from God. Theirs, they claimed, was a prophetic word directly from heaven. *"They say Johovah saith, when Jahovah hath not sent them, and they caused others to hope that their word would be verified"* (Ezekiel 13)

The multitudes of God's people who run about to hear only soothing messages need to take a second honest look at what they are hearing and believing.

"Have ye not seen a deceiving vision and spoken a lying divination when you said Jehovah saith whereas I have not spoken." (Ezekiel 13:7)

"They have seduced my people, saying, Peace, when there was not peace." (Ezekiel 13:10)

Their message was, *"God told me all is well. No trouble ahead. Good times! No trial or tribulation. God's desire is that all be happy, prosperous and at ease."* **Jahovah calls that deception!** I don't think ministers are taking seriously enough the tragedy of preaching the wrong message. How dare we preach peace and endless good times to a nation and a people on the brink of judgment!

Israel's sin was about to explode in unbelievable fires of divine wrath. Ezekiel did not want to preach such a disturbing message, especially to a people who had heaped to themselves pillow prophets who went about telling God's people that all was well.

Listen to what God was trying to say to His people. *"Therefore thus saith the Lord Jehovah: like as the wood of the vine amongst the trees of the forest, which I have given unto the fire to devour, so have I given the inhabitants of Jerusalem. And I will set my face against them: from one fire shall they escape that another fire may devour them....I have set my face against them....I will make this land desolate, because they have trespassed a trespass, saith the Lord Jehovah." (Ezekiel 15:6-8)*

The people rejected the true Word of God. The masses ran off after their favorite teachers to hear the deceptive message: *"God is not that kind of God. He desires only the best for us all. Great peace and good times lay ahead. Don't listen to the old prophets of doom. God told me, right from His throne room that the best is yet to come."*

I ask you, what will those pillow prophets do when God begins to judge the sins of this nation and cut off its bread and its fullness? Think of the unprepared multitudes of sincere Christians who should be repenting of lukewarmness; who should be weeping because of compromise and covetousness; who should be forsaking all rather than accumulating.

Thank God the Holy Spirit is rising up a holy people who are sick of all the self-centered ministries, and their cry is: *"We would see Jesus."* The man-centered gospel cannot last much longer. A time of purging is ahead. We are heading into refining fires. While the covetous lounge on their beds of ease and comfort, themselves with luxuries, a remnant will break away and go out seeking the Bridegroom. Christ is going to reveal Himself to the humble, the poor in spirit, and the true Word of the Lord will flow forth with unction and power. Union with Christ will become the pearl of great price.

2) *The true man of God preaches and practices self denial. Compare this with what the pillow prophets focus on! God said of them,* ***"They pollute me among my people for handfuls of barley, and for morsels of bread....they lie to my people"*** *(Ezekiel 13:19) A modern translation is: "These pillow prophets have money on their minds. It has made liars of them."* Here is the full picture of a pillow prophet. *He lets his imagination run wild. He operates on the idea that prosperity will last forever. He builds on dreams and schemes. To do it, he needs money—lots of it. His need for money becomes the focus of ministry. He ends up telling lies to God's people to get it.* ***Then he pollutes it all by saying: "God told me."***

The message of Jesus Christ is painfully blunt—deny yourself and take up your cross.

"Then said Jesus unto his disciples: If any man will come after me, let him deny himself and take up his cross and follow me." *(Matthew 16:24)*

Self denial—is a foreign-sounding concept in this day of self-pampering and ease and self-esteem and "it's all about me" importance. The pillow prophets have rejected self-denial flat out. Self denial is the giving up and forsaking of all and everything that hinders the constant presence of Christ.

There is no merit in self-denial. We are saved and secured by grace alone. It is not to be entered into to earn benefits from God. But self-denial removes hindrances to constant communion with Christ. Paul said: ***"I bring my body under...and bring it under subjection, lest by any means, when I have preached to***

87

others, I myself should be a castaway." *(1 Corinthians 9:27)*

We are not bringing our bodies under control; our passions and appetites are not under subjection. Sensuous television programs now whet the appetites among Christians for pornography. Lust is nearly out of control, even in the ministry. Almost daily I hear of ministers that are spending hours viewing X-rated movies and cassettes.

Multitudes of God's people, including preachers of the gospel, waste precious hours lounging before the TV idol. Like Lot, our minds are getting vexed by the things we see and hear.

Food is becoming the narcotic of believers. We don't need cocaine or alcohol, we have a legalized sedative— food. Never in all of my ministry have I seen so many Christians with appetites out of control.

The deepest truth about self-denial goes beyond giving up material things. You can sell your TV, shun all erotic sights and sounds, and bring all appetites under control, and still not have denied self.

What Christ is calling for is a kind of devotion to Himself that expels everything in the heart that hinders. It is a commitment to becoming absolutely nothing before God and man. It is being able to say with Paul: *"I no longer live; it is Christ living in me."*

The world must lose its charm to us. We must die to all self-ambition, to all attachments to earthly things, until we can honestly say: *"I am dead to this world and all it represents. I no longer live."*

Physically alive, yes! But I must die to all that hinders my vision and love for Christ. Whatever it is, it must go. Lust? Self-made plans? Bitterness, grudges? Recognition, self-esteem? I must die to it all. I must bring it all to the cross and execute self-judgment.

Why is it that Christians who are about to die become so detached from the world and material and physical things? It's because eternity is in view—and it all pales in comparison to the joy ahead. Why can't we live like that all the time? Why not keep our minds fixed on Christ at all times?

3. *A true man of God has a holy boldness against sin— he never whitewashes evil. The pillow prophets have no foundation of holiness upon which to build. Ezekiel said:* **"Their foundation thereof shall be discovered."** *(Ezekiel 13:14)*

The pillow prophets were building walls with un-tempered mortar and painting the flaws over with whitewash. Worst of all, their message and manner: **"...grieved the hearts of the righteous because of their falsehood."** *(Ezekiel 13:22)*

And they "strengthened the hands of the wicked." God accused them of damning souls by ignoring sin. It grieved God that compromising children of God were being encouraged rather than exposed. Lightness about sin only confirmed them in their compromising.

God will not let any minister of the gospel grieve or trouble His chosen and devoted ones without His express permission. But neither will He permit prophets of ease to call evil good and pamper backslidden Christians who need to repent.

Certainly we are called to proclaim the gospel of grace, mercy and pardon. But that the man of God is also commanded to *"Lift up his voice, cry aloud, and spare not—showing my people their sins."*

Could it be we can't lift up a holy standard because of corruption in our own hearts? Have our own sins robbed us of holy boldness? Do we wink at the sins of others because of besetting sins in our hearts?

Do you know of a man of God who boldly thunders against sin? Does his message ring, not of legalism, but of deep personal purity? Then run to his feet—sit under his message, for he has the truth that will set you free. He is the true prophet of God, and he makes all other prophets tremble and fear. The pillow prophets despise him because he walks with truth in the inward parts.

Seek out a man of God who makes Christ real! One who makes you sit up and take notice that he has been with Jesus. One who convicts you for wasting time and for becoming earthly minded. One who will point a finger in your face, discern sin, and cry out: *"Thou are the man."* He is the one who truly loves you and looks out for your soul.

The pillow prophets are building their huge walls. They look very successful and blessed. But Jehovah says: *"Your walls shall fall. I will bring it all down with my stormy wind. I will demolish your wall and level it to the ground."* *(Ezekiel 13:11-14)*

God has told us that in these last days our young men shall see visions. Not of success, of prosperity or of great achievements. <u>There will be but one vision for all</u>—**CHRIST!**

Thank you, David Wilkerson, for being a bold man of God. We learn so much about God from you, dear brother in Christ.

Chapter 3

Minutemen United

"Ye that love the Lord, hate evil" (Psalm 97:10)

Your Command is to love God and hate evil. Did you hear that?
No evil can stand in the presence of God. If you love God, you
cannot compromise with evil. You do not love God, if you
endorse and love abortion, sodomy, or any radical religious lies
like Islam, or any other Eastern religion or the New Age
Religion, because all are evil and not of God. They are all
religions—not the relationship with the Almighty One True God,
and they can never be.

As I indicated when I started this book, I was blessed by all those
vessels that God put into my path who contribute so much to His
kingdoms work. Men that were once like the majority of
Christians today, that were once *traitors* to God by disobedience,
family, and country, through repentance and surrender to God,
they now obey Jesus as they run to the battle lines to stand
against the evil God and they hate, because of their love for the
Lord. They are part of a remnant that exists in the Christian
church of America. Pray for them, and seek to have them come
into your churches to give a warning from God's Word. They are
awaiting your call. Don't be known as a backslidden Pastor with
a dead pew-sitting, dormant flock. Call on these people who are
waiting to serve you so they can help refresh your ministry and
that of your church family.

These Christian leaders, and those from all walks of life, will
benefit from the vigilant watchmen that have been called to warn
the children. You find these **Minutemen United** in Christian
ministries that boldly proclaim the Word of God with no

compromise. Leaders in these organizations, Pass The Salt, America ASLEEP kNOw MORE, Operation Save America/Rescue, Abiding Truth, James Hartline Report, What's Right What's Left, Elijah, Restoring America, Vision America, Jericho Riders, and others, have no fear and do not Retreat. You can Google them on the internet and get immediate response from them.

As I ask you to listen to their words, know that some offense/conviction may take place within you, if any reader has any strongholds in their life that keep them from following the commands of Jesus. It has been said: *The sting in any rebuke is the truth.* These words are not for the faint-hearted. The majority of Christians sadly stop following Christ once they find out where He expects to take them. The men that will speak to you now, love Christ so much that they have a cross on their back—as Jesus commanded: ***Take up your cross and follow Me***. It is not pretty—this is grueling work—but the most fulfilling and rewarding work. Pray for these Gideons, Davids, Daniels, Esthers, Ruths, Peters, Pauls,and Johns. They understand what the ***men and women*** in the Bible did when it was their turn to say *yes* to God. They also understand the times and have said *yes* to God now, for this is their time. Just as God is waiting for each of you to say *yes* when your eyes open to recognize that it is now your time to work with and to support each other in the battle. It is very exciting to be in it.

The first *Minutemen United,* ***man*** of God, who all Christians and especially Christian leaders and pastors should pay close attention to, is Dr. Dave Daubenmire, Founder of Pass the Salt Ministries, a.k.a. "Coach Dave" and is a Christian Radio Talk Show host. Listen to the Good Lord speaking through his commentaries, then pray for him and join him and the others in the action, the remnant that understand the times. We will start with some things that Christian leaders and all Christians need to hear.

93

Good for Nothing Christianity
Dr. Dave Daubenmire

"Ye are the salt of the earth; but if the salt have lost his savor, wherewith shall it be salted, it is thenceforth good for nothing but to be cast out, and to be trodden under foot of men."
(Matthew 5:13)

(Author's note: In early Christian times, when salt had lost its usefulness, it was placed on the roads/pathways, for people to walk on.)

"Better warn you up-front. This is not for the easily offended. If you are looking to "feel good" you'd be better off reading something from Rick Warren or Joel Olsteen. And please don't send me any emails telling me how mean-spirited I am, that I need more love, or that I need to meet Jesus.

If that is your inclination, do us both a favor. Stop reading right now. There. You've been warned.

To steal a phrase from a popular radio-host, I need some duct tape. I really don't know how much more of this I can take.

Waah! Waah! Waah! Make them stop saying such bad things about Christianity. That is what I am hearing from the big-time Christian pundits. *"Boycott the advertisers, Write the networks. Call your congressman. Waaaah!"*

First it was the hub-bub a few years ago about Andres Serrano's "Piss Christ." You remember that, don't you? The picture of a crucifix of Christ submerged in a bottle of urine, funded by your tax-dollars through the National Endowment for the Arts.

Next was the piece of work by Nikos Kazantdazis, "The Last Temptation of Christ," which Martin Scorsese turned into a movie, and depicted a married Jesus getting it on with his wife Mary Magdalene.

Recently, we have weathered The Book of Daniel, an NBC mini-series depicting Christians as hypocritical and unbalanced.

And now, "The DaVinci Code, which many Christian pundits claim questions the deity of Christ. Millions of books have been sold and a feature movie has just been released.

"Waaaaah! Make them stop being mean!"

A few months ago, the world almost erupted into war over the unflattering depiction of Mohammed in a series of cartoons.

The Muslims took to the streets. They defended their (pretend) god. They threatened violence, even death to those who published the pictures. I don't approve of their tactics, but I respect their indignation. Major media blinked, newspapers and magazines refused to show the pictures and they wrote about the need to be "sensitive" to the Muslims concerns.

The reaction of the leaders of the two religions has been stark. While Christians retreated into their churches and sucked on their thumbs, the Islam leaders spoke out boldly and clearly in defense of their (pretend) god. The Muslims took to the streets. The Christians depended on Republicans.

It is time that modern Christians asked ourselves some hard questions. Why is it that the American media fears and protects Islam, but knocks itself out throwing mud at Christianity? What has happened in America that the media no longer fears the reaction of the Christian Church? Why do the media view us the way they do?

What happened to the salt? Have we lost our savor? Have we become, as Jesus warned, good for nothing?

Good for nothing Christianity—that's what the media sees. They see a Church that no longer fears God, so they no longer fear the Church. Can you imagine the reaction if someone had dared submerge the Muslim prophet (a liar and a lunatic) in a jar of urine? Cities would still be burning. Which commands more respect, a snarling bulldog or a lazy old basset hound?

Let's face it. Most of the unsaved-world sees us as weak, ineffective, money-grubbing hypocrites. Might as well face facts—we're void of savor, and trodden under by man.

Perception is reality. A wise man once said, "Your actions speak so loud I can't hear what your mouth is saying." Instead of being mad at the Christian bashers, perhaps we should start with the man in the mirror. Why is Christianity so mocked?

May I offer a few snapshots, a series of pictures stuck in the minds of those who don't understand us?

We fight amongst ourselves. Pastors don't work together, denominations think they have a corner on Truth, and we can't agree on what the Bible says. A house divided against its self cannot stand.

We strive for the things of this world. While we watch millions of the poor languish in the depravity, we've turned their care over to the government, while our churches and church leaders build opulent ministries, including turning basketball arenas into sanctuaries, oblivious to the condition of those around us. While the Islamofacists willingly lose their live for their (pretend) god, Christians aren't willing to lose their "stuff" for theirs (the Alpha and the Omega).

We ignore the beam in our own eye. Fighting to "defend" marriage from the gays, we look the other way at the mess Christian heterosexuals have made of "one man-one woman for life." We declare the sanctity of life, yet warehouse our parents in nursing homes. <u>We uncompromisingly-defend our denomination's "theological purity," while we send our children to government schools where they grow in the Devil's theology.</u> We declare we are "one nation under God" but act like He is one god under the nation.

We defend the ungodly fruit of Republicanism. More has been done to destroy America under this Republican administration than any president since FDR, all with a wink and nod from our Christian leaders (are the Christian church leaders giving aid and comfort to enemies against God, family, and country on purpose or by ignorance). The defenders of Republicanism chortle "the Democrats are worse," because they have a Communist platform) as if being the lesser of two evils is somehow honorable. (both parties have been infiltrated by evil—would Jesus support evil at any level?)

We accept sin in the Church. We idolize sports, possessions, and our children. We seek "all of these things" more than we "seek first the Kingdom." We covet the same things our un-saved neighbors covet. We lie and cheat on the job. We dishonor our Lord, the Sabbath, our wedding vows, and our parents. We tithe to the Cable TV company but hoard money from those who do the Lord's work. We have a "form of Godliness, but deny the power thereof." We take the name of the Lord in vain by accepting Him as Savior, but not as Lord. The god of self sits on the throne.

I could go on, but you get the point.

So, what is the image that the Church is projecting to our enemies? Do they see a Church sold out to the cause of Christ, or a Church sold out for the material blessings of Christ? What images do Sunday morning preachers on your local TV project? Is it a *"best-life-now, Jesus-wants-to-bless-you, turn-the-other-cheek, Christian-psychology,"* kind of Gospel? Or is it a *"fall-*

on-your-knees, repent-of-your-wicked ways, be-ye-holy, judgment-begins-in-the-house-of-God," kind of Christianity? (What is your church leadership involved in, because the feel good preachers are giving aid and comfort to the enemy, and you need to pray for them to change, *"or dust your feet off"* and go somewhere where Jesus' command to follow Him is lived)

Who do the media think is more committed to their faith? Muslims who pray five times a day as they fall prostrate before Allah (a pretend god), or Christians who pray on the way to their Sunday morning Little League baseball game? Those who will strap a bomb to their body to die for their god, or Christians who retreat into the safety of the church to be hidden by theirs? (Are church leaders giving aid and comfort to the enemy on purpose or are they just (backslidden) cowards?)

I am always struck by something that David said before he acted and dropped Goliath in his tracks: **(I Samuel 17:26b)** **"For who is this uncircumcised Philistine, that he should defy the armies of the living God?"**

David wasn't upset that they were defying God; he knew God could take care of Himself. David was concerned with the *"armies of God,"* that they would allow their God to be spoken of in such a way.

To put David's statement into modern language, **"Ain't anybody gonna stick up for Him?"**

If the Church won't call evil what it is, if the Church won't rebuke the wicked, if the Church won't stand for Christ, how can we expect the world to fear our God? **If the Church won't** clean up its own mess, how can we demand others clean up theirs? **If the armies of God** won't stand up to the giants of the day, why should they respect us? **(If the Churches won't, why should God go on protecting us, in our disobedience?)**

(Psalm 94:16) "Who will rise up for me against the evildoers? Or who will stand up for me against the workers of iniquity?

One final question: If you weren't already a Christian, what is it about modern Christianity that would make you want to join?

Good for nothing Christianity, that's what the world sees: Salt without savor, easily trod upon.

Oh, Christ is so much greater than we have allowed Him to be! *"Waaaaah!"* (End)

Listen! Pastors, Church Leaders, Ministry Leaders, God is speaking to you in love to turn away from man's wisdom, all those things that give aid and comfort to the enemy of God, family, and nation. Even a loving rebuke can be perceived as offensive (stings) to those that do not want to step out of their comfort zone. Since you have taken on the role of teacher, you are called to know that there is only One True Teacher, and if you do not teach and work His way, then you again are giving aid and comfort to the enemies of God, family, and country. You must heed His call to you during this great time of need for your service to Him. Jesus calls you to be a *man* of God, not a male that looks for an excuse to cower. Listen to His question to you and all Christians*: "Why call me Lord, Lord, and then not do what I say"?*

Knowing that Jesus said that, knowing He is the Son of God, knowing that he is indeed our Savior, but also knowing He is Lord and we will some day kneel in His presence, do you want to have that knowledge and then have to answer that question? If we continue not doing what Jesus says enables the enemies to make swift and easy progress in their evil works and goals in our God-given nation.

Jesus was also a *man*. He offended the immature males. He loved the Father and wanted those that had been given to Him, and all people, to know the Truth. Jesus wants to gather each of you to Him, as He loves you so much, and He wants you to hear His words so that you will lead as a *Mature Christian Man*. The undisciplined male leadership who lacks devoted and dedicated servanthood is the reason the enemies of God, family, and country can look on Christianity in America as a **Dead Faith**. At this time, they expect no confrontation as they work out their New Age Religion for the masses and wicked plans, in total dedication, for the nation. There hasn't been any battle for themthus far—they just march strongly and boldly on—which is what we are supposed to be doing. I pray that you are convicted and become a dedicated, surrendered **man**, *putting on the whole armor of God as you join the army of God.* If you refuse this, the following commentary by Coach Dave may, again, offend you.

Dead Faith
Dr. Dave Daubenmire

(James 2:20) *But wilt thou know, O vain man, that faith without works is dead?*

Do you consider work a bad thing? Isn't it something we all do to "earn a living?" If you were recruited and trained by a CEO wouldn't you be expected to do something to earn your reward?

Why then is work such a bad word in relationship to our faith? Can you imagine telling your boss that you don't have to produce anything because you have been hired "by grace?" Grace got you hired alright, but you have to work if you want to be paid.

Spiritual welfare, living off of the efforts of others: That is how most Christians live out their faith. Church is the one place you can be a member and never have to do anything. It is sort of like a Greyhound bus. Get your ticket to Heaven, and "leave the driving to us."

"It is by grace, Coach, how you get to Heaven. It is a free gift. You don't have to earn your salvation. Jesus purchased you at the cross," they tell me.

OK. So, why did Jesus purchase me? If it is all about getting to Heaven, why did He leave me here? Why doesn't He take me now and set me on His trophy case?

For we are His workmanship, created in Christ Jesus for good works, which God prepared beforehand that we should walk in them" (Ephesians 2:8-10) Created for good works? Hmmm.

(James 2:17-18) *"Even so faith, if it hath not works, is dead, being alone. Yea, a man may say, Thou hast faith and I have works: shew me thy faith without thy works, and I will shew thee my faith by my works..*

What does faith look like? It must be possible for us to see it, or Paul would not have asked us to "show" him our faith. We all have faith (Romans 12:3), but is yours dead or alive?

I'm not talking about salvation. That is a free gift, one you cannot earn. No my friends, we're talking about faith. Salvation is not faith. It is the fruit of faith. Confessing with your mouth, believing in your heart brings salvation. Actions are evidence of faith.

Works are an outward expression of what you believe. We will be saved by grace, but judged by our works. You do have works, you know? The question is, will your works endure? (Are your works and/or lack of them giving aid and comfort to the enemies of God, family, and country?)

"If anyone's work which he has built on it (faith) endures, he will receive a reward. If anyone's work is burned, he will suffer loss; but he himself will be saved yet so as through fire." **(I Corinthians 3:11-15)** Receive a reward? Hmmmm. I thought it was by grace?

I smell smoke.

"And I saw the dead, small and great, standing before God, and books were opened. And another book was opened, which is the Book of Life. And the dead were judged, each one according to his works." (Rev. 20:12-13) Judged by works? You gotta be kidding?

I was wondering the other day what Heaven will be like. Will my dog be there? Will I actually see my Dad? Will Peter really be standing at the gates? Are there Gates?

Will there really be a *"crowd of witnesses there?"* (Hebrews 12:1) If so, witnesses to what? Witnesses testify. What will the witnesses testify about? Could it be works?

I love to get together with some of my friends and tell stories. Each guy brings his own story, his own perspective on what he witnessed. Reminiscing is fun and it solidifies a group's special bond.

Imagine you're in Heaven sitting around a campfire (probably where the works are being burned) and you notice a familiar face reflecting the light of the dancing flames.

"Hey! Aren't you Moses?" you ask the majestic looking man, as he nods his head. *"Man, tell me your story. What was it like to see God part the Red Sea? Weren't you scared of the chariots? What about all of the people grumbling in the desert? How did you put up with it? And the frogs...and locusts...What did the death angel sound like as it passed over? Wow, Moses. I got to hear your story."*

"And aren't you David? What was it like to kill Goliath? Where did you learn to use a slingshot? How did it feel to cut off that dude's head? Did you really kill a lion and a bear with your bare hands?"

"Samson? Oh my goodness! What was it like to pull those pillars down? Was Delilah really that beautiful? How could you let her trick you like that?"

"Daniel—Oh! Danie!. Man you had guts. What made you open the window and defy the authorities? How did it feel to walk down the runway to the lions den? Were you scared? Did you really sleep like a baby? Tell me at least that you kept one eye open!"

We will hear the stories of God's heroes—Saints known, admired, and made famous by their works.

For centuries we will sit around and listen to the tales, the stories of the great men of faith, testified to by the crowd of witnesses that are present. Your heart will leap out of your chest as the stories of courage, conviction, and self-sacrifice are re-lived. And then all eyes will turn to you. Shadrach, Meshach, and Abednego, will be there. Stephen, the nameless Saints of Hebrews 11, and those martyred for their stand for Christ will all look your way.

"So, tell us your story. What did you do when you were on earth? If we remember right you were there at one of the most cataclysmic times in history. Mothers were killing their unborn children, homosexuals were demanding to be married, they were teaching God's children lies in school, and they were even attempting to remove the mention of the name of God from the nation. What did your faith cost you? What works did you perform for Christ?"

"Me?" you'll embarrassingly respond, as the eyes of the martyrs burn in on you. *"Well, let me see. I gave to missions, paid my tithe, served as an usher, and gave to the building fund. You see, when I was on earth, we were all waiting to be rescued by the rapture, and we weren't much interesting in fighting. We were taught that the end was near and that there wasn't anything we could do about it. Plus, we had a government that didn't allow us to mix religion with work,"* (that will surely cause Daniel to perk up). *"Much of our time was spent reading books about living a better life, our pastor suggested them, and we were learning to be more accepting and diverse. Besides, we had so much more to lose than you all did—we had houses, and cars, and IRAs, and vacations, and our reputations—and our children....."*

Allow me to be frank. Someday they are going to dig a hole, put you in a box, and cover you with dirt. Your big house, nice cars, reputation and worldly riches will be left behind. All that will endure is what you did for Christ.

Hebrews 11 is the Faith Hall of Fame. <u>It is a litany of men and women remembered not for what they said or believed, but for what they did.</u>

Isn't it interesting that in our churches today we are encouraged to *"share our faith?"* Paul said to ***"SHOW"*** *it.*

A picture is worth a thousand words.

(Matthew 5:16) "Let your light so shine before men, that they may see your good works, and glorify your Father which is in heaven."

Want to glorify God? Show me your works.

(John 9:4) "I must work the works of Him that sent me, while it is day: the night cometh, when no man can work."

It's getting darker and darker. It's time to get to work. (end)

No one can tell it or help us hear and see it quite like you, Dave.

In speaking to congregations (around the nation, our having been invited by their Pastor to do so), the first action that I always request that they do is to pray for their Pastor and leaders. Satan is aware that if he can influence the Shepherd that the sheep will be led astray, or lulled to sleep, which will enable him to do the work that he does, very well—kill, steal, and destroy. Let your sheep entrusted to you be witnesses that you were truly a *man* that led into the battles instead of a male-child that talked.

The times are so urgent, and so many children, and young adults, are going to hell daily, and you can make a difference in the number headed to hell if you will actually do what He says. Listen for His voice. Jesus is asking that you no longer give aid and comfort to the enemy by inaction. Invite our group to minister at your church as a starter in the process.

Wait a minute! Did I say that people are going to hell daily? Are there some pastors that would claim to be Christian leaders, yet by their action or inaction could be looked at as *traitors?* This inaction is, actually, actively working with and for the enemy— which is *treason.* Do Pastors have some responsibility for what is happening now, to the next generation in our nation and schools, which would reflect on where those they could have touched may spend eternity? One of the popular silent messages taught by some so-called Christian church leadership is to call Jesus a liar by saying there are many paths to heaven (inactivity, holy non-judgmentalism, non-accountability, fear), and some even say that everyone goes to heaven. These people aid and comfort the enemies of God, family, and country and insult the name of Christ by claiming that false teaching. Where will Christians who are taught these untruths and their leaders be when they die? How about I share some insights on Heaven and Hell. I will once more let you hear from this sold out warrior for Christ.

Does Everyone Go to Heaven?
Dr. Dave Daubenmire

You don't hear much about hell anymore. It is not a very popular subject. In today's *"Who am I to judge?"* America, it is unusual to hear a Pastor speak on this most important of all issues.

Because of the influx of Humanism into the Church it seems as if most of the messages that we hear today focus on how Christianity can make your journey here on earth a little more enjoyable. I contend that seeker-sensitive churches are a good thing. We are all seeking. My concern is not that the churches are seeking the seekers, but what are they seeking them for? This brings us to the unavoidable question: "What is the purpose of the cross?"

The recent abduction of two Fox News reporters by Palestinian extremists and their alleged conversion to Islam really caught the eye of the world. Many of the radio talk-show hosts focused on the "conversion" to Islam of Steve Centanni and his cameraman Olaf Wiig. I listened in amazement as I heard caller after caller explain why they too would have "converted" in order to save their skin. In a society where we worship entertainment and those who provide it, it is frightening that even those who call themselves *"Christian"* do not really understand what that term means. Is it possible to deny Christ and go to Heaven?

Jesus died on a cross, not to give us a better life here, although that might be a by-product of His crucifixion, but to give us a path to Heaven. Why do Christians call Him *"the Savior?"* If He died on the cross to "save" sinners, what is it He has saved us from?

The answer is obvious, but rarely mentioned. Jesus died on the cross not to save us *TO* Heaven, but to save us *FROM* Hell!

Perhaps the question the seeker-sensitive churches, as well as the tradition-worshiping mainstream ones, need to ask those sitting in the pews is this one.

"Does everyone go to Heaven?"

Hell is the farthest thing from the minds of Americans. In fact, I have heard the mantra many times that *"this is hell right here on earth."* Funny, that isn't what

Christianity teaches. No, most "Christians" today think that they are going to go to Heaven because they are "a good person," or that they "go to church," or that they "try to do what is right," or my favorite, *"I was born a Christian."* How can any Christian study the Bible and come to that conclusion?

Right there is the answer. Christians today don't study the Bible. They take for granted what others have told them about it. The fructification of Christ, the central event of Christianity, is not understood by most church goers. Christ died to save us from our sins and an ultimate eternity in Hell. That message is lost on most Christians today.

Forever is a long time. A man once explained it to me this way. If a bird were to land on a beach and pick up a piece of sand and fly away to the farthest star in the universe and drop it off, and then return to the beach and pick up another piece and carry it off to that same star, that would take a long time. But imagine if that same bird were to repeat that trip until he had carried every piece of sand on every beach, and on every desert, to that far away star, how long that would take? And yet, we still would not have begun to touch eternity. Yes, forever is a long time.

Where will you spend it?

There is hope for America, but that hope lies only in the cross of Calvary. **Jesus told us, "And as Moses lifted up the serpent in the wilderness, even so must the Son of man be lifted up: That whosoever believeth in him should not perish, but have eternal life. For God so loved the world, that he gave his only begotten Son, that whosoever believeth in Him should not perish, but** *have everlasting life. For God send not his Son into the world to condemn the world; but that the world through Him might be saved. He that believeth on Him is not condemned; but he that believeth not is condemned already, because he hath not believed in the name of the only begotten Son of God. (John 3:14-18)*

The American culture today is hell-bent (sorry) on convincing you that *"I'm OK, You're OK,"* when in fact we are not! America is sick because Americans are sick. We are sin-sick, whistling past the graveyard, oblivious to the impending doom waiting at the end of our journey. We are a nation of "Christians" careening towards hell—truly living our best life now. Not concerned about eternal life? How about eternal death?

Sorry, but someone has to speak the Truth.

That brings me back to Steve Centanni and the talk-radio crowd. If this life is all there is, if Christianity is nothing more than one of the world's great religions, if our purpose here on earth is only to enjoy our life here on earth, then we are, as Paul said, *"of all men most miserable."*

I pray you will never have to make a choice between claiming Christ and dying, or denying Christ and living. If confronted with a sword will your set of religious moral codes give you something to die for? Is living a "good life" really what it is all about?

If you really knew Christ you would never deny Him. If you are merely following a religion then you are not a Christian. Christianity is not a Religion. *It is a relationship with the triune God.* Would converting to Islam to save this life on earth really be worth it? Would you trade an eternity in Hell for a few more years here? What if Steve Centanni had been beheaded after he converted? Where would he be today?

The Bible is filled with the names of those who did not flinch, and did not bow in the face of death. Hebrews 11 lists the *Faith Hall of Fame*, those who did not deny Christ, even though it cost them their lives.

Let's assume for a moment that Jesus is real and that He really did die for our sins. Let's also assume that what He said in Matthew 10: *"But whosoever shall deny me before men, him will I also deny before my Father which is in Heaven,"* is the Truth. Let's assume that there is a Heaven to gain and a Hell to shun, and let's assume that Jesus IS who He says He is, and that He IS the only way to the Father.

"And fear not them which kill the body, but are not able to kill the soul: but rather fear him which is able to destroy both soul and body in hell. Are not the two sparrows sold for a farthing? And one of them shall not fall on the ground without your Father. But the very hairs of your head are all numbered. Fear ye not therefore, ye are of more value than many sparrows. Whosoever therefore shall confess me before men, him will I confess also before my Father which is in heaven." (Matthew 28:33)

Jesus said: *"I am the way, the Truth and the Life. No one comes to the Father except by me."* (John 14:6) I think He meant it.

You shall know the Truth and the Truth shall make you free. Do you KNOW Him? Have you received Him into your heart, or are you burdened down with a "moral code" that you can never quite live up to?

Yep. Everyone is going to Heaven. Unfortunately, not everyone is going to stay.

Death awaits us all at the end of this earthly journey. Hell is real. What will you do with Jesus? (end)

Now stop and passionately pray for your Christian Church leaders, because they will deny Christ rather than physically die, just like Peter did, if they are not filled with the strength of the Holy Spirit. In denying Christ, they will spiritually die. So death will come in one way or another. Pray also that the Holy Spirit will give them the strength to be true *men*-servants of God that boldly proclaim Christ and lead their flock into the battles that rage for the souls of His children, holding up HIS banner, and engaging the enemies of God, family, and country.

Jesus has already given the command to follow Him. We are always very much aware of how much He loves us—this is something we are told over and over again—how much do we love Him? As a Christian Church or Ministry Leader, if you have been a *traitor* by your actions or inactions, and you are sorry for what you have done or failed to do, no matter how small a part you played, and are burdened by the souls that are going to hell because of your neglect, ask Him for forgiveness, and Jesus will tell you to go and sin no more. Say yes to Jesus, pick up your Cross, and make some life-stories that they can talk about in Heaven for eternity. Your eternity and the eternity of those you shepherd are depending on your choice.

Remember these words of Jesus: *"He that is not with me is against me; and he that gathers not with me scatters." (Luke 11:23)* There is deep and profound truth in His statement.

Chapter 4

Worldviews: Comprehensive and Exclusive
TRAITORS WITHIN

"Be ye not unequally yoked together with unbelievers: For what fellowship hath righteousness with unrighteousness? And what communion hath light with darkness? And, what concord hath Christ with Be'-li-al? Or what part hath he that believeth with an infidel? And what agreement hath the Temple of God with idols? Ye are the Temple of the living God. As God has said, I will dwell in them, and walk in them and I will be their God, and they shall be my people. Wherefore come out from among them and be ye separate." (II Corinthians 7:14-17)

America, once a strong Christian nation, was a beacon of light to the world, but has been infiltrated by *traitors* against God, family, and nation. This enemy that is within is rotting the nation internally, and has been aided and comforted, sadly, by Christian Churches, Christian Teachers, and Christian Parents. Ironically, by not committing to change our nation by battling the enemy within, these Christians are truly enemies of our Nation, too. But this can be changed. We can help to expose the enemy and shine light on its deceptive practices and its goals for those willing to see. If your aid and comfort has been because of ignorance, you join most everyone that has gone before you for decades. The enemy has been exceedingly, subversively deceptive, with hidden agendas, unwilling to be seen by the masses of Christians or unbelievers. The enemies have made enormous progress because of the unwillingness of our pastors to confront them in a battle for truth, morality, and keeping God as the foundation of our nation. What culpability do Christian leaders and lay Christians in every walk of life have in giving aid and comfort to the enemy, *traitors* if you will, which furthers the worldviews of anti-Christian, anti-family, and anti-country factions and organization and politicians, that continue to cause death and decay?

A worldview is comprehensive in that it is part of every element of society and it is exclusive in that it cannot co-exist with other world views. Cultures are formed by the *worldview* that is embraced or forced upon the peoples. The only *culture of life* is connected to the Christian Biblical *worldview.* All other *worldviews* are cultures of decay and death. In the United States we were once a great nation because our culture of life embraced and was driven by the faith of Christianity and was influenced by the Christian Biblical *worldview.* Today Christians are influenced by the culture of death, brought into being by the Secular Humanist Socialist infiltration into all parts of American society of *worldviews* against God, family, and country. We will look at the enemy, who are the players, and what is necessary for the future safety of the souls of our posterity. *Indifference* will be the cause of further decay and death, and it is touching and will continue to touch every family.

The Primary Enemy of a Christian America is Satan. Under his influence are Atheistic international one-world globalist economists and bankers, who support the Atheistic and Pagan Marxist Communism/Socialism, Humanism, The New Age Globalism and Islam. Under these you will find their dupes. Here are a few organizations: American Civil Liberties Union (ACLU), National Education Association Teachers Union (NEA) that dictates the socialist agendas via K-12 core-curriculum (in every subject/theme) in public schools, American Association of University Professors (AAUP) that continue this subversion on college and university campuses, Planned Parenthood Federation of America (abortion mills) (PPFA), Council on American-Islamic Relations (CAIR), Americans United for the Separation of Church and State, Southern Poverty Law, People for the American Way, Students for Democratic Society, numerous radical Homosexual Organizations, American Defense League

(ADL), Democratic Party, The Sacred Cow of Government Education—the U.S. Department of Education, National Organization of Women (NOW) and many other radical feminist organization, A.L.A., socialists, liberals, progressives, collectivists, some liberal churches that embrace the agendas of these organizations, Liberation Theology and their Social(ist) Justice programs, environmentalists, globalists, and some infiltration of wolves into the neo-con Republican party. These are some groups that are enemies against God, family, and nation.

The dangerous element of Socialism/Communism is that to an *unbeliever* it is a very appealing compassionate-appearing ideology—they are unaware that it is disguised under the Atheist Religion. For *believers,* they are sold the bill of goods that Communism/Socialism fit like a "hand in glove" movement—it is not until later, that the believer realizes he has been sucked into a movement that claims later that, "really, to be a Communist/Socialist, one must give up most of his Christian beliefs—ultimately all of them if they wish to remain a member. This is how so many caring people are sucked into these organizations. They truly believe they can create peace on earth. Without the indwelling of God's Holy Spirit, they are, as Jesus said: *"Blind and Deaf"* to the deception until it is too late. What they cannot see is that they and their families will have to live under tyrannical violent slave-dictatorship, too, along with all the rest they cause to suffer under it. I would not want to live with their consciences once they realize their goals have been accomplished. Since they refuse to know God's Word, they cannot have His wisdom or truth. Rebelling and refusing to accept the Lord, the One True God, they are easily lead astray and begin to think they can create a utopian peace on this earth— in the world—on this planet. **They are the enemy's army—and it must be asked:** *"Where is the army of God?"*

The majority of Christian leaders and Christian laity have given aid and comfort to one or more of these enemies, because of wrongful action, inaction, fear, ignorance, not knowing what to do, and/or sleep. Perhaps if this is mentioned over and over—which you can see that I do—it will sink into the minds and hearts of God's people. Repetition is helpful in internalizing and memorizing a fact. Christians need to be brainwashed with their Christian duties, too. Because of the enormity of this cancer within our country, our only hope is for Christian leaders and their flocks to repent, surrender, obey Christ, and restore Jesus as the foundation of this once great country. And this will not happen without intense, passionate involvement and dedicated devotion by God's chosen people/servants, who are willing to work under Christ's leadership, and His Holy Spirit's counsel. *"If My people who are called by My name* (that's us, folks) *will humble themselves and pray and seek My Face, and turn from their wicked ways* (inactivity and ignoring His command can be wicked, too) *then I will hear from heaven and heal their land."*

Here are some Communist goals: Promoting Homosexual Lifestyle goals (33 different abnormal lifestyles) via NEA's mandated pro-homosexual curriculum, K-12. Likewise, militant and radical Homosexual Organizations and NEA Teachers as well as AAUP Professors Unions are devoted and dedicated to the Liberal Socialist Democratic Party and donate generously to their campaigns, while not supporting conservative politicians at all. These Socialist politicians, in turn, owe many favors to their generous supporters, which furthers this death-to-our-nation cause.

Supporting and furthering the Pro-Islamic-Fascism goals will also help these unions to produce the future Communist/Socialist/Progressivist/Collectivist/Environmentalist/Globalist (call them whatever they wish to be called from one year to the next—we must stay "on" to them and know who they hide behind!) One-World Dictatorship through rewritten History/Geography texts used in public schools. Four decades of this planned deception has been very effective. Socialists/Communists are very patient and very hard-working—and *extremely deceptive—always*

working subversively, destroying from within! They have to be!
If the general public knew what has happened/is happening to
our country they, at this point, might run and hide. Our silence
has helped them tremendously.

In addition, all of the previously mentioned groups' agendas are
Socialist and these are front organizations to promote
socialist/communist goals, slowly at first and now fastly eating
up and chipping away one freedom after another that we have
always enjoyed. Just now, after years of this we wring our hands
and are beginning to see *"the writing on the wall."*

Socialists/Communists have seduced unknowing gullible
Christians through *Social Justice and Liberation Theology*
ideologies and talk which is Socialism/Communism and even
many in the evangelical community now are being manipulated
into the movement(s), because they have rebelled and/or refused
to be warned of the anti-God philosophies of these groups. These
groups with their false compassionate caring are very appealing
to un-churched or mildly-churched people. Therein lays the
danger. This happens because Pastors have not been warning
their flocks and Socialists/Communists have convinced many un-
discipled Christians to take part. Pray that God will help you see
and then give you the strength to take the actions necessary to
stop giving aid and support to the enemies of God, family, and
country.

Added to the above Communist/Socialist goals that are
constantly, feverishly and passionately, ongoing, are those goals
that have been already fulfilled These are: Steering children into
the total degradation/decadent lifestyles they have produced
through sex education in the National Education Association
Public School mandated curriculum. In addition, they have
taught four decades of our children to "hate America and
everything about her" including the Constitution. They
manipulate and brainwash the minds of our children K-12
incrementally unbeknownst to parents, totally submerging them

in the Socialist philosophy of one-world global society—one-world religion—one-planet-under-man ideology—as core-curriculum in every subject (now called themes). Included in their curriculum is the intentional dummying down of our children (50% dropping out of school and not graduating high school) so that they will only be left with the ability to obey the Nanny State and be ruled by an iron fisted dictator. As God as my witness, this has truly happened—all the while conservatives wonder why we lose so many elections these days. Simply put, any one under 45 who has had nothing but a public school indoctrination-education, absent any Christian influence, is a *Liberal Democrat Voter!*

*Pastors! There should be no mystery in this outcome for you, if you have been paying any attention at all to the National Education Association Teachers Union and the Federal Government ownership of the public schools. First and foremost, our Pastors should have been aware and warning their congregants for four decades! Socialism DEMANDS atheism! You should know that! You should combat it! The souls of our children are **in your hands first**, and **then your congregants**! God is watching. God is allowing the enemy to gain ground because His people are doing nothing! The Old Testament is full of God's wrath toward His people and their nations when His people do not stand for His righteousness and by so doing they participate in the enemies' follies. His wrath is meted out always in response to His people's laziness, rebellion and stiff-necked slothfulness.*

Congressional Record—Appendix pp.A34-A35. January 10, 1963. *Current Communist Goals* put together by a top FBI agent and brought to Congress by Mrs. Nordman.

Mr. Herlong. Mr. Speaker. Mrs. Patricia Nordman of DeLand, FL., is an ardent and articulate opponent of communism who has been alerting the public to the dangers of communism in America.

At Mrs. Nordman's request, I include in the Record, under unanimous consent, the following *"Current Communist Goals."* (The author will extract some of these communist goals of the culture of death to our nation. They are being realized in America because of a growing Communist influence in all three branches of government, infiltration of both major parties with dominate control of the Democratic party, indoctrination in the government controlled school system, and Christian leadership and lay support through ignorance or prior indoctrination and propaganda.)

Goal #11. Promote the U.N. as the only hope for mankind. If its charter is rewritten, demand that it be set up as a one-world government with its own independent armed forces. (This is being supported by some in all three branches of Government and some in both political parties, the government school system supports this in their indoctrination, and Christian leaders have been inactive except for a remnant.)

Goal #12. Resist any attempt to outlaw the Communist Party. (The ones that came over on the Mayflower would have already tarred and feathered them and sent them packing. But Christians today are silent.)

Goal #13. Do away with all loyalty oaths. (Ruth Bader Ginsberg and some of the other communist traitors in the judiciary gave a loyalty oath to support and uphold the Constitution of the U.S. but have looked to put forth their own whims and agenda instead, Ginsberg also has started a precedent to go to the international community/courts instead of the Constitution, when she worked to overturn the Sodomy laws in 2003. She was an attorney for the A.C.L.U. and put in place by the Democrats to further the Communist agenda.)

Goal #15. Capture one or both of the political parties in the United States. (In 1972 in a Communist publication, the communist leader spoke of working with the liberals in the Democrat party for 25 years. And spoke of how Lenin said it was their duty to take positions of influence in the legislature.) The Communists have been very successful in determining the platform of the Democratic party to further their goals. It has happened progressively/incrementally as the Christians have been sleeping or convinced to join their ranks. Christians should pray and then look at how their platform consistently supports evil that is against God, family, and country. Be aware also, that the Republican party has also now been infiltrated with liberal agendas, although the influence is with more stealth as they seek to mask themselves whenever possible to carry out their goals.

Goal #16. Use technical decisions of the courts to weaken basic American institutions by claiming their activities violate civil rights. (Judges across the country have been making decisions against God, the family, and the constitution, some controlled by the communist agenda, and the Christians have been sleeping or convinced that it can't happen here.)

Goal #17. Get control of the schools. Use them as transmission belts for socialism and current Communist propaganda. Soften the curriculum. Get control of teachers and professors union associations. Put the party line in textbooks. (What a success they have had in goals 15, 16, & 17. They have softened the curriculum and dumbed down our nation to being almost at the very end of the world list in intelligence and literacy. We're so sorry, Lord, we used to be first when You were still with us and when Your people cared.)

Since *the 1960's* they have controlled and *become* the leadership in the N.E.A. and Federal Education Department. The government school indoctrination of our children has: socially engineered and taught them to kneel to a one world community; not only tolerate, but *approve of and accept* homosexuality and encouraging students to "try it;" and force-fed the *unproven theory* of evolution education into them—parents liking it or not.

They have skillfully and forcefully eliminated God from the minds of Christian children who are attending the public schools, through their Atheist Secular Humanism Religion themes.

All three branches of government and both political parties support this sacred-cow-idol of government public school education K-16, and the majority of Christians in leadership and those under their influence, have been blinded for various reasons, in this regard. The educational system now in place is the indoctrinating/brainwashing establishment (liberal military campground) for the current and future recruitment and training of Liberal Left Voters—our children—like it or not—without our permission or in most instances, without our knowledge. **Hitler promised:** *"I'll control the schools and I'll own Germany."* He not only said it, he did it! The Communist Liberal Left educational elite salivate as they so easily use the educational system to further their agenda and reach their silent revolution goal, with nary a whisper from the Christian Church, to combat this evil. It is Atheism folks—if Christians don't stand up and fight to protect our children and demand that our country remain "one nation under God," who will?

The kicker is that the Christians not only willingly give their children to this system that is anti-Christian, anti-family, and anti-country, we actually pay them to indoctrinate the children in a climate that leads them, and thereby our nation, to hell. And we keep on paying them—more and more and more. They have totally broken our educational system *purposefully* and are now ready and demanding to "rebuild" it according to the *gospel of Socialism's final stage*. At the rate the Christian Church is accommodating them by their lack of involvement and shameful uselessness, it won't be long until the dictator is well in place in our nation. It will be too late then, Pastors! The souls you were responsible for will be lost. Where, oh where are the alert and caring Pastors of the flocks?

Goal #20. Infiltrate the press. Get control of book-review assignments, editorial opinion writing, and policymaking positions. So much could be said here, but lets look at it this way. Are any of these entities using their resources in an effort to help restore God as the foundation of this nation? Of course not because 95% are not Christians—it's *not their job!* We must remember and internalize: "*....those who are called by My name....*" are the ones responsible for Christian work and obedience. Are these people lying to the masses while they disseminate socialist propaganda, abusing these avenues of imparting information to the citizenry, ultimately using these tools to further their agenda against God, family, and country? Remember: If no one stands in the gap for God, the evil one has free reign. The answers reside in the fact that Socialism/Communism can only exist in an Atheistic nation since the State is the pagan god that everyone MUST worship. Hence the takeover of these areas by the Liberal Socialist Leftist party taking advantage of Christians leaving these areas unattended.

Goal #21. Gain control of key positions in radio, television, and motion pictures. Again, these immoral entities have not been used to honor God at all—it is their combined focus to eliminate God and morality in our nation. They HAVE to. We might ask—though anyone paying any attention at all already knows the answer—why are these avenues used primarily now to promote rotting trash? They keep pushing the envelope of vileness and mindless idiocy aimed at morally decaying our children and families while destroying the true male image of Godly men, to a level of depravity that seems to have no limit. Knowingly they are secure that at first we resist, then tolerate, and then accept their garbage. Always, for the past four decades, they have had free reign as they destroy all morality and ethics. It's the new progressivism used to force us into collectivism— with no individual rights. The answer to the previous question is, of course, only a decadent and degraded, government-dependent, people/society will embrace Socialism/Communism. The masses, at this point, are demonstrating that they cannot and will not take care of themselves—enter the dictator who will gladly make them his/her slave while giving them barely enough to eat because they have engineered out all their abilities to individually take care of themselves, via the public school system. It's a well-constructed and socialistically engineered trade-off. The government owns you—you become its slave.

Goal #22. Continue discrediting American culture by degrading all forms of artistic expression, (and)
Goal #23. Control art critics and directors of art museums. "Our plan is to promote ugliness, repulsive, meaningless art."
I combined these two goals and ask that you pray and stand back to look at their success in this endeavor. Lenin would smile upon his little "useful idiots" that pulled this one off. Art has become so offensive that one has to take great care that the children are steered away from it, because pornography and decadence rules within its halls.

Goal #24. Eliminate all laws governing obscenity by calling them "censorship" and a violation of free speech and free press, (and)
Goal 25. Break down cultural standards of morality by promoting pornography and obscenity in books, magazines, motion pictures, radio, television and the internet. For hundreds of years after Christians started this country they looked to a Higher Power for decisions that would affect the children and the families, and they did not tolerate anything that would harm the tender virtues of the young, seeking to protect the children and the family. Once-safe and innocent magazines produced for home and teens are now not recognizable due to the near nudity and suggestive, to the point of demanding, premarital sex-promoting articles, and featuring, almost entirely, indecent clothing styles. Jesus was always the founders go-to person for any decision, and they in no way intended to put freedom of speech and freedom of press in place to protect filth and anti-Christian agendas, and to say otherwise with any type of rhetoric to disarm, is a lie from the pit of hell.

Goal #26. Present homosexuality, degeneracy and promiscuity as "normal, natural, and healthy." Scripture states these are sins before God and He calls such things abominations. We cannot argue with God regarding this matter. The atheistic Communists, who are Relative Secular Humanists, many who are now teachers in public schools, and the National Education Association Teachers Union, have been so successful at teaching these behaviors, at tax payers (and Christians) expense to five and six-year-old little children, (K-12) in the public school classrooms, as core-curriculum in many subjects, now called themes. They have taught toleration but now they *mandate* that toleration is not enough—that these "behavioral choices" MUST be *accepted and promoted, and encouraged.* However, they do not teach that these behaviors are choices—they teach that the person is born a homosexual/lesbian., and the students are encouraged to question themselves along this line of thinking.

Along with the mandated pro-homosexual classes, the mandated unhealthy sex education classes nearly push our young children into having premarital sex. The texts for these classes can justifiably be called pornographic. They mention not a thing about love—only sex and it being a totally expected "natural" thing to do—are provided by, interestingly, Planned Parenthood Federation of America. Needless to say, this is very transparent as the next step for the poor innocent young girl who finds herself pregnant, will most assuredly be strongly "guided" to the "Counselor" at the School clinic located conveniently right on the school grounds. The next "logical and right thing to do," for the young girl is the eventual "guided" trip to the abortion mills of the well-financed-by-tax -dollars, PPFA—parental consent or not!

Once a child has practiced homosexuality or promiscuity, they rarely back out of it but go deeper and deeper into it. He/she eventually loses all of their self-worth and self-respect, and most teens then resort to illegal alcohol/drug useage, and even abuse of each other,—leading to drop-out-of-school consequences. It is a known researched fact that many of these "children" are suicide prone, too, as noted in researched facts. These children are just too young to handle this abnormal "guided" engineering of their lives alone and they should not be held responsible for what has happened to them. We, as Christian people, called by His name, are the responsible ones for having allowed all of this to happen to them, as we slept or honestly, did not want to be bothered. What an avoidable insane tragedy for our children. We can no longer avoid doing the responsible things now to result in helping our children obtain a decent future.

Goal #27. Infiltrate the churches and replace revealed religion with "social" religion. Discredit the Bible and emphasize the need for intellectual maturity which does not need a "religious crutch." (and)
Goal #28. Eliminate prayer or any phase of religious expression in the schools on the grounds that it violates the principle of "separation of church and state."
Although not being stated until the 27th Goal, this goal and the goal to takeover the schools, to eliminate the influence of the Son of God, Jesus, from all parts of society have been the most successful ways to destroy America. The Designor, Jesus, sugar-coated, has been relegated "in place" where everyone is comfortable with their sins, and discrediting the Word of God. Most Christians are blind and asleep, and kept that way, as they sit in the pews of many churches. With few true mature MEN of God serving as shepherds in the pulpits, the children and families are being devoured, because they are not fully discipled and taught to cherish and protect Christianity. I pray that the Holy Spirit will open our pastors' eyes and ears to this truth before it is too late for you and your family. Pray that your pastor becomes a real MAN of God and obeys the commands of the Lord of Lords.

It must be made known and crystal clear that *Liberation Theology* (or) *Black Liberation Theology* is a totally Socialist/Communist

Religious Movement, secretly hiding behind the smooth and innocent sounding "Social Justice—Social Religion" title—or LaRaza—right within the Christian community. It is a radical activist "revolution-minded" secretively organized movement having been working actively in coups in third-world countries and actively working in that regard, within the USA for decades. The modern Illegal Alien Immigration problem has been actually ushered into the USA by these groups, intentionally. This is possibly the most important thing to realize and know regarding our Illegal Alien Immigration atrocity that debilitates our economy and causes such unrest among our citizens. It is a well-planned quiet Revolutionary War going on, right now, in our country.

This movement, infecting some mainly Catholic and also some Liberal Christian Churches now (also can be known as the enemy within) is extraordinarily dangerous to our free Nation's wellbeing and is completely abhorrent of the *individualist* capitalist American way of life, liberty and pursuit of happiness freedoms. Liberation Theology (LT) is a totally racist belief system that abhors the "white" race for they mistakenly, passionately, hatefully, teach that *the white capitalist* is guilty of all injustice in the whole world, ignorantly ignoring the fact that the predominantly white West capitalist portion of the world has been the life-sustaining-blood of Third-World countries. Ironically, most leaders in the LT movement are themselves "white," and belong to some Catholic Seminaries and some Orders of Nuns, and they have been almost single handedly the most radically activist organizations behind the Hispanic Illegal Alien movement, *the La Reconquista* movement, along with *Reparations Movement* for the Black people in the USA.

Taken right from the wikipedia wiki/reconquista_(mexico) web site, is this: LaReconquista (defined as a Spanish/Mexican and Portugese word for reconquest) [of the Southwest USA, and now even more parts of USA]; and further: "Modern Definition of the LaReconquista: North America, or Anahuac (ah-NAW-wahk), the future "indigenous" nation as described by the *web site Mexica Movement:* In more recent times, the nation of Indigenous Liberation has become popularized by the Mexica Movement, a group based in LosAngeles. Whereas previous and continuing groups (LaRaza and Liberation Theologists and Social Justice groups—my comment) have advanced the notion

Liberation Theology (LT) is an appealing forceful movement and it makes up several spokes in the wheel of Socialism—it is a huge quiet revolution that is prepared to use force when necessary and when the timing is right. Good-hearted people are first sucked into it with a false sense of compassion, until the member realizes, too late, that it is completely evil—and most cannot escape it for fear of elimination). It is attractive to the "do-good" mentality of the unbelievers as well as misguided believers, who do not realize what they are becoming innocently involved in. They are very community minded until one disagrees with their philosophy—and then that person is "legitimately," strongly, not tolerated or shunned, and is considered the "enemy." LT has been able to maintain a very secretive and subversive strong negative influence on our national way of life and is out to destroy it. In their minds, ***America is evil and they hate her with a passionate hatred and anyone who does not hate her is looked upon with great disdain and considered totally ignorant of America's horribly hateful ways***. The "revolution" mentality of the illegal aliens in our nation today has been strong and is gaining influence, guided into that frame of mind by the Liberation Theology Movement. Few, if any, pastors know about this movement.

That sounds like a strong condemnation—but it is the truth. Liberation Theologians cannot tolerate the Biblical Christian viewpoint (it is the passionate hatred at work here), therefore the person who professes it, and teaches that fundamental Biblical Christianity is (again passionate hatred here), at the least, part of all that is wrong in North America, due to their *imagined erroneous belief* that Fundamentalists are totally intolerant. In the real world, *in which Liberation Theologists do not live,* research proves that Fundamental Christians are the most tolerant of all people. (Sometimes we tolerate too much!)

Goal #29. Discredit the American Constitution by calling it inadequate, old fashioned, out of step with modern needs, a hindrance to cooperation between nations on a worldwide basis. You need to only listen to the rhetoric and watch the decisions of Comrade Judges from the Supreme Court, to many jurisdictions across the nation, to see those who do not want to uphold the Constitution as it exists, because it stands in the way of furthering atheistic Communism goals, if it is upheld in its true form.

It is appropriate here to mention, that the misinterpretation of the Constitution almost daily in the courts result in what Christians today believe and the founders maintained to be immoral decisions against God's commandments.

Goal #30. Discredit the American Founding Fathers. Present them as selfish aristocrats who had no concern for the "common man." (and)
Goal #31. Belittle all forms of American culture and discourage the teaching of American history on the grounds that it was only a minor part of the "big picture." Give more emphasis to Russian history since the Communists took over. Jesus and the Scriptures was the center of our heritage as a nation, and that is the only reason that we were once a great nation. To lie about the Founding Fathers of this country falls in line with the atheistic Communist agenda to get God out of everything and weaken the family and nation. Knowing our past is so important for the present and future, and impugning the Founding Fathers coming from those that do not speak truth and could not carry their shoes is evil.

If U.S. History is taught, the bias against America through the re-writing of American History and Geography to suit the Socialist globalist viewpoints of the NEA and Federal Education Department's goals, and subsequently taught to our children in the public schools, incrementally over the years, destroys pride in America in the students' minds. Conversely this teaches a "hate America" philosophy, and falsely brainwashes students into believing that relinquishing the sovereignty of the USA is the only moral thing to do. This re-written history, with hidden globalist teachings inserted within it, results in the students' acceptance in their minds and hearts that ONLY a global, one-world-citizen frame of mind is the ONLY "good" and "acceptable" and "just" way to live. This, by itself, will enhance and speed the loss of the sovereignty of our Nation, making all the lives lost for defending our nation in all past wars, of no significance—while at the same time fostering an unpatriotic mindset in the child—who would find it against his conscience to ever join the military to defend this "awful" country. They produce these kinds of feelings and thoughts of guilt in our children by relentlessly, repeating over and over, the mantra that American citizens are responsible for all the inequality and injustices and imagined environmental woes of the third-world countries and that they, as American citizens, must assume the "guilt for the world's poverty and sicknesses." Therefore, the only solution is to "join the world as a *one-world-global-citizen*."

(Author: I must insert here the following from one of Phyllis Schlafly's Monthly Newsletters.)

What's Happened to College History and English?
From: March 2008 Phyllis Schlafly Report

In 1995, the Federal Government gave $2 million to leftwing professors at UCLA to write *National Standards for United States History*. The *Standards* were filled with so many attacks on Western civilization that American Federation of Teachers chairman Al Shanker said, *"this is the first time a government has tried to teach children to feel negative*

about their own country." **The U.S. Senate voted 99
to 1 to repudiate the *Standards*, but that didn't stop
the book from being distributed nationwide and
having a profound effect in rewriting American
history textbooks to *comport with liberal revisionism
and feminist ideology.*** (end) Thanks so much, Phyllis
Schlafly.

**Goal #32. Support any socialist movement to give centralized
control over to any part of the culture--education, social
agencies, welfare programs, mental health clinics, etc.** The
Bill of Rights was put in place because the people rightfully
knew the heart of man to be deceptive above all things, and that
centralized power was inviting corruption. The Founding Fathers
would not have signed the Constitution without a Bill of Rights
that limited the powers of the Federal Government and left the
important matters to the people and the states. Communists have
pushed the agenda of centralized control very effectively to the
point of tyranny. Can you imagine for a moment someone in
Washington, or in the Dept. of Education or the NEA/AAUP,
loving your children more than you do, or making sure that your
children retain their faith, ensuring a relationship with Jesus
Christ for eternity? They will tell you that you have local control
of your schools, and then they have great belly laughs as most
people across America actually believe what they have been told.
At the same time, they are teaching lies to children that they
came from green algae pond scum, abortion is a right, sodomy is
natural and healthy, and Islam is a religion of peace—all as core-
curriculum, thirty-three hours a week, in the classrooms. One or
two hours a week of Christian Sunday School is not enough to
combat the daily brainwashing and indoctrination they receive in
the public schools, and the confusion it causes in the minds of our
immature children is nothing short of *abuse* in the classroom.

**Goal #33. Eliminate all laws or procedures which interfere
with the operation of the Communist apparatus. (and)**

Goal #34. Eliminate the House Committee on Un-American Activities. This is partially caused by attacking anything Christian, and putting laws in place to cover murder, lies, obscenity, atheism, paganism, along with causing dissatisfaction and violent uprisings and riots for any reason and eliminating patriotism, and taking away laws that hold lawbreakers accountable or shine light on their evil. These things have been put into effect by the efforts of the Liberal Left Democratic party over the past five decades, and now, over the past few years, even some in the Republican party have been swayed by the Liberal Left.

Goal #35. Discredit and eventually dismantle the FBI. There have been increased efforts over the past several years to discredit the work and limit its effectiveness of the Federal Bureau of Investigation, (and the Central Intelligence Agency [CIA]), however, they have not been able to completely dismantle them as yet. Efforts to discredit, thwart or limit their abilities to keep our nation safe by endless and lengthy hearings are continuously being sought by the Liberal Left. Many good patriotic Americans have worked for the FBI; what we must be vigilant for is any control of that organization by anti-USA and anti-God influences.

Goal #36. Infiltrate and gain control of more unions. The atheistic Communist agenda is firmly in place in the N.E.A., and though they have had huge success in other unions and still have people in place to cause dissatisfaction and chaotic unrest, they have cherry-picked the most desired union which put them in a position to control the education of the children. Most of the N.E.A. teacher-members are innocently ignorant and decent people, but give aid and comfort to an entity that is against God, family, and country, by not becoming more vigilant in what activities they support with their union membership dues. No Christian or Christian teacher can look at the N.E.A. Annual Convention Agendas and say that they are what God would concur with, and with the knowledge that it is anti-God, stay in support, no matter what propaganda the union uses to keep you supporting their traitorous goals.

Goal #37. Infiltrate and gain control of big business. The Communists are experts at giving pressure from above and below, pressuring business and unions into hostile opposite camps. The atheistic Socialist Progressive Communists have actually convinced many innocent Americans that moving jobs out of this country into other Communist countries is good for Americans. The hundreds of thousands of jobs lost by Communist influence as a result of Trade Agreements is against God, family, and country, and affects millions of lives and hurts workers in many unions and, subsequently, their families.

Goal #38. Transfer some of the powers of arrest from the police to social agencies. Treat all behavioral problems as psychiatric disorders which no one but psychiatrists can understand [or treat]. Be vigilant, as both of these are incrementally being implemented without general knowledge of the citizens, without having to go through the due process system to protect the unalienable rights of citizens. Nowhere is this more evident that in the government public schools across America where only school counselors may recommend children being put on hurtful medicines to behaviorally modify them and make them more compliant to receiving the relative, liberal, socialist indoctrination.

Goal #40. Discredit the family as an institution. Encourage promiscuity and easy divorce. (and)
Goal #41. Emphasize the need to raise children away from the negative influence of parents. Attribute prejudices, mental blocks and retarding of children to suppressive influence of parents. Next to getting God out of everything by attacking Christianity at every opportunity, the Communists have gone after the Christian family because they cannot accept any rival power base. They know they can pick off individuals that have no back-up system, very easily. Look at every law that was

put in place to protect the family that has been cleared off the books by the anti-American Communists that have worked within our legislative and judicial system since the mid 1940's.

Over the past five decades, Socialist educators and the NEA have purposefully caused the decadent nature of promiscuity to reign in our nation's schools, through mandated sex education classes resulting in fractured families. They did this on purpose to further their "cause" of Socialism and to bring our nation down. They also worked in concert with radical feminist groups and Planned Parenthood Federation of America, and now with the radical activist Homosexual groups.

Exactly as they planned, they will now offer the citizens the "answer" for fixing the problem. Step up to bat now, NEA, to "help" the weakened family that you intentionally created via the NEA socialist agenda within the schools. Cradle-to-grave-education is a Communist MUST to gain total control of your children and your nation. Great rhetoric and front people like Hillary Clinton, who pretend well that they love the children, are deceptively convincing unknowing parents to give the children up at an earlier age, and demanding that preschool be mandatory.

The NEA literally claims that children raised in Christian homes are mentally ill by the time they reach kindergarten so, therefore, they must remove the children from the home. It is their social duty. These are the verbal seeds they are planting now in the minds of young single parents and working parents trying to convince them to voluntarily register their babies in preschool. Voluntarily, they say now to the parents, but demanding they confiscate the children from birth to five years old, will come in the future. Translated, that means simply this: Children living at home being brought up in a Christian home with good, strong Christian influence in their lives and minds must be rescued from this psychologically ill environment. Period, no ifs, ands or buts! It is actually stated that way in the NEA Convention Agenda. Yes, people, it is their "plan"—their "stated goal." Another way they are pushing to gain control of the youngest children is their raising the question of the low academic outcomes in the classrooms, which, of course, they socially engineered in the first place, to dumb down our nation (this goal completed). Now they come along and want to "solve the problem" by claiming that children just aren't ready for kindergarten because "single and working parents aren't readying them for it" and, therefore, preschool must be mandated. And gullible, vulnerable, unknowing and too-busy (most single parents) are buying this lie hook line and sinker—and I do mean "sinker"—as a good deal. This is how they will ultimately "sink" our nation in the abysmal socialist global ocean. It certainly worked for Hitler and his cronies—tried—tested—and proven to work. All the ground work has been done for the NEA/ACLU/PPFA/AAUP—they just have to follow the same path. Let me remind you once again: Hitler: By controlling the schools I'll own Germany. And he did! Sadly, as millions ended up being murdered by force under his dictatorship. We must be very careful not to allow this same thing to happen here.

Goal #45. Repeal the Connally reservation so the United States cannot prevent the World Court from seizing jurisdiction over domestic problems. Give the World Court jurisdiction over nations and individuals alike. Get on your knees and pray, because this has been in the works to implement as soon as they can. The government has Communists within that are working to make this happen; the media has Communists within working to make this happen; the schools are indoctrinating the children with teacher change-agents, socially engineering them into this type of system; and the Churches have been infiltrated by humanistic feel-good teachings that encourages them to stay silent, to make this happen.

Already is has been seen in newspaper reports that some Supreme Court Justices want to use the European Court system's precedents for some of our cases. Can you imagine someone in Sweden, heading up the influence on that court, a country that is

70% atheistic and agnostic and who believe it is permissible that brothels be open for people to have sex with animals, having a say-so in our Courts? Or someone from Iran's Courts, who thinks that everyone should be Muslim, or be inferior, pay a tax, or die because they are considered infidels, should influence our Courts? Or how about an atheistic Communist Russian, that does not believe in a higher power, so it is alright to kill any opposition? Or a Communist Chinese judge who rules that people should be tortured or put in prison if they have a Bible, and force the killing of babies if you have more than one? Bottom line, do you want anyone to make a decision about you, your family, or your country, that does not seek wisdom and justice from a higher power—namely God? There are traitors amongst us, many, in this country that are giving aid and comfort to the enemies of God, family, and country working tirelessly to make this happen. Our Supreme Court is making new laws and rewriting the Constitution every day, taking away our freedoms.

One last thing that must be addressed because of its success in breaking down the Christian family as the greatest source of strength in our country is the Communist goal for the women of America. Their goal has infected every family in some way. Karl Marx and Friedrich Engels wrote in the Communist Manifesto, "The bourgeois family will vanish as a matter of course." Noting that the parent/child relationship is disgusting, their desire was to destroy the center of power that existed in the Christian family home. To do this, they worked to weaken the family by getting the women (the heart of the family) out of the house (also see above section on NEA's goal for preschool for baby-to-school plans).

In America, the Communists/Socialists used a plan by William Foster, who was the head of the Communist Party, USA, serving as their General Secretary. He was a founder of the *American Civil Liberties Union* (ACLU) and worked with Roger Baldwin to promote communism and attack Christianity, because Communists hate God, and must have a Godless pagan society.

Incrementally, they started to convince the women that they were parasites or oppressed slaves. Because of how Christians have been taught to honor mothers, you would naturally look at this as an impossible task to convince anyone that Mom or Grandma was a parasite or oppressed slave. Not in America. Telling the housewives and mothers that they were oppressed by their men, and doing a worthless and thankless job in the home, and that true satisfaction could never happen for her there, she must get out for her own self worth and sanity. She must free herself from exploitation and drudgery. Put down the most beautiful job given to a woman from God, to be a house wife and mother, make such a person feel like a second class citizen—this is how the subversive movement of "dissatisfaction sowing" works to further their cause. They use this effective method in every realm. Free women from ongoing housework, the enslavement of children, and offer her free love, easy divorce, and independence. This could not happen overnight, but the

Communist-feminists have known that they would have to do things incrementally/progressively over decades, their slogan, being: "Make haste slowly." The Communists put into effect the last obstacle to getting the women out of the home, like they had done in Russia. They developed a system of kindergartens and government-run and Union-run daycare centers, where they herded the children. So, instead of Mom giving Godly wisdom to her children, they convinced her that the wisest thing she could do was work outside the home. Through high taxation, *also known as income redistribution*, (now happening in the USA) working outside the home became a necessity.

Look at the Communist Manifesto, and as you see Socialism/Communism's successes in this country, know that it is no accident that Jesus has been attacked by their 'useful idiots," as similarly, now, the Christian family has been broken down, and the Christian Mothers have been convinced and forced to work outside of the home.

The atheistic Communists have had "useful idiots" in our government, 'useful idiots" in the media, "useful idiots" in education, and even "useful idiots" in many of the pulpits, all of whom have given aid and comfort to enemies of God, family and country to help make these things happen. With great sadness we must admit that the Christian shepherds have such great culpability with their silence, apathy, and indifference in furthering atheism in our nation. Christian Mothers, you are called to go back home, do with less, and love your children so much that you are a slave to the commands of God. If you truly love your children you will need to do this if you want their soul to be with Jesus for eternity. Satan will give you many excuses to keep working outside of the home, to stay enslaved to him through man's wisdom. This is another time for you to choose. Please help save this country by turning back to God's ways. There will be sacrifice, but the result of having your children living in freedom in our nation, and in Heaven for eternity, is worth all costs. In doing so, you will be in the front lines of this silent revolution that is occurring now in the USA.

As you look at the above goals of the atheistic Communists for America, and notice how many things have been implemented already over the last few decades, there are still some of you that will convince yourselves that it can't happen here, so let's eat, drink, and be merry. Then there are the young pastors that won't even understand what is happening—they don't know what Socialism/Communism is, a.k.a. Progressivism/Populism/ Liberalism//Humanism//Environmentalism—Manmade Global Warming/Globalism/ Collectivism/ Liberation Theology/Social Justice movement/Evolution Theory that destroys the belief in God! Socialism/Communism hides behind all of these titles— they are all one and the same—Atheistic One-World Dictatorship! It is taught subversively hidden under these titles in public schools. In the same way that Socialism has taken over other nations—by taking over the schools through Teachers/Professors Unions and the Federal Government Department of Education variety of programs: Global 2000, No

Child Left Behind, School-to-Work, Life Long Learning, and so on and on and on, along with the UNESCO and Global-International One World Education system.

Can't you see our ancestors in this once Christian America as you look back over the last 100 years? They knew it could happen here and they fought and *warned* us to be watchful and fight against it. They would have said there is no way that in America anyone can 'choose' to murder a baby. It can't happen in America that our children will be taught that they came from green algae pond scum. It can't happen in America that the children will be taught to accept the sin of homosexuality as natural, normal, and healthy. It can't happen in America, that kids will kill kids in schools and that the school children will be getting pregnant, have abortions, with millions living in fornication and disease, as it increases daily. It can't happen in America that they will attack Christianity openly, and take Scripture and prayer out of the education of the children. It can't happen in America that Pagan religions would be openly embraced, placing other god's before God. It can't happen that our children will be molested and raped in the schools, and that there would be video cameras and armed guards. It can't happen that they have dogs sniffing our drugs in the public schools. It can't happen in America that our government could be infiltrated and influenced by atheistic, humanists and Communists. It can't happen in America that our media would be infiltrated, influenced and owned by atheistic, humanists and Communists. It can't happen in America that our education system, textbook publishers and teachers unions could be infiltrated by atheistic, humanists and Communists. It can't happen in America that the pulpits could be influenced by the atheistic humanists and Communists.

You could indeed go on and on about the *"it can't happen here"* attitude as Christian leaders helped their flocks sleep. Don't any of you men-children at least want to become mature *men*? Jesus has always had the invitation there for you. Will you turn away and sleep at the most critical time in your nation's history, and put your children and families at risk of going to hell for eternity? Nine out of ten children from Christian homes are leaving their faith after being indoctrinated in an Atheistic Pagan education system, but hey, *"it can't happen here." **"Judgment begins in the house of God." ** (1 Peter 4:1)*

Chapter 5

It Can't Happen Here

As Paul stated: *"And so I solemnly urge you before God and before Christ Jesus, who will someday judge the living and the dead when he appears to set up His kingdom. Preach the Word of God in season and out of season, being persistent, whether the time is favorable or not. Patiently correct, rebuke, and encourage your people with good teaching of sound doctrine. For the time is coming when people will no longer listen to the right teaching of sound doctrine. They will follow their own desires and will look for teachers to tickle their ears, by telling them whatever they want to hear. They will reject the Truth and turn aside to fables, following strange myths." (II Timothy 4:1-4)*

What great timing to hear from another true MAN of God, Pastor Rusty Thomas, a warrior for the Lord, who will indeed have stories to talk to Moses and David about when he gets to Heaven. Listen to the wisdom of the Holy Spirit working through him to speak to you about the *"It Can't Happen Here"* attitude that always helps evil *"To Indeed Happen Here."*

It Can't Happen Here?
By Rev. Rusty Thomas

I'm sure the title of this message has been a phrase that has been uttered in many nations throughout mankind's bloody history. Perhaps the Czar of Russia, the King of France, and the nation of Germany all were convinced that the Communist revolt, the French Revolution, and the Nazi holocaust would never happen, especially, under their watch. Their one common denominator, however, is they were all dreadfully mistaken. The unspeakable did happen and when it did, unprecedented bloodshed and injustice ran rampant.

As one looks at history, how can we account for a nation like Germany? They reached the heights of the Reformation and then descended into becoming the land of the holocaust? How did this civilized, sophisticated nation become reduced to brutal barbarism? What created the climate that allowed a demonic madman like Hitler, to convince the German people to cooperate with his "Final Solution?"

I believe we live in a time in America when we need to pull our collective heads out of the sand and answer these historical questions before we are condemned to repeat this same folly. For years, Hitler indoctrinated Germany and cultivated the culture to follow his vision from Hades.

He captured the civil government, attacked the Bible, silenced the Church, captured the youth with Nazi propaganda, and dehumanized the Jewish people. (author's note: Does this sound familiar as you looked at the above goals of the Communists, different players and different names with the same intent, power?) Thus his dream of the "thousand year reign" of the Third Reich turned into a nightmare that catapulted the entire world into a bloody war.

Whether or not we want to face reality, America is in the process of following this same primrose path that leads to perdition. For decades, there has been a systematic assault against America's Godly heritage, the Christian faith, and the Biblical principles that has produced the freest, most blessed, and prosperous nation on the face of the earth.

Since the turbulent 1960s, the Supreme Court has used their considerable power to perpetrate a social experiment on America. They have repeatedly rendered one disastrous decision after another. Their judicial activism has paved the way to remove the knowledge of God from the public life of our nation. As a result, the bible is attacked, the Church is threatened to keep silent in public affairs, American youth have been indoctrinated with humanistic propaganda, pre-born children have been dehumanized in the womb, and the vilification of Christianity increases with each passing day. Sound familiar?

Consider this:

Today, there are more books from American authors warning our nation against the dangers of Christianity, than there are those warning against radical Islam.

General Pace mentions "Homosexuality is immoral" and the *"powers that be"* bear tooth and claw to suppress his free speech. Clearly, this censorship sends a distinct message that the Christian worldview will not be tolerated in public discourse. Thus it appears that if you desire an influential job, a greater position, or hope for advancement in America, you must sell your soul to the devil, deny the Christian faith, and dare not introduce moral absolutes that may offend America's immoral sensibilities.

World Net Daily posts article after article demonstrating how evil is being codified into law and our culture is unraveling before our very eyes. One headline reads,

"District gags 14-year-olds after 'gay' indoctrination. 'Confidentiality' promise requires students 'not to tell their parents.'" In essence, the Deerfield High School coached the children to lie to their parents in order to avoid parents being upset by the school's homosexual indoctrination.

In another article, WND reported, "In Massachusetts, after a school repeatedly advocated for the homosexual lifestyle to students in elementary grades, several parents sued, only to have the federal judge order the 'gay' agenda taught to the Christians. The conclusion from **U.S. District Judge Mark L. Wolf** found that it is reasonable; indeed there is an obligation, for public schools to teach young children to accept and endorse homosexuality. Wolf essentially adopted the reasoning in a brief submitted by a number of homosexual-advocacy groups, who said "the rights of religious freedom and parental control over the upbringing of children …would undermine teaching and learning…"

(Author's note: You must understand teachers' and professors' unions and the ACLU are indoctrinating your children, and **all** government schools have been ordered by the NEA to start this promiscuous sex education and homosexual indoctrination all across the country, K-16. The atheistic humanists and Communists are hurting the children of America while apathetic and pusillanimous Christian leaders and Christian laity sleep. The NEA is supposed to be a teachers union to protect the benefits of its teachers—it has become, over the past several decades, the DICTATOR AND MANDATOR of all public school curricula and textbooks, and generous financial supporter of only Liberal Left Socialist Democrats running for all State and Federal offices. These people on both sides own each other and owe each other Socialist-agenda-driven favors.)

You read this right. According to the inmate running the asylum (Judge Wolf, which is an appropriate name), Homosexuals know, better than parents, how to teach and what is best for the learning of our young. And Christian, in particular, must submit their children to this indoctrination with no opportunity to opt-out (of the classes). Dare anyone say "tyranny?"

Another case in point is the Southern Poverty Law Center, headquartered in Montgomery, Alabama. Their stated goal is to monitor hate groups and extremist activity in the United States. In times past, they have been champions against racial discrimination. In recent days, however, their focus has dramatically changed. No longer do they seek to just prosecute the KKK. No! Their new enemy to prosecute is fundamental Christians. They send out reports to our civil government, (Authors note: The Communist dupes that have infiltrated the civil government), listing Christian groups who are actively engaged in our culture as the new "hate groups" that promote "extremist activities."

Just the other day, a New Jersey School held a mock drill and staged a "hostage situation." Care to guess who the enemy was? Care to know the fanatical terrorists that attacked their school? If you guessed Muslims, you would not only be politically incorrect, you would be factually incorrect as well. No! The psychos were portrayed as, you guessed it: Christians.

The TV sitcoms and Hollywood movies continually spew out their hatred against God and the Christian faith. When confronted, they claim artistic freedom. Why doesn't their artistic freedom extend to other religions and philosophical groups? What makes the Christian faith, the only acceptable faith that can be publicly maligned, mocked, and censored in the land where tolerance is the new idol before which America bows?

Our culture, government, schools, and media are being dominated by the faiths of Humanism, Evolution, and Hedonism. They are following the same pernicious path that has diminished the glory of every nation that has been dominated by these idols fit for destruction. They instinctively know they cannot allow the Christian worldview to see the light of day in America again, lest their house of pagan cards collapse about them. This is what drives them to promote their godless worldviews at the expense of the Christian world-view. They have a huge problem, however. If they remain consistent with themselves, their godless worldviews will consume themselves, and every American will be forced to sludge through the fall out of their refuse.

Church in America, we must not remain silent anymore. It is time to break out of the Christian ghetto America has become. The religious apartheid must end. I don't care if you lose your job, are passed over for a promotion, or go to jail. We must reclaim our prophetic voice and engage our culture, government, schools, and media with the claims of Christ and the truth of His Word. This is the faith and worldview that founded our great nation and it's the only faith and worldview that can sustain our great nation. All else is sinking sand and broken cisterns that can't hold water.

If we fail in this hour, when the enemies of the cross are emboldened to the degree they are in our nation's history, we will have not one person to blame, except for ourselves, when they come for our children and our grandchildren. *Can't happen here?* Tell that to Russia, France, and Germany. I'm sure they will understand our deception.

In King Jesus name, Rusty (end)

Where is the warning, and where are the Watchmen? *"Unless the Lord watches over the city, the watchmen stand guard in vain." (Psalm 12)* We are being led by selfish leaders in the government that do things man's ways instead of God's ways; a government education system that tells lies with a hidden agenda (and all schools are infected); and a media system that is run by and serves those against God, family, and country. So where is the church God? We have so many pulpits that think they are smarter than God by referring to man's wisdom rather than God's Word, and rather than engage or resist the evil, they rest in a false peace, not backed by God. Listen to God's word about such leaders and shepherds: *"His watchmen are blind; they are all ignorant, they are all dumb dogs, they cannot bark; sleeping, lying down, loving to slumber. Yea, they are greedy dogs who can never have enough, and they are shepherds that cannot understand, they all look to their own way, every one for his gain, from his quarter. Come ye, say they, I will fetch wine, and we will fill ourselves with strong drink; and tomorrow shall be as this day, and much more abundant."* (Isaiah 56:10-12)

With the authority of God's Word, *"it CAN happen here"* and it *is happening here*, so weep for your children, get on your face and cry out for their present and future now, and for their eternal souls.

Chapter 6

Heaven or Hell for Eternity

"My people perish for lack of knowledge. Because you have rejected knowledge, I also have rejected you as my priests; because you have ignored the law of your God, I also will ignore your children." (Hosea 4:6)

All of us are ignorant to some degree about something, yet to stay ignorant on purpose about those things that affect souls for eternity, enters the realm of blindness. Through ignorance, I repeat again, we give aide and comfort to the enemies of God, family, and nation. Do you want this to be a part of your life? This day you are given the knowledge and hopefully you understand at this point why the moral decay is happening in this country today, where is has come from, and where it is leading. Hopefully, you are ashamed because you have done nothing to stop the evil because of that ignorance. Most of us have had to go through this *shaming process*, repent, pick up the cross and begin actively working against the evil. Are you ready to begin?

As I continue, I must also give you the goals within the agendas of the Atheist Humanists, lies of radical Islam, and the sinful plans of the Homosexual agenda. **Know this!** The Atheistic Communists, Humanists, Islamists, and the Homosexual agendas are all anti-Christian and *traitors* to God, family and country. In love I ask those shepherds that claim the name of Christ: *Do you give aide and comfort with your silence and inaction, to these dupes of Satan that are against the one you claim to be the Son of God?* You know this: That the sins of your past or present, can be repented of, and you know that Jesus is calling on you to be a *man* of God. Jesus commands you to hate evil, as He defines evil, so do your job or take responsibility for the souls that you are putting at risk of going to hell for eternity. If you are part of His remnant that engage the evil and defend Christianity, *then I ask God to increase your talent and expand your territory* because you are needed, and know the heroes of the Bible would welcome you into their company. May God deliver each of you from having to hang your head in shame when asked: *"What did you do when you accepted Christ and heard His command to follow Him to the cross?"*—and you responded by doing nothing?"

Abbreviated version of the Humanist Manifesto I

1. Man gradually emerged by chance from lower forms of life over millions of years.
2. Man creates god out of his own experiences.
3. Man is his own authority and is not accountable to any higher power.
4. There are no absolute rules to live by.
5. All men should be exposed to diverse 'realistic' viewpoints, including Profanity, immorality, and perversions as acceptable modes of self-expression.
6. All forms of sexual expression are acceptable.
7. Government ownership or control of the economy should replace private Ownership of property and the free market economy.
8. 'Global Citizenship' should replace national self-determination.
9. There is no hope of existence beyond the grave--no heave or hell.

Humanist Manifesto II

As shown by Dr. Stanley Monteith's research in *Brotherhood of Darkness*, Francis Schaeffer studied the decline of Western civilization, and he came to the conclusion that Secular Humanism is responsible for our problems because secular humanists advocate abortion, homosexuality, prisoners' rights, socialism, and world government, and deny the existence of God. Every Communist and every Socialist is a Secular Humanist, and although every Humanist is not a Communist, every Communist is a Secular Humanist. In order to exist, Socialism/Communism MUST eliminate God from the nation's culture.

The beliefs of the Religion of Secular Humanism were codified in the *Second Humanist Manifesto* where seventeen concepts were presented that changed the world. ***Humanist Manifesto II*** proclaimed that secular humanists:

1. Reject traditional religious beliefs, and seek "new human purposes and goals." Humanists proclaim there is "no divine purpose or providence for the human species…No deity will save us; we must save ourselves."

2. Reject as both illusory and harmful the "promises of immortal salvation or fear of eternal damnation…" which are the basis of both Judaic and Christian beliefs.

3. Believe that "moral values derive…from human experience. Ethics is autonomous and situational," and that we should "strive for the good life, here and now." Thus humanists believe that individuals determine what is right and wrong.

4. Believe that "reason and intelligence" will guide mankind to a better world.

5. Stress individual freedom without moral restraints.

6. Recognize "…the right to birth control, abortion, and divorce," and that "…the many varieties of sexual exploration should not in themselves be considered

'evil.'" The humanists condone homosexuality and their other forms of sexual perversion.

7. Support concepts of individual freedom such as "an individual's right to die with dignity, euthanasia, and the right to suicide."

8. Advocate democracy and participatory democracy rather than a republican form of government. (author's note: especially if they control the media propaganda)

9. Advocate "the separation of church and state and the separation of ideology and state." This program was designed to remove both God and prayer from public schools as well as from the nation..

10. Advocate "alternative economic systems," and the need to "democratize the economy." Humanists promote Socialism.

11. Advocate the "elimination of all discrimination based upon race, religion, sex, age, or national origin," and the right to universal education." (now known as Globalism and/or Socialism—author's comment) They also oppose "sexism or sexual chauvinism." This requires government control over every aspect of our lives. (Again, author's comment: Their goal is to sow discontent and dissatisfaction—from radical feminism and union pickets—to every level of society—leading to riots and resultant violence. Look for an increase of this happening more and more often.)

12. Support the ending of nationhood and national sovereignty, and advocate a "world community." (author's comment: The "it takes a village to raise a child" mentality—again a.k.a. Globalism)

13. State "this world community must renounce the resort to violence and force (author's comment: this supports the furtherance of their evil unabated by wars of good vs. evil) as a method of solving international disputes." They want a world government which includes an international court.

14. Advocated that "the world community...engage in cooperative planning concerning the use of rapidly depleting resources...population growth must be checked." This is the basis of modern-day environmentalism (a.k.a. Socialism) and population control (via abortion and euthanasia—mercy killing).

15. Propose foreign aid and birth control for developing nations.

16. Since "technology is a vital key to human progress..." they oppose "any moves to censor basic scientific research on moral, political, or social grounds."

17. Call for "...international cooperation in culture, science, the arts, and technology across ideological borders. We must learn to live openly together or we shall perish together. (Please note by author: Remember, most of these areas have been discovered and furthered almost exclusively by the West, and paid for by the citizens of the West. We must now be forced to share all knowledge acquired through our Democratic/Republican system with the world, to be used in whatever manner the Socialist countries wish to use it—*even when they wish to use it against us t*o force us to adhere to their Atheistic Socialism

Their plans, and most of them have been implemented already, to introduce Socialism to our United States of America and to create a One World Government, undermine and gradually eliminates the Judeo-Christian God and beliefs and foundation of our nation. Most Democrats, a growing number of Republicans, and all Communist movement's Leaders should be in line fighting to get the *Humanist of the Year Award.* They would have competition for this Award by the leaders of the NEA, AAUP, PPFA, American Library Association, ACLU, many Judges, and all the bigoted Christian-hating organizations.

Demands of Sodomite Movement
(Distributed at their Gay Pride March in Washington, D.C. April 25, 1993)

(Note: It has gotten so much worse since then as they announced they intend to sodomize your sons wherever they find them—they state that they will turn your children to their ways, whether you like it or not. They are now in many schools K-12 indoctrinating the children and desensitizing the teachers and parents to the SIN of sodomy)

1. That all sodomy laws be repealed and all forms of sexual expression (including pedophilia) be legalized.
2. That defense budget funds be diverted to pay for AIDS patients' medical expenses   and sex'change operations.
3. That same-sex marriages and adoption, custody, and foster care within these Structures be legalized.
4. That homosexual education programs be offered at all levels of education, including elementary schools. (Author's note: They have accomplished this via NEA Teachers Union.)
5. That contraceptives and abortion services be made available to all persons, regardless of age.
6. That taxpayer funding be made available for artificial insemination of lesbians and bisexuals.

7. That expression of religious-based concerns regarding homosexuality be forbidden That organizations like the Boy-Scouts be required to accept homosexual Scoutmasters.

DefendTheFamily.com Alert

Matthew Shepard: The Horst Wessel of the "Gay" Movement
Scott Lively, J.D., Th.D.

It was **1930** and a culture war was raging between the Fascists and the Communists in Germany. The growing Nazi Party was strong, but the people still favored the Communists. It fell to young Josef Goebbels to win hearts and minds to the Nazi cause. How could this be done? The Nazis were newcomers, trying to change the Social Order, and their aggressive tactics were offensive to many people. But in a move that would establish him as a master propagandist, Goebbels turned the tables by casting the Nazis as victims of the Communists. The key was Horst Wessel.

Horst Wessel was just another Nazi street thug, but on **February 23, 1930** he was murdered by a militant Communist. Wessel wasn't killed over ideology; it was a matter of unpaid rent to his landlady. However, the timing was right for Goebbels' scheme and so Horst Wessel became the first martyr of the movement: the symbol of Nazi victim hood at the hands of the evil Communists. The "Horst Wessel Song" became, literally, the anthem of the Nazi Party, and Wessel assumed mythic stature as a figure of near-religious worship.

In **1998** a culture war was waging between the homosexuals and the Christians in America. The growing "gay" movement was strong, but the people still favored the Christian values of marriage and the natural family. The leaders of the "gay" movement needed to win more of the public to their position. How could this be done? The "gays" were still relative newcomers, trying to change the social and moral order of the nation, and their aggressive tactics ("We're Queer, We're Here, Get Used to It!) were offensive to many people. But in a move that would confirm their reputation as master propagandists, the "gay" leaders turned the tables, casting the homosexuals as victims of Christian "homophobia." The key was Matthew Shepard.

Matthew Shepard was just another self-identified "gay," but on **October 12, 1998**, he was murdered by two men. He wasn't killed because he was homosexual it was a matter of robbery. And the robbers obviously weren't Christians. However, the timing was right for the "gay" scheme, and so Matthew Shepard became the new martyr of the homosexual movement: a symbol of "gay" victimhood at the hands of the evil Christians. A play about his death, "The Laramie Project" became the showpiece of the "gay" movement, and Shepard himself assumed mythic stature as a figure of near-religious worship. (Author's note: This play is now being presented by High School Drama Clubs.)

Matthew Shepard is the Horst Wessel of the modern "gay" movement. He was probably a fine young man, despite his lifestyle, and his murder was certainly a deplorable act. *However, his legend is a lie.* Its purpose is to deceive and manipulate the public. And its proponents are Fascists.

Indeed, the American "gay" movement is as Fascist as the German Fascist movement was "gay," and there are many links between the two. For example, the first U.S. homosexual organization, **formed in 1924,** was the Chicago Chapter of the German Society for Human Rights. The most prominent member of the German parent organization was Hitler's closest friend, openly homosexual Ernst Roehm, head of the Nazi SA (also known as the Brown Shirts). Interestingly, Horst Wessel, as a member of the early SA under Roehm, was probably homosexual or bisexual as well.

And yes, Hitler was "gay."
http://observer.guardian.co.uk/international/story/0,6903,56489 9,00.html

Just how closely were Nazi Fascism and homosexuality linked? It was Soviet author Maxim Gorky who observed: "There is already a saying in Germany. 'Eliminate the homosexual and Fascism will disappear.'" This citation and additional proof of the assertions made here may be found in my book, co-authored by Jewish researcher Kevin E. Abrams, *The Pink Swastika: Homosexuality in the Nazi Party*, published online at www.defendthefamily.com.

Several years ago Eric Pollard, a "gay" founder of the radical AIDS Coalition to Unleash Power (ACT-UP) made a startling admission in the *Washington Blade,* a leading homosexual newspaper: "I sincerely apologize for my involvement in and my founding of...ACT-UP DC...I have helped to create a truly Fascist organization....[which uses] subversive tactics, drawn largely from the voluminous book *Mein Kampf,* [Hitler's autobiography], which some of us studied as a working model (*Time to give up Fascist Tactics*: *Washington Blade*, **January 1992).**

Prominent homosexual writer Randy Shilts labeled another "gay" activist group, *Queer Nation,* "brown shirts" and "lavender fascists." These admissions were surprising because they directly contradict the goals of the "gay" propagandists, who campaign incessantly to define "gays" as exclusively victims of society. But such confessions are rare, and never reprinted in mainstream publications, so the public never learns the truth.

It is a testament to "gay" propaganda that much of the American public now thinks of Christians as the aggressors and homosexuals as victims. But it is the "gays," not the Christians, who are trying to overthrow the traditional, family-centered society. And it is the Christians, not the "gays" that are being silenced and marginalized for their views: in government, mass media, academia and corporate America. Adolf Hitler would be proud. (end)

I think all can agree that sometimes we give aid and comfort to the enemy because we are more afraid of man, than we are God. Accusations flung at Christians will cause them to sometimes hide or decide not to act in love as Christians, and let those caught up in a sin like homosexuality, that will take them to hell, continue in their lifestyle without warning them, (and there are many other sins that Satan will make look inviting), rather than stand up and speak the Biblical truth in love so that a person may possibly be saved. To hide or not show Christian love and point out a sin, shows no love to those caught up in any sin and it is another way that we are a traitor to God and His children by our silence. I want to again thank Dr. Scott Lively for his ministry, *Defend the Family,* and his work to show the common sense logic in a Biblical way that destroys all arguments of those that are against God, family, country, and specifically Christianity.

Is Hating "Haters" Hateful?
Scott Lively, J.D., Th.D.

(An essay on the double standard being used by the Left in the public debate on homosexuality.)

Hate has a pretty bad name in the world today. No one wants to be called a hater, especially Christians, which is probably why we get accused of it all the time by our opponents. Homosexuals are especially fond of calling people haters. They even invented the word *homophobia,* which means *hate and fear of homosexuals*, envisaged as a mental illness (a phobia is an anxiety disorder).

I hate being called a homophobe. It has such an ugly connotation. It's especially unpleasant because, as a Christian, I'm supposed to have a reputation for loving people, not hating them. So I've worked really hard over the years to try to get the homosexuals to stop calling me a homophobe. I've pointed out the difference between hating people and hating their behavior (loving the sinner but hating the sin). They hated that. Then I tried "walking my talk" by taking an ex-"gay" man who was dying of AIDS into my family. My wife and I and our children loved and cared for him during the last year of his life. T hey hated that even more.

Then I began asking for guidance from homosexuals themselves: "Tell me, where is the line between homophobia and acceptable opposition to homosexuality?" I asked. "What if I just agree with the Bible that homosexuality is a sin no worse than any other sex outside of marriage?" "No, that's homophobic," they replied. "Suppose I talk only about the proven medical hazards of gay sex and try to discourage people from hurting themselves?" I asked. "No, you can't do that," they said. "How about if I say that homosexuals have the option to change if they choose?" "Ridiculous," they answered. "Maybe I could just be completely positive, say nothing about homosexuality, and focus only on promoting the natural family and traditional marriage?" "That's really hateful," they replied.

After I while, I realized that the only way I could get them to stop calling me a homophobe was to start agreeing with them about everything. But here's my dilemma: I honestly believe the Bible which says that homosexuality is wrong and harmful and that all sex belongs within marriage. I've also read the professional studies and know that "gay" sex hurts people because it goes against the design of their bodies. And I'm friends with a number of former homosexuals who are now married and living heterosexual lives. Do I have to give up my religion? Ignore scientific facts? Betray my friends? Is that the only way to avoid being called a hater and a homophobe?

There's no escape. A homophobe is anyone who, for any reason, disapproves of homosexuality in any way, shape, manner, form or degree. This leaves me with just two choices: agree that everything about homosexuality is natural, normal, healthy, moral and worthy to be celebrated OR be labeled as a mentally ill, hate-filled bigot.

Am I wrong? Is there any way to openly disapprove of homosexuality without being a homophobe? "Gay" leaders, please set me straight on this.

Because if I'm right, that means the "gay agenda" is to stop everyone from following the Bible regarding sexual matters. It is, after all, their stated goal to "stamp out homophobia." No more religious freedom. It's also to suppress scientific research that has reached conclusions they don't like, especially if it helps people to change their homosexual orientation back to a heterosexual one (ask the doctors and scientists at narth.com what they've had to endure). If it discourages homosexuality, even by implication, it's homophobic and can't be used.

There's a queer reasoning behind all of this. Homosexuals call me names like bigot and homophobe, condemn my religion, mock my rational conclusions about social issues, impugn my motives, display intense hostility toward my actions, and curse my very existence, all under the justification that I'm a "hater." But if I'm a "hater" for civilly opposing what they do, why aren't they haters for uncivilly opposing what I do? Such a double standard, in the context of a public debate on "civil rights," is not just hypocritical, it is surreal.

I admit I have some hate. I hate watching people kill themselves with preventable diseases like AIDS. hate seeing children being steered toward unhealthy lifestyles. I hate having my pro-family views distorted by dishonest journalists, politicians and academics. And I hate seeing my God being treated like a homophobe for what He teaches in His Bible.

So if you're not going to stop calling me a "hater" for wanting homosexuals to be saved and healed, or for opposing their political agenda, let's at least see a little more of that famous "American sense of fair play" in the public debate on this issue. Hatred of "haters" is hateful too. (end)

Radical Islam—Religion of Death

1. Mohammed told his followers of his man-made religion that it is OK to lie to your wives, OK to lie in battle, and OK to lie to further Islamic take over of the world, and OK to lie as they sign "peace" accords and agreements which they never intend to keep. (Now when they open their mouths, we cannot believe what they say. Let us listen to what God says: ***"Thus says the LORD; Cursed be the man that trusts in man, and makes flesh his arm, and whose heart departs from the LORD." Jeremiah 17:5.*** While this is talking about all men and can be used to wake people up to hear the Word of God, it also speaks clearly about a false religion like Islam that was birthed out of the mouth of the liar, Mohammed.)

2. Muslims are told in Surah 5.51: "Take not Jews and Christians as your friends."

3. Muslims are told in Surah 3.151: "We shall cast terror into the hearts of those who disbelieve."

4. Muslims are told in Surah 9.123: "Believers, fight those disbelievers who are near you. Deal harshly with them."

5. Muslims are told in Surah 3.14: "Women are possessions."

6. Muslims are told in Surah 3.826: "The majority of people in hell are women."

These and many more statements in the Koran, specifically by Mohammed, did not come from God, but are the self-made delusions of an imposter. Because it is a lie from the pit of hell, it has caused the death of multi-millions, and demands primary allegiance of all those calling themselves 'Muslim.'

How deep is our *Treason?* How much should we be ashamed? Listen to the wisdom of the Holy Spirit working through Coach Dave Daubenmire who understands these times and the legacy we will leave the children that are left after the slaughter of the innocents. Once again, we continue to offend God by doing things man's ways instead of God's ways. One day our posterity will shout back at us: *"WHY?" did you allow this to happen. WHERE were you? WHAT were you doing? HOW could you have been awake when we were losing our country and they were taking away our God?"*

Are we awake yet, or is the church still sleeping? If I listen carefully, I think I can hear the heavy breathing of people who are soundly sleeping. We know that there are church communities that are disobeying God by refusing to wake up. This leads to Hedonism in society that causes a rotting cancer that destroys people and nations. We worry so about Socialist Environmentalism and a sighing tree and turn our backs and plug our ears to the crying out of our weary and our beaten down children.

Christian Hedonism
Dr. (Coach) Dave Daubenmire

Barack Obama recently called abortion a *"difficult issue."* That is a nice way of saying you must ignore all of your moral instincts. Killing an unborn baby is not a *"difficult issue"* if your conscience still works.
Everyone knows the "fetus" is a human being, unless, of course, you are looking for an excuse to do wrong. *Going against your conscience is difficult business.*

He called the miraculous creation of a baby *"punishment."* I know you think I am making this up. Watch for yourself. And this man is being considered as president of the United States?

This is where moral relativism has brought us. When you turn from God-created standards of right and wrong you are sure to end up in a moral swamp laden with *"difficult issues."* When right and wrong become an opinion, rather than truth, the swamp gets muddied. *The truth is not difficult to believe, but it is difficult to obey.*

Obama is no exception. Most of our leaders swim in the backwash of truth that did not make it down the toilet when God's standards where flushed out of America. Septic waters are difficult to swallow.

What has happened to us, America? How have right and wrong become so cloudy? *Could it have anything to do with the moral-relativistic religion of Secular Humanism that we have allowed three generations of Americans to be brainwashed with in our government schools?* Could it have anything to do with the unwillingness of the pulpits to draw a line in the sand, based on God's moral law*? Are the pulpits complicit by encouraging public school attendance?*

Look at this! How can anyone call a precious baby "punishment"? How could anyone who would not defend precious unborn babies even be considered for ANY leadership role at ANY level?

Hillary says she is a Christian. Barack's church has received national exposure recently for racist and unbiblical views. They both claim to follow a holy Jesus! If no one else will say it, I will. Hillary Clinton and Barack Obama are not Christians. They are pagans.

I feel it coming already....the *"who are you to judge"* emails....usually from other brain-washed, brain-dead Christians. Let me put it another way. Hillary's and Barack's lives do not bear the fruit of Christianity. Not real Christianity. They bear the fruit of paganism.

Oh, they want to protect the environment, feed the poor, and provide healthcare, which ARE Christian values. But they want government to be God. They want government to play the role of provider and protector. They want government to have some Christian characteristics. But they do not want righteous government. They want a government where the standards of right and wrong can be voted on. They are doing all they can to push God out of government so that those in power can play god.

Because of "elected officials" like them, having a baby is now considered *"punishment."*

Hillary and Barack may go to church and they may claim Christianity but they don't obey God nor do they expect others to obey Him. Think I am wrong? What about this:

"If you love me, keep my commandments." And this: *"Thou shalt love thy neighbour as thyself. There is none other commandment greater than these."*

I used to tell our football players that you can judge a person's character by the way he treats the *"least of thy brethren."* Jesus said: *"And the King shall answer and say unto them, Verily I say unto you, Inasmuch as ye have done it unto one of the least of these my brethren, ye have done it unto me."*

Who is more defenseless than an unborn baby? I don't know what Jesus thinks about government healthcare, or fighting so-called man-made global warming, or government relief (rather than His Church) for the poor. But of this one thing I am sure, God hates the killing of unborn children. God gave us a choice all right, and He told us what to choose.

"I call heaven and earth to record this day against you, that I have set before you life and death, blessing and cursing: therefore choose life, that both thou and thy seed may live:" (Deuteronomy 30:15-19)
How did we reach the point where protecting the environment is more important than protecting babies? How can a man be found guilty of murdering a baby in the womb but the mother can do the same deed with impunity? Murky moral waters, my friend.

Can one call himself a Christian if he can't pass the life test? *"....that you and YOUR SEED might live."* Shouldn't a Christian agree with God on the issue of life? Can a true Christian be pro-death to the innocent?

Barack is for death. Hillary is for death. They are of their father, the Devil. Read it for yourself. They worship death and everything that leads to death. They promote death, defend death, and spread death. (Author's note: This brings to my mind *Darwinian Evolution* and 1850s agnostic English philosopher Herbert Spencer's book *Social Statics* and his back-then new term *survival of the fittest* that Darwin subsequently adopted.)

Before you go there, I am also sick of the "war" party, so don't throw that in my face. If the "war" party was as serious about saving babies as they are about spreading an always doomed democracy, maybe God would be able to smile upon us once again. Remember this: *God hates hands that shed innocent blood.* Read this list. God is angry with the wicked every day. If we want terrorism to stop in the world we must stop the terrorism in the womb.

Secular Humanism is a Religion where man is god. It is based on "reason, logic, and justice." It is *Paganism* and *Paganism* is now the *Religion* of America. Pagans are hedonistic. We have become a selfish, self-indulgent lot, we Americans. We abort babies because that innocent baby might *"mess up our lives."* We are *"lovers of pleasure more than lovers of God."* A baby is created in the image of God, but we love ourselves more than we love God, and that's why babies are now called *"punishment."* God called them ***"a blessing."***

Our leaders call themselves Christian but they are hedonists. Hedonists believe in the glorification of nature and pleasure. Our courts are pagan, our schools are pagan, our entertainment is pagan, and our government is pagan. Our leaders spout the name of Jesus but they only *"have a form of godliness."* Let's face it. We are voting for pagans, not Christians…both Donkeys and Elephants. Is John McCain a servant of Christ?

In all of your life, have you ever done anything more important than being a parent? Before you were a parent did you ever think it was possible to love another human being so deeply? *"Greater love has no man than this than he would lay down his life for his friend."* Five thousand American babies will be sacrificed today as we argue over health-care, the environment, and the economy. **Will no one fight for the babies?**

Pro-abortion politicians do not have the love of Christ, no matter how much they talk about "their religion." They love themselves, their careers, and their agendas more than they love others. They won't stand up for the helpless.

Again, thou shalt say to the children of Israel:
"Whosoever he be of the children of Israel, or of the strangers that sojourn in Israel, that giveth any of his seed unto Molech; he shall surely be put to death: the people of the land shall stone him with stones. And I will set my face against that man, and will cut him off from among his people; because he hath given of his seed unto Molech, to defile my sanctuary, and to profane my holy name. And if the people of the land do any ways hide their eyes from the man, when he giveth of his seed unto Molech, and kill him not: Then I will set my face against that man, and against his family, and will cut him off, and all that go a whoring after him, to commit whoredom with Molech, from among their people. (Leviticus. 20:2-5)

Abortion is hedonistic, pagan, and demonic. Abortion is child-sacrifice. God specifically condemns it. Humanism teaches us that sometimes in order to be happy we must sacrifice our offspring to Molech, the god of self.

Our leaders support it, are complicit in it, and encourage it. They teach it to our children (in the public school classrooms) and they teach them the doctrines of demons—*the "I wills"* right out of the Devil's mouth.

Which view do Hillary and Obama hold? Obviously, hedonistic humanism! Hillary and Obama serve Molech, not Jesus. How can we even dare ask God to bless America when we sacrifice our children on the altar of pleasure?

Terrorism in the womb leads to terrorism in the world. (end)

Thank you Coach Dave. Although, this is not the only evil that is taught to our children, it is key to our culture of death, taught by those against our God, our families, and our country in public schools. Stand up Christians; Speak up Church, or we will be responsible for the enemies who continue to kill, steal, & destroy the babies, and in the future the elderly and physically impaired/challenged, and Godly foundations of our once great country.

A Liar that Kills, Steals, and Destroys

Satan is the father of lies, and uses lies as the primary tool as he seeks to kill, steal, and destroy. His dupes—also known as *"useful idiots"* of the Communist Movement so-named by their superiors in the Party—are rotting our country from within it. Hopefully, *truly hopefully*, you now see their goals and know their successes. Again I will repeat: they seek to kill, steal, and destroy Christianity, the family, and our nation, and put our children at risk for eternity. They cause dissatisfaction and cause riots as they persist in stirring up hatred and unrest and dissension among the citizens of our nation in every area and realm of our lives. They are relentless in the pursuit of causing chaos in our country. Satan's other dupes—the sodomites—are helping to rot our country internally, you see their goals and know their successes; they seek to kill, steal, and destroy Christianity, the natural family, and put our children at risk for physical and psychological illnesses now and for eternity. More of Satan's dupes—through the radical religion of Islam—are helping to rot our country internally, you see their same goals and know their successes; they seek to kill, steal, and destroy Christianity, the family, and put our children at risk for eternity. Satan's Socialist/Communist dupes—the Humanists—are helping to rot our country internally, you see their goals and know their successes; they seek to kill, steal and destroy Christianity, the family, and put our children at risk for eternity. Now, after *clearly restating this*, I think you can connect the dots.

Let us also remember that when the United States falls into a Socialist dictatorship, the whole world will suffer as we support almost all of the third-world countries now. When a disaster happens anywhere in the world, who is it that rushes in to help rescue the people of other nations? Is it one of the third-world countries? No! it's the USA! Where will they be when we become a third-world country living in self-imposed poverty?

Christian leaders of the people have always been looked at as the watchmen, yet His Shepherds are many times seemingly blind to every danger. Scripture talks about many of them as *silent* watchdogs that *give no warning when danger comes.* Ones that love to lie around sleeping, greedy dogs but never satisfied. They were stupid Shepherds, all following their own ways and all intent on personal gain. (Isaiah 56:9-11)

Pusillanimous Christian leaders may each of you repent. Ask God to deliver you from the evil of apathy, fear and laziness, as being one like many that are behaving this way during these tragic times. All Christians should **hate** the evil in these agendas and if you have been silent and inactive against this evil, there should be repentance and a cry to God to *"deliver us from evil"* as *we work under His command. Faith without works is truly a dead faith.* Make no mistake, to be silent and inactive is giving aid and comfort to these enemies, and something that should cause great shame to any Christian behaving this way.

If you claim Jesus, and call Him Lord, then follow His commands and stand up as a **man**. Engage the enemy for love of God's at-risk children who are at risk of going to hell for eternity. Start speaking about it; from the pulpit. Encourage leaders in your Church to form groups to decide what action could be taken by your Church members. Form committees and seek out other Churches in your area and ban together for group thinks and plan activities. My hope and prayer is that you are restored to your first Love, to live out your faith with conviction to follow Jesus to the cross, even to the point of death.

(Psalm 94:16) *"Who will rise up for me against the evildoers? Who will stand up for me against the workers of iniquity?*

Chapter 7

Christians--Traitors?
How Can That Happen?

Can Christians be Giving Aid and Comfort to the Enemies of God, Family, and Country?

(Matthew 13:25) *"While we were sleeping, the enemy came and sowed weeds among the wheat."*

HOPE!!! I start with that word to let you know that there is hope, even though the pain you will have to endure, by receiving the evidence that shows many Christian teachers, parents, and people from all walks of life are *traitors,* most out of ignorance, will be great. Please know that Jesus would forgive your repentant heart and have mercy on you, and tell you to go and sin no more, if you would choose to repent. He would want you to *know* these truths, so that you may be set free and become real *men* and *women* of God. All of us have different gifts, God is using this vessel to warn, love, and restore His children. Don't take a chance by ignoring the evidence and find that you or a loved one is called home by God in the morning, or even five minutes from now. This is a serious sin of negligence on the part of Pastors and all Christian adults.

Listen to the words of one of the greatest Christian *men* America has been able to call one of her sons, **Patrick Henry:**

> **"Are we disposed to be of the number of those who having eyes, see not, and having ears, hear not, the things which so nearly concern their temporal salvation? For my part, whatever anguish of spirit it**

may cost, I am willing to know the whole truth; to know the worst and provide for it."

This is also true about our Spiritual Salvation, and we must pray for God's Holy Spirit to impart His wisdom and understanding to open our eyes and ears; we must be willing to receive it, no matter how our prideful spirit may resist hearing it.

Pray not only for yourself, but for your friends, family, and neighbors, so that you and they will ask the Holy Spirit to give them the strength to read, see, hear, and understand the truth that you see in God's Word through His watchmen, because the enemies of God, family, and country have been convincing you otherwise for generations now. Ultimately, you will choose God's ways or man's ways. One gives life, the other death. One offers heaven, the other hell. If you, yes YOU, are able to get through this book and do what God asks of you, then you can be used to save the children, families, and country from certain destruction.

Hold on!!! Where are the mature Christian *men* and *women* (and) What are they doing as we pay tax dollars for government public education to kill children in Spirit, Mind, and Body? Do we love God if we have the children in an Atheistic and Pagan education system that is anti-God? Do we love the children and family, if we have the children in an atheistic, pagan education system that helps send them to hell for eternity? Do we love our country if we allow our children to be indoctrinated in an education system that is fulfilling the Communist agenda? Remember what our Leader said: *"If anyone harms the least of these....."*

"Learn not the ways of the heathen." (Jeremiah 10:2)

This system of Federal Education Programs and NEA/AAUP education dictatorship kills over fifty percent of our children's futures by dumbing them down and causing them to drop out of school because it kills their *individual* incentive to dream to become all they can become. It kills all the children's national pride in America. These "children" become America-hating "adults." Practically all the curriculum from K-12 is utter fuzzy confusion or sex ed classes or meaningless social(ist) science classes which their minds cannot comprehend, or collide with the ideals their parents try to instill in them—causing even more confusion or humiliation if they try to state their moral or historical beliefs. Because of this, the children do not know what is happening to them and why they "just don't care or are depressed" or "why they cannot learn the subject matter" or "why they have the internal struggle by the time they are teens that causes them to rebel." Teenage rebellion is *not normal*—we've bought that lie from the behavioral scientists that are purposely causing it—the same as we bought the ADD lie caused by all of this so-called "education." Children (and parents I might add—who are unaware of what is happening to their children) unjustly accuse themselves and suffer much guilt by what they are forced to endure and also forced to "learn" that is so much against what their parents have taught them to believe. It is indeed a tragedy of great magnitude. This kind of mental torture and abuse is enough to drive many over the edge, into alcohol and drug abuse, promiscuous sex or pornography, and even suicide. Consider all the "legal" drugs the children are subjected to in order to help them cope through this misery—also known as ADD and ADHD.

I think that this may be the time to include the following assignment paper that a young man wrote during his first year in college, for his English class, which he wrote concerning his education experiences. Having attended three types of educational systems throughout his young life, it is quite revealing though the young man did not even realize what insight he was giving into the public school educational system, by what he wrote. I saw it immediately. It does reveal that he suffered from the "rebellion" phase that most teenagers go through during those traumatic public school years, and that parents have been made to believe and accept as "normal behavior" but is thoroughly misunderstood. Having been in the public school system as educator, administrator and Superintendent, I contend that it is not normal for a child to have to experience rebellion during those years as is the claim of most psychologists today and for the past few decades. It has become a predictable force as a result of the public school educational system, itself. Students in home schools or private schools and most charter schools are hardly touched by the phenomenon. In reality, students in public schools are not rebelling so much against their parents, *as it has been preached to us*, as they are against the NEA and AAUP liberal humanist socialist amoral education agendas which conflicts with their internal codes of morality and ethics—particularly if the student is a Christian—*but for all students in general*, as God has placed in every human being the conscience to know right from wrong, Christian or not.

It should also be noted that this student suffered from blaming himself for this injustice that he was subjected to—as he watched his grades fall from excellent to barely getting by and as his admitted LOVE for learning changed into apathy. What guilt he suffered! that should not have had to be borne by him (or by so many of our precious students who suffer from this). Being a Christian young man, he was able to "hang in there" and complete his High School education, against the odds. The influence of his Christian parents, though they, too, considered Matthew's rebellion one of his own making, helped in other ways to encourage him to say in school. We really do need to help parents understand that they *should undertand* this "new," but decade-old phenomena of rebellion, produced by public-education. *We could save a lot of children if they did understand it—but we won't unless we all wake up and march to the schools and demand that they stop their hidden agendas-curriculum.*

Today, everything around students is in chaos, with no discipline, as well as confusing chaos in most of the subjects they are forced to learn. This is a critical paper in that it shows, as we follow the student as he progresses from Christian School to Public School to Charter Middle School and finally to Public High School, the state-of-mind experienced, from wanting to learn, and being allowed to learn academically, to not being challenged or receiving meaningless, confusing curriculum in most classes, along with truly stupid books that were assigned to be read. Remember as you read, the student is oblivious as to what his schooling is producing in him—and do remember, the process is called "intentional dumbing-down—and his glorified opinion of the education system has been well indoctrinated into his thought processes." For background purposes, Matthew is a born-again fundamental Christian young man.

My Personal Relationship with Education
Matthew Curtis, College Student

The American education system is the most vital part of this country's foundation. The American people rely on this important system to educate future presidents, doctors, businessmen, and our working class. Without the educational system in this country there would be social and cultural problems. To me, it is an experience, one that I must devote most of my time and effort to. It shapes and molds me into a knowledgeable, intelligent citizen. As I went through the system, I had a few similarities with Rodriguez (paper on Rodriguez follows) and how he thought about learning. The American education system has affected the relationship with my family and culture as well with how I view myself as an individual.

My family originally comes from Poland and Germany. They immigrated to America in the late 1800's and started out in the working class society. (Author's note: I have learned that Matthew's German grandparents were large and small business owners upon coming to this country.) They brought their Christian (Catholic) beliefs with them. Education has always been a big part of my family's culture. Every succeeding generation has been more prosperous due to the big push on education that influences my family. There is never discouragement on learning, instead, the constant encouragement to learn more has been a part of my family's culture. It is this importance on education that has brought our working class family into the upper-middle class. The sacrifices my ancestors took to insure proper education is why I am able to go to college and write this paper on my own computer. Without the advocacy my ancestors gave their children, my parents might not have been able to provide me with the education I need to be more prosperous than them. My experience began when I was five years old.

My first experience with the American education system was when I started kindergarten. It was different than most children however, because the first school I attended was First Assembly, a private Christian school. During my years at First Assembly my appreciation towards learning was I couldn't get enough of it. I "...hoarded the pleasures of learning." (Rodriguez 626) I was exposed to the wonders of education and all it had to offer. After the price of tuition became too expensive, I spent the last half of my fourth grade in a public elementary school. There I saw the true (public) educational system at work. The learning was not as accelerated as the private school. Because the style and speed of learning was different, during the time I spent at the elementary school I lost my zeal and enthusiasm I had for learning. I thought that learning was dull and dry. (As a result I was shortly removed from that school and) it wasn't until (Charter) middle school that my fire for learning was rekindled.

At Paramount Charter Academy, my relationship with education greatly improved. Like Rodriguez, I was always wanting more, sucking up information like a dry sponge. My hand was the first raised at questions; I would sometimes even shout the answer out in eagerness. I read books for fun and was in Science Olympiad; I couldn't get enough of it. Like Rodriguez, I was: "Too eager, too anxious—an imitative and unoriginal pupil." (Rodriguez 622) During my middle school years I was very much like Rodriguez, except I knew my family was behind me all the way.

Once I moved on to (Public) high school, I went through a stage of rebellion. Instead of rebelling against my parents, I rebelled against my education. I became the best slacker I knew. I could sleep through school, do 50% of my homework, and still manage to pass my classes, even if it was by a half percent. (Believe me, it happened!) Unlike Rodriguez, my appreciation towards learning went downhill. I lost all drive and passion I once had for it (again). (Author's note: At this point, this is Matthew's second experience with NEA Public Schools—coincidence? I do not think so!) This time, it wasn't the change in schools or the style of teaching, I just felt like rebelling against something. My parents were disappointed in me for choosing this lifestyle, but still pushed me, which is probably why I am not still in high school with tons of credits to make up. (Author's note: Notice the "guilt" and "rebellion" against learning that this student was experiencing—and "boredom.")

In Rodriguez's story he did not think that his parents helped him much through school. He thought that his family was distant from him and chose rather to spend his time in books rather than with his family. It was not until he had realized that he was a "scholarship boy" that he was finally able to go home and appreciate his family. He still had the appreciation towards learning but felt that he had enough of his intensive studies out of the way and he was ready to live his life.

In the first part of Rodriguez's paper his relationship with his family was very poor. He criticized them in negative ways for not getting the education they needed to have better jobs in America. I do not think this criticism was necessary and that he was just being selfish and immature when he thought about his parents. In the last part of Rodriguez's paper he feels a sudden urge to go back and rethink his education history and how it affected him. He went home and noticed things about his parents that he hadn't picked up on before. He found that his parents were not complete strangers after all, but similar to him in many ways. He realized that it was because of his education that he was able to draw conclusions about how his parents lived based on how much they let education influence culture. The same education that had made him bitter towards his parents now let him see clearly as to how his parents lived. He appreciates this knowledge that he has acquired through all of his long years of study. I can't relate to this idea that Rodriguez had about his parents. I knew from the start of my education that I owed it to my parents and family to help me through the learning process. I did not criticize them, but was thankful for their support.

Now my appreciation and relationship with education is improving. I am finding it easier to appreciate learning as I once did. I am not back to the student like Rodriguez, but hopefully I will be able to bounce back into the swing of things very soon. Education is the single most important component in our modern lifestyles. Without the American Educational System, our country would be in shambles and poverty.

(Author's comment: This statement is innocently lacking in mature wisdom—our country is just that—because of the dummying down and demoralizing of most of our students.)

It is this educational system that has shaped and molded not only me, but has done the same for every person who has gone through it. The American Educational system has affected me in the most positive of ways towards my relationship with my family, culture, and myself.

Works Cited: Rodriguez, Richard. *The Achievement of Desire*. College English: Nov. 1978 (end)

(Author's note: It is obvious to me, having been part of the Public School system, that Mr. Curtis' experience in high school is what most of our students go through—and that they truly do not know why they have the feelings and thoughts that they do. He states that the American Educational System has been "good for him" because he is not old enough or experienced enough to understand that this philosophy has also been drummed into him by his teachers. Students are simply too young, and most parents are not aware of the depth of the negative indoctrination the students must mentally and emotionally deal with and try to live through, the lack of challenge, and the fight they have to go through within themselves to stay in school, amidst the chaotic atmosphere, and the struggle to maintain their Christian worldview. Parents and pastors also have been sold the lie that rebellion in the teenage years is unavoidable (as stated above but bears repeating)—and they do not realize that the rebellion has been manipulated into the student's life by the subversive NEA and AAUP curriculum to cause dissention on so many fronts, for their ultimate goals for their Socialist cause. Thank you, Matthew, for this insightful paper and your permission to use it. My heart bleeds for these students whose inner turmoil is very great.)

I would also like to include the following paper by Matthew Curtis simply because it is background information on the authors that Matthew quotes in his first article. I am not cognizant of the fact whether Matthew was assigned his topic or if he chose the topic for his papers. Nevertheless, this second paper is one that shows the dramatic "conflicts of thought" that are held within the educators' minds of today, and what they are purporting to the students. You will read more along these avenues of thought, in great detail, later in this book.

Nonetheless, I am glad that Matthew, whether he chose the subject or not, has shed some valuable light here. Gone are the days when students were taught basics and good literature—what we have today is the intentional indoctrination/brainwashing of our students into a political system that is geared almost entirely toward the NEA and AAUP's goals for a Socialist United States of America through the elimination of our past culture history and belief systems, through the intentional and systematic dummying down of our students, and demoralizing and desensitizing them to accept decadent lifestyles. Whether these students-become-adults will ever be able to understand what has happened to them is questionable—since the very brainwashing they have received in the government schools may never allow them to do so. That's the goal of the brainwashing system. Seeking the Holy Spirit's Truth will enlighten and enable them— but the masses of our students, never being evangelized, will never have the benefit of learning His Truth. The Atheistic Humanist educational system itself will prevent evangelizing them—which is why we Christians must jerk ourselves awake and begin praying and repenting so God will hear our prayers and have mercy on us. Let's move along now into Matthew's second paper:

Rodriguez and Freire on Education
Matthew Curtis, College Student

Education is the cornerstone in today's society. It influences and alienates people so that they may be successful in the world. This influence and alienation that comes from the modern education system affects humans and how they live. Paulo Freire and Richard Rodriguez both agree that the popular educational system causes alienation, but have different ways of how this problem should be solved. The banking concept and the problem posing method are two forms of education that Freire and Rodriguez both have strong opinions about. The idea of this paper is to explain their differing ideas and to compare and contrast them.

Rodriguez argues that education changes people by separating the student from his family and culture. The student must decide *(sometimes subconsciously) whether to embrace the alienation and grow farther from his family and culture, or to deny his teachers and stay with the family's lifestyle. The student must "...take his first step towards academic success, away from his family."* (Rodriguez) *His idea of the "Scholarship Boy" is an example of how a person who embraces the education and at the same time denies his ancestors, can be successful in the world we live in. "A primary reason for my success in the classroom was that I couldn't forget that schooling was changing me and separating me from the life I enjoyed before becoming a student."* (Rodriguez 623) He believed that in order to be successful in life, you must learn to become a *cultureless* individual. (Author's *emphasis added*)

Growing up as a scholarship boy showed Rodriguez the true nature of the modern educational system. By taking in all of the opinions the teachers gave him and believing it as facts, he would then start "...to idolize my grammar school teachers, imitating their accents, using their diction, trusting their every direction." (Rodriguez) *Instead of having the teachers show Rodriguez how the real world worked, they told him opinions about how they thought the world worked and with that denied Rodriguez and other students from the truth, their individualism.* (All Author's *emphasis*)

There are certain aspects about Rodriguez's education theory that Freire would encourage and discourage based on his own model. The idea of the Rodriguez's "scholarship boy" ties in closely with Friere's banking system style of teaching, where "the student records, memorizes, and repeats" (Freire 1) what the *teacher's opinions are. This banking system causes students to lose their individualism and their culture. Without the students own ideas and praxis, "individuals cannot be truly human."* (Freire) (Author's *emphasis*)

Freire counters this banking system with the problem posing method. He believes that the teacher as well as the student should be actively involved in the teaching. By having the class involved in discussion, both the teacher and the student will have their chance to speak and teach. Through this problem-posed discussion, the student can take in the information and analyze it, then share their own opinion with the teacher and the rest of the class. "The teacher presents the material to the students for their consideration and re-considers her earlier considerations as the studiers express their own." (Freire) This method keeps the teachers opinion from swaying the students idea's about the world and helps the teacher learn from the students opinions as well.

The problem posing method also brings out the idea of

praxis. Praxis is the process of application of what you have been taught. Freire believes praxis important to the student and how they will live their lives after the teacher has finished the curriculum. Freire believes that through the dialog that comes with praxis, students will be more likely to understand, and want to make a difference. "Dialog wasn't just about deepening understanding—but was part of making a difference in the world." (Smith 2) "The process is important and can be seen as enhancing community and building social capital and to leading us to act in ways that make for justice and human flourishing." (Smith 2) However, for a dialog to happen there must be respect from either side of the dialog. There must be understanding from either side when the dialog is engaged. Without respect for another, people will not be able to have a successful dialog with each other.

Both Freire and Rodriguez have valid points to make on the modern educational system. The influences that education brings can be seen as both positive and harmful to developing students. The banking concept of teaching is discouraged by both Freire and Rodriguez because it is an impersonal, alienating form of education. The problem posing method, suggested by Freire, is a better way to teach both students and teachers in an open, respectful way. Both of these models of teaching have their own positive and negative aspects, but both work towards educating the student. It can make a student academically successful by memorizing and restating everything that the teacher says, or learning through dialog in a respectful environment. **Though Freire and Rodriguez may not agree on all ideas of education, they both understand that education leads to *alienation from your culture*. (Author's emphasis added)**

Works Cited

Reese, Robert. *The Relationship of a reader and a writer: Rodriguez and Hoggart.* 2002.

Lantengo. 22 October 2006.
http://writing.lantengo.com/rodriguez.php7>

Smith, Mark. *Paulo Freire.* 30 January 2005. Infed. 12 October 2006, http://www.infed.org/thinkers/et-freir.htm
(end)

Pastors, are you willing to be reviled for Christ? Are you willing to even encourage your congregants to be willing to be reviled for Him?—for that is what He has called us to be willing to suffer for His name's sake, and for the keeping of or the furtherance of His good news. Are you willing to be unpopular to those that are of the world and apart from Jesus?—to be known as a "peculiar person or people. Are you willing to speak the truth no matter what the cost? Are you too timid to bring up evil controversial issues that plague our lives and nation to your sheepm for fear of alienating them? Are you willing to go past the point of no return for the souls of His children and for the freedoms we enjoy in our nation? Are you willing to pick up a Cross because you love God and love the children and fight for saving their souls for eternity? If you have answered *yes* to any of these questions, thank God. If you were prompted by the Holy Spirit to say *yes* to all of theses questions, then the Bible and this book will prepare you for what you can do to combat the enemies within. I think it has been emphasized quite clearly what we as a nation are headed for if Pastors and Christian families continue to do nothing. Be comforted with these words of Jesus, if you decide to step out of the boat.

(Matthew 5:10-12) ***"Blessed are they which are persecuted for righteousness sake; for theirs is the kingdom of heaven. Blessed are you, when men shall revile you, and persecute you,*** *and shall say all manner of evil against you falsely, for my sake. Rejoice, and be exceedingly glad: for great is your reward in heaven: for so persecuted they the prophets which were before you."*

Job Description: Needed: Mature Men and Women, Leaders for God, seven days a week. Christians are needed who understand the times and know that our children and most of their neighbors and friends are at risk every moment that the disciples of Jesus are asleep and silent. Are His children going to hell for eternity because of your action or inaction? Pray for Wisdom. Hard work ahead—Apply now.

Listen to the words of Jesus: *"But whoso shall offend one of these little ones which believe in me, it were better for him that a millstone were hanged about his neck, and that he were drowned in the depth of the sea. Woe unto the world because of offenses! For it must needs be that offenses come but woe to that man by whom the offense comes."* (Matthew 18:6-7)

STOP!!! Are you aware that children are growing up to go to hell because Church leaders and Christians in general have allowed Satan and his dupes to control the education of the young? As written above—are you one of those who are willing to continue to listen to beautiful sounding rhetoric, while it produces rotting fruit, from males and females that wish to control you, as they vomit words that are like the changing wind, while our posterity faces an eternity out of the presence of God? Remember these words from the Lord and apply them to every male and female that speaks of the written word to you, which includes church leaders, government leaders, educators, and even me.

Thus says the Lord: *"Cursed be the man that trusts in man, and makes flesh his arm, and whose heart departs from the Lord." Jeremiah 17:5,* and remember also these words of the Lord: *"The heart is deceitful above all things, and desperately wicked;*

who can know it? I the Lord search the heart. I try the reins, even to give every man according to his ways, and according to the fruit of his doings." Jeremiah 17:9.

LISTEN!!! To paraphrase part of the sermon, *"Sinners in the Hands of an Angry God,"* by Jonathan Edwards:

Man's prudence and care to preserve his own life, or through care of someone else to preserve him, does not secure him for a moment. God in His Divine Providence and universal experience from the time of Adam and Eve bear testimony to this. Man's own wisdom does not secure him from death; if it were otherwise, we would see some difference between the wise and shrewd men of the world, and others. Perhaps wise and shrewd men would have less liability to early and unexpected death. But, how is it, in fact? *"How dies the wise man? Even as the fool." Ecclesiastes 2:16*

As Edwards continues:

Noting that the heart is deceitful above all things and desperately wicked as stated in Jeremiah, men take great efforts to escape hell, even though they in some ways and to differing degrees continue to reject Christ and thus remain wicked men, even though they would convince themselves otherwise, and none of these plans secure them from hell even one moment. Most men and women who hear of hell convince and flatter themselves that they will escape it. Most men and women depend on themselves for their own security and flatter themselves because of what they have done, what they are now doing, or what they intend to do.

And further: When people know that hell exists, whether you believe it or not, hell is an absolute, and each person lays out in their own mind how they will avoid damnation, and oh how they flatter themselves that they have a well laid plan and that their scheme will not fail. Even though we hear in Scripture that the path is wide that goes to hell and that there are few who are saved, and that more have gone to hell than to heaven out of those that have died before him, yet each person imagines that they lay out matters for their own escape better than others have done. Also, because of the torment of hell described in the Scriptures, people will tell themselves that they will not fail in their efforts to lay out plans that will keep them from this lake of fire. Being far too confident in their own schemes, the foolish children of men will miserably delude themselves into thinking their own strength and wisdom will prevail, yet it is indeed no more than a shadow. Most people who have lived before each of us, that are now dead, and thought that their scheme in their own power and wisdom would work are probably, even undoubtedly in hell. Do not think for a moment that they were not as wise as you or anyone else alive today, or that they did not lay out matters to escape hell as well as those alive today. If we were able to ask each person in hell if they ever expected to be in this torment, they would say that they had plans never to come to such a place, and even as they relied on their own wisdom and strength to lay out plans to escape hell, they would tell us how God's wrath was too quick for them, like a thief in the night. Remember this, God is not obligated to keep you from eternal destruction in hell for even a moment of time until you believe in Christ, and follow His commands, that is your only security and that is the only security for those you love and touch in this life."

So what do Christian leaders in Christian churches and ministries, Christian educators in the government schools, and Christian parents and neighbors have to do so they and those around them are assured of hell for eternity? **NOTHING!** Yes, if we continue not raising the banner of Christ, if we continue not standing up for Christ to those around us, if we continue not to surrender and submit ourselves and repent to Christ, if we continue in disobedience to Christ's commands, then our willingness to do nothing will help to send many to hell for eternity. This is seen by the enemy as your being ASHAMED of the Gospel of Jesus. Eternity is for a long time—and it could start before your next heartbeat—or one of the children's..

Atheistic Communists, Humanists, Pagans, and other traitors that kill, steal and destroy, walk amongst us and control the education of our young. They are against God, family, and country, and those that call themselves Christians, from all walks of life, naively give them aid and comfort on a daily basis. It seems as though God's Spirit has me repeating this over and over—to the point that I am tired of hearing it myself, but trusting His Spirit, I will continue to say it as many times as He imparts it. I won't question Him; perhaps it really needs to sink into the minds and hearts of the readers.

If you desire for the children to be in the presence of God for eternity, you must see through the eyes of Jesus by His Holy Spirit He has placed in you as a believer, and know with His wisdom. You must kneel down right now while it is in your power through the Grace of God, before you go further in this book, and pray that the Holy Spirit will be your Helper, Counselor and Comforter, to let your eyes see and your ears hear. Why this prayer, and why this cry? Because so many children and that includes Christian children's souls, are being lost. Christian Pastors and their people, while the government education system is wide awake and working feverishly, are soundly sleeping. They depend on you to stay asleep! Know up front that as you read the truth in this book, that you will face choices you must make (don't delay choosing to say *yes* to the Son of God).

> *"Be not conformed to this world; but be ye*
> *transformed by the renewing of your mind."*
> *(Romans 12:2A)*

Knowing the truth will set you free, note the operative word *knowing*. In 1 Chronicles 12:32 it talks about the men of Issachar who had understanding of their times and *knew* what Israel should do. So listen carefully to these words,

> *"Study to show thyself approved unto God, a workman*
> *that needs not to be ashamed, rightly dividing the word*
> *of truth."* (II Timothy 2:15.)

Know the primary source evidence and study the facts, never exaggerating, and although feelings are important, they become an opinion, so stay with the thinking facts which become the foundation of truth.

Is it offensive to us to ask ourselves, "Am I ignorant or stupid?" People are many times offended when asked that same question by others. We are all ignorant in some way, but can we be called stupid if we choose not to know something just so that we can selfishly stay comfortable in ignorance? Is it stupidity when Christians pay others to lie to our children, rape our children, kill our children, infect our children with STDs, indoctrinate the children to kneel to a one world government rather than to God, dumb down the children, indoctrinate the children that man should be able to marry man, teach our children that all religions are to be considered as just different ways to God, indoctrinate our children that God did not create, propagandize our children to accept the atheistic communist, humanist, pagan ways, teach our children that parents should stay out of education and let the school socially engineer their children away from God, family, and country, and finally, should we pay the government to school our children in such a way that puts them at risk of going to hell for eternity? What do you say to Christian leaders, Christian teachers, Christian parents and neighbors that say "LORD, LORD" to Jesus, yet know that Jesus would ask them, ***"Why call me LORD, LORD, and then do not what I say?"***

May the Holy Spirit open your eyes and ears to God's Word. May I not give you any words of myself that do not come from our Lord and Savior's Word. Those that are His children, hear His word, and know it is required of you to be like Jesus, i.e., kneel down and pray, and then get up and ACT. Can you hear your children, your grandchildren, your neighbor's children, the posterity of this nation, crying out to HIS men and women, to stand for them? I hope so.

If you are interested in having a true ***man*** of God in your church, standing and acting as an example of Christ, then *pray* for your Shepherds, and *encourage* and *demand* them to do God's will, stay in His Word, and act on His command to disciple the men in their flock to "go ye!" Many Pastors do not have the courage, and whether it is lack of trust in Jesus, or fear of losing members when they speak against the public school system, or too complacent or lazy, or whatever the reason he or she may have for refusing to do so, they need to be prayed for and uplifted for a change of heart, so that they can join that remnant of MEN and WOMEN of Christ, that understand the times and look for the opportunity to engage, like David, the enemies standing against the armies of God. Oh, how we need them! Or perhaps the Pastors are not aware that their congregants will stand with them if they do engage in the battle.

With great sadness, many that call themselves Christians have made all kinds of excuses because of fear, not to follow the commands of Jesus—*forgetting to remember* that He *is* the Son of God—and that He does not *ask us* but He *commands us* to protect the innocents.

Jesus said, ***"All power is given unto me in heaven and in earth. Go ye therefore, and teach all nations, baptizing them in the***

name of the Father, and of the Son, and of the Holy Ghost;
Teaching them to observe all things whatsoever I have
commanded you; and, lo, I am with you always, even unto the
end of the world." Amen. (Matthew 28:18-2)

Did you hear, really *hear* the words of Jesus, the Son of God,
who said that *all power is given to Him in heaven and earth?*
Now *how much power?* Did you hear Jesus say, **"Go ye...."** or
did He say, "sit ye" or "sleep ye?" **"....and teach them to**
observe all things whatsoever I have commanded you,*" teach*
them whose commands? And in addition, **"I am with you**
always," did you *hear* Jesus say that He was with you always?
OK, let's do one more recap. This guy Jesus, who you say is the
Son of God and who you claim as your Savior, tells you He has
all power, *commands* you *to go and teach others to observe His*
commands, and lets you know *that He will be with you always.*

So why are you afraid? If you are the Shepherd of His flock, or if
you are a member of the flock, does Jesus give you the "choice"
of whether or not to protect his sheep or your children? Do you
think that Jesus is a liar? And if not, you must know that going to
church every Sunday as part of the flock to sit in a pew within
four protective walls, listening to a feel-good message from a
pastor who may redesign God so that you are comfortable, or
throwing a few dollars into the basket for the missions, is not
what God is telling you to do. Of course, you should not neglect
the missions, but He is calling you to obey Him and do so much
more than that. With love, the truth must always be spoken, and
if the truth *convicts* you, (be careful because Satan uses
condemnation to anger you), know that you have been blessed by
the grace of God, and you are repentance-ready, and then
submission-ready to perform His demanding works. Aren't you
ready to be a real MAN or real WOMAN of God? Pray right
now for the strength to be a 'go ye' person that follows His
commands and cry out to God to be used by Him to stand in
harm's way for His children. They truly have no one else but us.

Satan is made very happy by our failures to act which is really an awesome act *for his success* in our children's lives.

While the majority of Christian church leaders are completely silent or fail to help parents, Christian brothers and sisters of our Lord are putting their children in harm's way when they send them to government public schools. Trust Jesus as He speaks again through eyewitnesses with His inspired Word.

"Be ye not unequally yoked together with unbelievers: (for too long we have taken this to mean in marriage only!) For what fellowship hath righteousness with unrighteousness? And what communion hath light with darkness? And, what concord hath Christ with Be'-li-al? Or what part hath he that believeth with an infidel? And what agreement hath the temple of God with idols? For ye are the temple of the living God; as God has said, I will dwell in them, and walk in them and I will be their God, and they shall be my people. Wherefore come out from among them and be ye separate." (II Corinthians 7:14-17)

The government public schools of America are breeding grounds for Satan's lies, as they yoke Christian children with unbelievers, as they fellowship Christian children with unrighteousness, as they give our Christian children communion with darkness, as they teach our Christian children the lies of infidels, and as they indoctrinate our Christian children to worship Atheist idols before God. Instead of being separate and teaching our Christian children God's teachings, which teaches us to be separate from these evils, Christian parents purposefully send their children to government public schools and give them over to be among the very things that God said not to be a part of. From the beginning we have had a sinful and rebellious nature. Do we continue, in our rebellion and disobedience, to think that we know a way better than our God's way? Do we live as though we are smarter than God? For in our disobedient actions or non-actions, that is exactly what we are saying and doing.

Are you aware that when you pay for and send children into the government education system you can be considered a traitor since you participate by supporting the enemy that is actively teaching our posterity to be traitors? Many are partakers of treasonous acts because of ignorance but there are those that act in a treasonous way on purpose. We are the first to call people traitors for acts they are performing to cause the downfall of our nation—when in reality, we are traitors too, who fail to act to combat the enemies' goals, and defend our Christian nation and our God.

Traitors walk amongst us. Many of them are in *control* of the education of our children, and they *control* and indoctrinate the teachers that teach our children, and they *control* the teacher unions like the NEA, and professors' union, the AAUP, and they *control* what goes into the textbooks, and they *control* the core-curriculum. This is also known as a *dictatorship* and this dictatorship is ruining our children and our nation. Can you see that we no longer *control* our children—the enemy does! We must not allow ourselves to fool ourselves. An all-out expose' of these unions must be made, nationwide, by every church and every home—with the unions' goals and end-results made public knowledge. That is what this book that is in your hands right now, is attempting to do.

God gave the children to the parents to train up. This means we must be very vigilant about *anyone* or *any institution* that is used to train them up, if we are not doing so ourselves. This is a huge job and a huge responsibility that we cannot pass off to Atheistic Humanist Socialist public schools. God told the fathers to protect the children and teach them all day long, in all ways and in all things, about Him. The schools are not allowing any teaching about God—they have removed him from every aspect of learning. You must not go on hiding from this fact.

In times past, the parents looked to the church for help, but always maintained control of the teaching of their children to make sure it was God-centered according to the Bible. When good Christian people became lax, they were fooled and mislead with lies regarding our Constitution, how children should be educated, and what the purpose of public education was, and its incredibly subversive end goals. As a result, progressively, gradually, incrementally, the government took over the total role of the teaching of our children. The Socialist motto is "move ahead progressively, slowly and swiftly." Prior to this takeover, for many decades it was rare to find someone who was illiterate. In the meantime, parents were lulled into believing public education was proceeding well as long as the name of God was left in the *Pledge of Allegiance* and *The Ten Commandments* and the *Bible* were not outlawed. They were unaware that in the hidden and secret places of the NEA and AAUP, plans were being laid to eliminate God from all aspects of our children's and nation's lives.

Then as usual, the heads of these man-made organizations, as part of the Socialist movement, the NEA and AAUP in our nation, believing they were smarter than God, turned their backs on Him. They began removing all aspects of God from the lives of the children in the public schools. This led them further, by the actual indoctrination of our young, socially engineering them subversively, manipulatively and incrementally, teaching them by self-proclaimed change-agent teachers, that they should be ashamed of the Gospel through humiliating them before their teachers and peers. Today, the goal of education has taken another detrimental turn away from knowledge, toward the de-humanizing of students into a national Atheist Secular Humanist Religion, which is part of the Communist agenda. This agenda permeates every part of the curriculum so that through this social engineering the children will kneel to the State instead of to God. There no longer is, nor can there be, any "choice" in this matter, for parents of these public school children. It has been and is continuing to be a *teacher union-led dictator-controlled* type of schooling. Yet is has gone even farther than that, to indoctrinate them to kneel to and believe in an Atheistic One-World

Government and Religion and all that that implies, with all its perversions, that is not of God. This, too, is incorporated into every subject, now known as "themes," as core-curriculum.

Jesus says, *"I am the way, the truth, and the life, no man comes to the Father, but by me."* (John 14:6)

Chapter 8

Trampled Under the Foot of Man

Christians what did Jesus say about you being salt? *"You are the salt of the earth. But if the salt loses its saltiness, how can it be made salty again? It is no longer good for anything, except to be thrown out and trampled by men."* (Matthew 5:13)

As mentioned before, in Jesus' day, when salt lost its saltiness, it was crushed and used in the roadway, where the people walked. Perhaps we should all pause and think about that.

Where is the Christian Church as Satan works through his dupes to KILL, STEAL, DESTROY, and DIVIDE? The targets?—The Church, American Families and our Nation by controlling the schools and children. Who are the players and why? Please look at the goals and agendas outlined already and those that will follow. Line of Evil plaguing America's families and children: Satan has ownership of the Atheistic Communist Party, the Communists control the Democratic Party Platform, which in turn controls the N.E.A. platform and vice versa, which in turn controls the education of the children. Some would argue that the N.E.A. controls the Democratic party, but either way they bring forth the Communist agenda and the end results harm the children, and decay our families and nation. Know also, the Republican Party has also been infiltrated.

Progressively marching onward....

You have seen the Communist goals and know that they are being implemented and met.

You have seen the Humanist goals and know that they are being implemented and met.

You have seen the Sodomy goals and know that they are being implemented and met.

You have seen the radical Islamic intent and know that it is being implemented and met.

Now watch as the N.E.A. does their part to implement the Socialist/Communist and other goals that are against God, family, and Country. Thank you to Phyllis Schlafly in her tireless work to expose those things that are against God, family and country, and to R.L. Beasley, a true MAN of God, who printed it in his publication "The Beacon." You will notice that many political goals of the NEA have nothing to do with and, in fact work against, giving children a better education—in fact, their goal is being realized more each day. But the Communists are proud of their own "useful idiots," as they call their workers, and their other puppets the Democrats, agree. Look at excerpts and paraphrases from the following article.

The NEA lists it goals and Democrats agree.
By Phyllis Schlafly

Democratic Senator Hillary Clinton told the NEA delegates that she will fight school vouchers with every breath in her body. Democratic Senator Barack Obama likewise inveighed against "passing out vouchers". Former Democratic Senator John Edwards also announced his opposition to vouchers. Democratic Governor Bill Richardson wants to steal more money from parents and raise teacher's average minimum wage to $40,000 a year. Democratic Representative Dennis Kucinich goes all-out for the Communist goal to have a universal pre-kindergarten system which will provide year-around day care for children ages 3-5. All Democratic candidates look forward to increased federal control of and spending for public schools.

The NEA demands a tax-supported single-payer health-care plane (socialized medicine) for all residents (a word artfully chosen to include illegal aliens). The NEA supports immigration "reform" that "includes" [note: this is a change from last year's verb "may include"] a path to permanent residency, citizenship, or asylum" for illegal aliens. This would also steal more money from you.

For many years, and again this year, the NEA urged a national holiday honoring Cesar Chavez. The NEA must have forgotten that Chavez, a strident advocate for farm workers, vehemently opposed illegal immigration because he knew it depressed the wages of U.S. citizens and legal immigrants.

The NEA supports a beefed up federal "hate crimes" law with heavier penalties. They know that this fits their agenda against Christ and supports the pro homosexual agenda. The NEA wants federal legislation to confer special rights on the basis of sexual orientation or gender identity and expression.

The NEA passed at least a dozen resolutions supporting the gay rights agenda in public schools. These cover employment, curricula, textbooks, resource and instructional materials, school activities, role models, and language (with frequent use of terms such as sexual orientation, gender identification, and homophobia).

The NEA enthusiastically supports all the goals of radical feminism, including abortion, the Equal Rights

Amendment, school-based health clinics, wage control so the government can arbitrarily raise the pay for women but not men, the feminist pork called the Women's Educational Equity Act, and letting feminists rewrite textbooks to conform to feminist ideology.

- The NEA supports statehood for the District of Columbia.
- The NEA supports affirmative action.
- The NEA calls for repeal of right-to-work laws, which allow teachers in some states to decline joining the NEA
- The NEA supports United Nations treaties, especially the UN Convention on Women, the UN Convention on the rights of the child, and the International Criminal Court.
- The NEA loves global education, which promotes world citizenship and taxing Americans to give away our wealth to other countries.
- The NEA has another favorite in environmental education, which teaches that human activity is generally harmful to the environment and population should be reduced.
- The NEA wants the right to teach schoolchildren about sex (all orientations) without any interference from parents.
- The NEA wants the educational bureaucracy to regulate all home schooling taught by parents.

Here are some of the things that the Communist NEA opposes:

- Vouchers (for Parental Choice)
- Tuition tax credits
- All parental choice programs
- Making English our official language
- The use of voter ID for elections

- Privatization of Social Security
- Testing of teachers as a criterion for job retention, promotion, tenure, or salary.
- Allowing homeschoolers to participate in any public school sports or extracurricular activities.

Two of the NEA's favorite words in its resolutions and policies are *diversity* (that means teaching that gay behavior is OK), and *multiculturalism* (that means stressing negative things about America and positive things about non-Christian cultures).

The exorbitant dues to the NEA enable its well-paid staff to lobby Congress and state legislatures in behalf of all these goals.

Thank you for your vigilance, Phyllis.

This agenda is financed by some Christian teacher's NEA or AAUP union dues in the public school system, Is their money paying for goals of the Communists, humanists, sodomites, radical feminists, anti-Christians, anti-American sovereignty, anti-moral agendas that are against God, family, and country? Is that giving aid to the enemy, and giving them comfort in your silence, as you bring to and enforce their agenda to an innocent child, putting them at risk of going to hell for eternity? Silly question—the answer is obvious—of course it is!

Scripture (GOD'S WORD) does not allow for Christians to send their children to the government schools that exist in America today. Scripture (GOD'S WORD) does not allow for Christian teachers to pay into a union like the NEA or AAUP that is against God, family, and country. May the Holy Spirit help you to see and hear His voice through those statements. Where are the church, the Christian teachers, and Christian parents in all of this? **It is sinful and tyrannical to**

steal money from Christian patriots to pay for an education system that is opposed to everything that we hold dear. Satan is made happy if you do not hear or see the truth in that statement. **There is one true Shepherd, there is one true Master, there is one true Teacher, and those that call themselves Christian know that to be Jesus. Jesus would command His followers to run as fast as they can from the government schools of America, and if your pastor is not leading this way, then he is not teaching like the one true Teacher.** Pray for your pastor, that the Holy Spirit will give him the boldness and courage that is needed for such a time as this, for many souls are crying out for strong leadership from a true Shepherd who is a mature Christian, who follows in the teachings of Jesus.

As Scripture states, "there is nothing new under the sun." Know that these traitors will destroy this once great country called America if they are allowed to take the Scriptures away from the education of our people. Listen to the wisdom of God through a priest named **Martin Luther, who stated, "I am much afraid that schools will prove to be the great gates of Hell unless they diligently labor in explaining the Holy Scriptures, engraving them in the hearts of youth. I advise no one to place his child where the Scriptures do not reign paramount. Every institution in which men are not unceasingly occupied with the Word of God must become corrupt."**

This is stated well and is truth from Scripture, yet many that call themselves Christians cannot see or hear these words because they are blinded by the world and in slavery to what the world offers. Can you not hear or see God's wisdom when he says:

"Train up your child in the way he should go: and when he is old, he will not depart from it." Proverbs 22:6

Do not the Scriptures cry out to you to raise children *"In the nurture and admonition of the Lord" Ephesians 6:4*

Can you not hear God saying in the Scriptures, *"And thou shalt love the Lord thy God with all thine heart, and with all thy soul and with all thy might. And these words, which I command thee this day, shall be in thine heart; And thou shalt teach them diligently unto thy children, and shalt talk of them when whou sittest in thine house, and when thou walkest by the way, and when thou liest down, and when thou risest up. And thou shalt bind them for a sign upon thine hand, and they shall be as frontlets between thine eyes. And thou shalt write them upon the posts of thy house, and on thy gates." Deuteronomy 6:5-9*

Can you hear God telling you that HE is to be a part of everything in everyway and always first, and would definitely tell those who believe in Him to never sacrifice the children on the altar of Be'-li-al by putting their children in the government schools of the United State? Where are your eyes and ears when God teaches you in *Psalms 127:3* that children are given to parents as:

Lo, children are a heritage of the Lord:"

The Lord would tell you to never put that heritage at risk of hell for eternity by sending them to a humanist, atheist government school in America. Do your ears not hear God speaking in *Isaiah 54:13?*

"All thy children shall be taught of the Lord."

The one true God would never have any of HIS children taught in a government school of the United States of America today.

Chapter 9

Tricks to Form a Communist Collective (Disobeying God by Consensus)

"Watch and pray, that you enter not into temptation; the spirit indeed is willing, but the flesh is weak." Matthew 26:41

Stay the Course—you have been duped along with the overwhelming majority of Christians in America, and I was duped for 52 years myself. Although there is more than one technique to incrementally turn America to becoming an Atheistic Communist country, you need to be aware of a technique that is 200 years old, and has been used for years by Communists, Humanists, and their puppets in the US. It is called the **Hegelian System of Dialectics** and is used in many parts of society today, to manipulate communities. Another great MAN of God will speak to you through his newsletter, and it would be good for you to sign up and get John Stormer's, "Understanding The Times" newsletter, Liberty Bell Press, P.O. Box 32, Florissant MO 63032. Read and reread the following if necessary, *because it was developed as* *a process to erode personal beliefs to achieve group consensus*.

As John States, *"America has lived through a revolution. In the last fifty years, American society, its culture, its churches, its education, its families, its politics, the understanding of the Constitution, economics and government have been transformed drastically.*

"The revolution has changed the way individuals think and live. To bring about the change people had to be moved away from the absolutes of right and wrong they had been taught and believed.

"The goal has been bringing them to accept a whole new set of group values—known as consensus. The change transforms individualists, people who think for themselves and have a firm body of beliefs, into people who fit into and respond as members of a group.

"That the revolutionary change has happened should be apparent to anyone who has observed the transformation of American values, morals, music, TV, etc., in the years since 1960.

"Has it just happened? Or have forces been at work in society which have moved individuals away from the absolutes of right and wrong they once received from parents at home, from teachers <u>through Scripture</u> at school, and from the Bible and the Lord at church."

Dean Gotcher, as a researcher, author and speaker, has effectively analyzed the forces bringing about the revolution and the process being used day-by-day in every area of society. Gotcher heads the Institution for Authority Research. He started his years-long study and research into the methods used to produce the revolution after he nearly lost his faith while attending what claimed to be a Christian college and later at a seminary. As he returned to the Bible-based faith in which he grew up, he started taking classes in secular institutions. He enrolled not to be taught---but rather ***to research how future teachers, administrators, preachers, and business leaders had their own thinking changed and how they were being trained to change the thinking of those who would come under their tutelage and authority in the future.*** He read and studied over 600 books by 250 ***different socio-psychologists and education reformers*** (authors note: Marxist/Communist dupes) **who advocated ways of changing people and society.** Some of the better known names include Carl Rogers, Abraham Maslow, Lawrence Kohlberg, Antonio Gramsci, George Lukacs, Gordon Allport, Erich Fromm, etc. Some like Herbert Marcuse and Theodor

Adorno **were** *part of the infamous German neo-Marxist Frankfurt Institute. They left Germany in the 1930s and came to America to gain positions of influence in universities, Hollywood, etc.*

Gotcher coined the term "DIAPRAX" to label the process the socio-psychologist "change agents' advocate in their writings and teaching to produce the revolution in America's schools, churches, and business. What he found and described is a process through which people are skillfully manipulated away from the "thou shalls" and the "thou shall nots" with which they grew up. The skillful manipulation, usually in group settings, bring individuals to replace the "thou shalls" and "thou shall nots" they've learned with "might be," "could be," or "ought to be." The *transition succeeds* Gotcher says "....*because man's sinful nature, inherited from Adam, resents having anyone in authority telling them what they must do. It is rebellion against authority--rebellion, at its heart, against God."*

For it all to work, the family, and its influence on its children, must be weakened. How the program works in schools to weaken family ties and values is detailed in a later section on education.

The process, which Gotcher has labeled DIAPRAX, is an implementation of German philosopher Georg W. F. Hegel's 200 year old application of the Theory of the Dialectic. DIAPRAX is the term Gotcher coined to characterize....

> *....a dialectical driving for unity, bringing together opposite views, facts or feelings through speculating, conjecturing, theorizing, reasoning, etc.*

What is this *dialectic? The Dictionary of Philosophical Terms and Names* described *dialectics* as: *"...the process of thinking by means of dialogue, discussion, debate or argument.*

From *Noah Webster's 1828 Dictionary* the following concerning dialectics can be developed:

> *The concept of dialectics goes back to the ancient*
> *Greek philosophers (Plato, Socrates, Aristotle,*
> *etc.) and refers to that basis of logic which*
> *teaches the rules and modes of reasoning.*

Gotcher says the *dialectic* is... *using dialogue as a means to resolve conflicting positions.*

> Because *dialectics* glorifies human reason and
> places reason above revelation, *dialectics* is a
> way for "...*moving people away from absolute*
> *truth or values toward group consensus in order*
> *to accomplish "group goals."*

Richard Paul, an influential socio-psychologist, in his book, *Critical Thinking: What Every Person Needs to Survive in a Rapidly Changing World* puts his finger on *reasoning* which is at the heart of dialectics. He said: *"We must come to define ourselves...as people who reason their way into, and can be reasoned out of, beliefs."*

MOVED FROM TRUTH BY FEELINGS

Summed up, *reasoning* seeks reconciliation of the conflict which develops between facts and absolutes (thou shall or thou shall not) and feelings (it could be or it ought to be). Gotcher says "...**such** *reconciliation* **or** *synthesis* **of a conflict is impossible for those who continue trusting and obeying God.**"

What did Hegel contribute to developing *"rules and modes of reasoning* which moves people from being true self-governing, God-fearing individuals to being members of a consensus-controlled group?" The on-line *MSN Encarta Encyclopedia* summarized Hegel's contribution this way:

> *The dialectical method involves the notion that all movement, or process, or progress [change], is the result of the conflict of opposites. Traditionally, this dimension of Hegel's thought has been analyzed in terms of the categories of thesis, antithesis, and synthesis. Although Hegel tended to avoid these terms, they are helpful in understanding his concept of the dialectic.*

Dean Gotcher provides a more down-to-earth practical illustration of the *dialectic* in a group. He wrote:

> *THESIS is what you believe is true for yourself. ANTITHESIS is what others believe is true for their selves [which produces conflict]. SYNTHESIS is the consensus that you and others, through reasoning, come to agree upon what should be generally true for everyone.*

He gives this illustration:

> *THESIS can represent your original position or fact on any issue such as-- "it is always wrong to lie." ANTITHESIS is a different position within the group on the same issue based on feelings: "It is all right to lie to get out of a bad situation-- or to avoid hurting another." SYNTHESIS would be a compromise, a finding of unity to resolve the issue and rationally justify behavior: "It is ok to lie providing it is justifiable in light of the situation, is beneficial to others, and doesn't hurt anybody."*

WANTING ACCEPTANCE BRINGS CONFLICT

Gotcher, in his writings and seminars, shows how for the last fifty or so years socio-psychologists, sometimes known as *"change agents,"* have *developed techniques for causing individuals as part of a group to question their own firmly held beliefs (their thesis).* After stating their view (their thesis), dialogue develops and conflict develops from the antithesis (or opposing possibility). Soon they can be moved along by the *facilitator---a manipulator---*until a consensus (group think) develops. That would be the *synthesis--*the completion of Hegel's cycle. Then it would start all over because everything, Hegel taught, is in a constant state of change.

CONSCIENCE SUBMITS TO GROUP ETHICS

For Hegel, *morality,* which starts as *individual conscience,* must move beyond this to a level of *social ethics.* For Hegel, *social ethics* is not the product of *individual judgment. Individuals can be complete only within social relationships—in the group.*

The on-line *MSN Encyclopedia* summarized Hegel's position this way:

> **Hegel considered membership in the state one of the individual's highest duties. Ideally, the state is the manifestation of the general will, which is the highest expression of the ethical spirit. Obedience to the general will is the act of a free and rational individual.**

In other words, to be "a free and rational individual" it is *necessary to put aside your own views and beliefs and submit to the consensus of the group.* In effect, this means that the individual has value and reality only as a part of a greater unified whole. This view permeates *totalitarian governments* and *much of education, politics, and media in the U.S. today.* (Authors note: The Communists in America are experts at this—it is the very life-blood of the movement.)

The *Grolier Encyclopedia* sees Hegel as saying that true freedom...

> *"...is achieved only as the partial and incomplete desires of the individual are overcome and integrated into the unified system of the state in which the will of one is replaced by the will of all."* **(Author's note: Notice that the wills of all become what the few in power say that it is, and manipulate their resources to make it so.)**

In his writings and lectures Gotcher shows how the process which he has called DIAPRAX—THE PROCESS FOR IMPLEMENTING Hegel's dialectic—is at the heart of change in the basic institutions of society today.

WEAKEN THE FAMILY'S INFLUENCE

Gotcher, from his research, quotes influential socio-psychologists—*change agents*—who advocate the weakening of the family and its authority as the key to changing society and its culture. (Author's note: This is part of the Communist agenda, humanist agenda, NEA agenda, and Sodomite agenda.) Influential socio-psychologist James Coleman wrote in his book, ***The Adolescent Society; the Social Life of the Teenager and its Impact on Education*** wrote:

> *The family must be prepared to deal with [the adolescent's] early social sophistication. Mass media, and an ever-increasing range of personal experiences, gives an adolescent social sophistication at an early age, <u>making him unfit for the obedient role of a child in the family...</u>*

Richard Paul, another influential socio-psychologist in his book, *Critical Thinking: What Every Person Needs to Survive in a Rapidly Changing World* wrote:

> ***Children can and should learn to make up their own minds thoughtfully and reflectively, but they will only do so if parents and teachers recognize the <u>problem created by belief inculcation.</u>***
>
> ***How can we teach dialectic reasoning and pave the way for human emancipation? The classroom environment would be structured so that students feel encouraged to decide for themselves ....<u>teachers should shield their students from the pressure to conform to peers or the community [parents, ministers, police, etc.]</u>***

(Author's note: Understand that the Liberals, Communists, Humanists, NEA and AAUP teachers and professors, ACLU, Sodomites, and other such ilk, must manipulate you as a parent into a no-influence-status in the child's mind and family, except what they deem to be good group-think, that furthers their cause. They have been very successful as Christians have turned their back on the Gospel, to become like the world—to the point that they do not recognize what has happened to themselves, either. They have become so engrossed in the *material* side of life, so busy, that they do not even wish to hear about what is happening in our nation. The process of changing citizen's thought patterns has been done so subtly, so progressively and incrementally, that the masses do not even realize they have been so gradually manipulated into a wholly new frame-of-mind control and way-of-life. Parents no longer have control over their children. Children and parents alike, hate this, and are frustrated by it, but they don't know what has happened to them and cannot correct it because the indoctrination is so thoroughly accomplished in both child and parent. They are told the same song and dance over and over again—"It's just the teenage years." This leaves both parent and child confused and unsettled and the parent, having lost control of their child, is fearful for the child. The child is extremely fearful inside also because he internalizes that he should not be in control, because the child needs the parent to be the parent—and he/she realizes that the state or the school has become the main authority figure in their life, and they really do not want this. This totally confuses the child. Most of what they are taught in school is contrary to what the parents teach at home. I believe this is part of the confused state of mind that is resultant from the usurpation of the parental role and ideals by the NEA and AAUP and ACLU that causes the child to have inner turmoil and anxiety—and the matter worsens as they grow older each year and not knowing or understanding what has happened to them—they only "feel" mixed up and uncertain and confused mentally. They feel intensely threatened and not understanding why, the only escape is to quit or drop out of school, become promiscuous sexually, turn to alcohol, or drugs to ease the pain. This end result is the goal of the Socialist change agents/manipulators. (More on this in the next chapters.)

That is also the basis of the DARE anti-drug program and most sex education, etc., in schools (*the mere innocent and naïve young child* has to decide what is right for him/herself with no parental *interference*). *Can you imagine the stress placed on the child?* It is also the philosophy behind Outcome-Based Education, School-to-Work, Mastery Learning, etc. and other school reforms (sic). Many of the *education reformers' (again, sic, what they **honestly** should call themselves are Social Engineers engineering our nation into Socialism/Communism) buzz words* are the keys to those programs. But honesty is a word foreign to them—their middle names are lies and deceit and manipulation. They include words and terms such as: *"Outcome-Based Education (OBE) "Values Clarification," (note: Values are subjective to the person or NEA/AAUP's desires—Virtues are unchangeable, concrete character traits; training children to "do higher order thinking," to be "critical* *thinkers" (**honestly** what they mean is how to go against parents or authority figures—and they wonder about the boundary-less undisciplined students who are now simply living out what they have so effectively been brainwashed to do for the past 40 years; and "lifelong-learners," (to prepare them to be constantly controlled by the State, throughout their lifetime, to do the bidding of the State career-wise—no choice for the individual's desires for career).* How can those education words, terms and movements which should be so reasonable be decoded and understood? They are so dangerous and so deceitful that there should be an outrageous outcry from the citizens and the Church demanding that all this nonsense should be stopped immediately. Let me explain some of these buzz-words a little more definitively.

To be "higher order thinkers' children must be challenged to think "outside the box" of rigid, traditional values and ways. To be "critical thinkers" they must be willing to challenge everything they have been taught and traditional ways of doing things. They must be "life long learners" because in Hegel's scheme of things everything—values, morality, traditions, etc.,-- are in a constant state of change so we must constantly learn new values, new ways of doing things, new approaches to government, etc. (Author's note: This flies in the face of God who is absolute truth as is His wisdom in the Scriptures. This is against the Christian family and all families and is against a Christian country. All of these concepts are tools the enemies use against God, family, and country. Also, *life long learning* is the way a nation living under a dictatorship, is controlled by the State—through *life long learning* requirements of every individual the State keeps tabs on all individuals and dictates what "knowledge" the people *must learn about the State and its demands.* The dupes are the Liberals/Progressivists/Socialists/ Communists/Globalists and their "useful idiots," the Liberal Left Democrats, Planned Parenthood, NEA, AAUP, Sodomites, Humanists, Radical Feminists, radical Islam, etc.)

Isn't that what is really behind so many education reforms? Benjamin Bloom is known as the grandfather of *Outcome Based Education.* His two Taxonomy books are widely used in training school teachers and administrators. Key people in business management, government and the military are also trained in Bloom's taxonomy concepts. Bloom has been quoted as saying:

> *"We recognize the point of view that truth and knowledge are only relative and that there are no hard fast truths which exist for all time and places...the purpose of education is to challenge students' fixed beliefs."* *(emphasis mine)*

(Satan would be very proud of Benjamin Bloom and how he has represented a rotting cancer in the academically failing education system in America. You see, for Socialism to arrive and thrive, the masses must be dumbed down and it certainly has happened in our country, as studies unequivocally evidence—and in looking back over the past three to four decades, the socialist engineers of the NEA have done a magnificent job in reaching their goals.)

LIFE-LONG LEARNING

In the Spring 1994 issue *of Education Record,* President Clinton said the same thing, stating: "For *Life-Long Learning* to become a reality, a whole new ethic will have to grip the American imagination." (Bill has been a good Comrade (a.k.a. *useful idiot*) to the Communist Party.)

Unless the "new ethic" and *Life-Long Learning* is based on seeking the absolute truth it will degenerate into what *II Timothy 3:7* says of people in "the last days." This scripture characterizes such people as: *"Ever learning, and never able to come to the knowledge of the truth....evil men and seducers shall wax worse and worse, deceiving, and being deceived."*

UNESCO and the UN have been pushing the concept of *Life-Long Learning* for over thirty years. A 1973 UNESCO publication *Towards a Conceptual Model of Life-Long Education* describes *Life-Long Learning* as the continual transformation of children and adults—***to be employed by the State in whatever work the State needs to have done***. There will be *no choice* for the individual. The UN and UNESCO see transcending national and cultural differences through *Life-Long Learning* as necessary for ultimately achieving *One World Government*—also known as Socialism/Communism/Globalism/Environmentalism/Collectivism/Progressivism/Populism/Fascism and other *isms*.

IT'S IN THE CHURCH

The *dialectic* approach is used in transforming traditional churches to make them part of what is called the church growth movement—the movement spreading like wild fire across America. It is transforming churches in the name or hope of "reaching today's generation." It often advocates putting aside bible words which can be intimidating. Traditional hymns and hymn books, and the song leader or choir are replaced by a "worship team." Pulpits, which connote authority, are "threatening" and are moved aside. Sometimes drama teams and skits replace the traditional preached sermon. Invitations to repentance and salvation and submission are eliminated or downplayed. Sunday schools downplay the teacher and teaching and focus, with a *facilitator*, on discussing what the class thinks or feels about God's Word. Do keep in mind that these "open discussions and group thinks" already have the "answers" that they "lead" the children to accept—making the children think they "arrived at the answers they themselves decided upon." Traditional denominational names are replaced with labels like "Community" or "Fellowship." In other words, do away with anything that divides—that keeps us all from coming together and being comfortable as *a group*. **<u>Divisive doctrines of the</u>**

Word of God--like repentance, submission, judgment and hell---are downplayed, ignored or given a negative connotation. Those who question the changes are labeled as "rigid," and "divisive" and as being "opposed to progress," and as unwilling to realize that "we live and minister in a changing world." Of course, it is mostly the "older" generation, trying to impart the Godly wisdom they have acquired to the younger generation, who are actually considered "foolish" in their outdated thinking. The younger generations of the past thirty years, having been educated in the public school arenas, have been subtly indoctrinated that the "older, parental" generation is not as "smart" or as knowledgeable about the times we live in. It is impossible to try to reason with these people and to try to educate or warn them as the older people are charged scripturally to do. The dialectic approach has been engrained in their minds and they turn to their peers for knowledge of discussion—who, in reality, know only what they know and can offer no real truth to the questions they may have. The parents or older generation, therefore, can have no input into their minds—they have been successfully brainwashed—and totally disregard any information the older generation has to offer no matter how desperately they need it..

BRINGING INDIVIDUALS TO A CONSENSUS

It's done in *groups.* It's done to bring **a *group* to *a pre-determined* "consensus"** that has been already determined and developed by someone else—and they are unaware of this! Implementation can take several forms. Two approaches are described in detail in the final chapter of ***None Dare Call It Education,*** which should be studied by every citizen in our country. (Author's note: This book was written by John A. Stormer and is a must along with his other books. *None Dare Call It Education* starts with a quote by author Cal Thomas that I will paraphrase: "If parents knew what was going on in the education of their children in public schools, there would be a revolution.") One technique is called the *Delphi Technique*. The process was developed by the Rand Corporation, an influential think tank, in the 1950s. Another note: There *is* a revolution going on—an uncontested one waged by our enemies—and they have nothing to fear because the silent Christian majority remains silent as the enemy progresses, rapidly, now.

Here's how what Gotcher calls the DIAPRAX process works:

> To deal with a crisis (real or manufactured) in a community, a state, a school district, a local church, a denomination or a mission board, a business, a trade union, a legislature, etc., a group is formed to study the problem.
>
> Someone (perhaps an "expert") presents the need for solving the crisis. The "expert" doesn't appear to advocate any particular viewpoint or solution. Then, small groups are often formed so, supposedly, everyone "will have an opportunity to have input into the solution. (That can also isolate the few people who have clear-cut positions so they can't take the group over.) Each small group has a *facilitator* and a *recorder*. (Author: a.k.a. teacher/change agent.)
>
> People who strongly advocate a solution based on real facts—are responded to with "that's one way of looking at it," or "well, that's your opinion," or "why do you feel that way?" or "how do you think you came to believe this?" When a strong point or statement of fact is made by a participant, an *expert facilitator* may say, "That's good, I believe what you are trying to say is…," or "could we say it like this…," moving what the individual said closer to the ***predetermined but unannounced consensus they***

want the group to reach. That's what the group's recorder writes down. People who express strong views will often be challenged to "set aside your differences so we can work together to find a real solution for the problem." The individual opinion must be eliminated or given up by the person. Those who try to go beyond the immediate "crisis" to look at what they see as the underlying cause of the problem may be told, "That's beyond the scope of our meeting today. We're just going to concentrate on..."

Author's note: This is how Christian opinions and beliefs regarding moral or ethical situations are gradually, subtly but forcefully eliminated in the minds of the young Christian child. For examples of just a few areas of concern, it is how lifestyles such as homosexuality, promiscuous sex, abortion, illegal drug usage and liberal democratic socialist political persuasions are now being taught in the elementary K-12 grades to captive audience children. It is total manipulation of the children's thought processes into a favorable and approving opinion of homosexuality, and the other areas mentioned, that the parents and their children do not agree with. (Please keep in mind that the parents are not aware that this indoctrination is even happening to their child.) Eventually the child is forced to adopt the NEA/AAUP dictated school's belief system which is directly in opposition to their own and their parents, they rebel and revolt against their parents, and the poor child is left totally confused and guilt ridden and utterly damaged—because, in reality, they DO NOT WANT TO GO AGAINST THEIR PARENT'S BELIEFS, but they are left no choice in the matters if they wish to receive passing grades and feel welcome in the group. We end up with VERY angry and confused young adults, many, many having to be medicated legally or illegally, who sometimes carry guns to crowded classrooms. What an abominable shame on us.

PRESSURES FOR COMPROMISE

The two biggest things the *teacher/change agent/facilitator or change agent/organizer* of the group has going for them is that, (1) few can clearly enunciate and defend their strongly held beliefs (thesis) in an impromptu setting in a meeting, and (2) those who know what they believe and have a desire to stand for what is right are also torn by the desire to be accepted—to have good relationships with others who appear to hold other views (antithesis). If no one else speaks up, an individual doesn't want to look foolish (pride). Temptation is great to *compromise* and go along so the group can come to a consensus (synthesis). Normally, the "consensus" will never be put to a vote-- a consensus will be *announced or agreed to informally* as the facilitator says, "It would appear in the interest of solving the problem that we all can basically agree that..."

Gotcher lays out six conditions through which the group decision making process develops the "consensus." He says:

(1) *The group environment must be "open-minded."*

(2) *It must be "non-directive," where rules and preset standards are not presented by the leader that might stand in the way of the person or group exploring and discovering new experiences together. [In other words, the announced purpose of the meeting should not be "How we can work together to pass a school tax increase." although that may be the desired ultimate consensus.]*

(3) *It must be adverse to any closed, black and white philosophical viewpoint.*

(4) *The group environment must be social in nature.*

(5) *It must use a social issue that the group has differing views or viewpoints about.*

(6) *It must use the social issue to allow all participants to come to a consensus or "group feeling" regarding a possible solution.*

(Author: Again, please note, that this is how they "teach and influence and indoctrinate" children to be more concerned about how their peers or teachers view them than about what their parents have taught them. This is an incredible pressure for children to bear so the easiest thing at the moment is to agree with the peers/teachers even though they may really and truly believe the opposite idea. As years go by the pressure increases and demands our children live in confused, tormented minds leading to promiscuity, alcohol and drug usage and even possible suicide to evade this pressure.

Gotcher breaks the process down into three phases:

*(1) **Thesis:** In this phase the participants are given the opportunity to state their position on the issue being discussed. This position is usually based on fact or experience.*

*(2) **Antithesis:** The facilitator, through casual dialogue, will create conditions that help participants feel the necessity to compromise or readjust their positions in order to be accepted by the group and/or build group cohesion. [IF we are going to solve this problem, we must all come together.]*

*(3) **Synthesis:** The facilitator helps the participants realize that peace and acceptance can only be accomplished through unity. The rigidity of "right vs. wrong" has been broken down and brought under an umbrella of ambiguity and paradox. **Final decision will be based on feelings and will no longer be grounded in absolute truth.***

The process works because most people are torn between what they believe and think to be true--and their desire to be accepted by the group. They hesitate to be an obstructionist and "stand in the way of progress" so they compromise.

Oh, my! Our own poor pathetic children's minds are stolen every day through countless hours in the classroom under NEA's own entitled "change agents."

HOW TO RESIST THE GROUP PRESSURE

Recognize that the on-going battle is not against flesh and blood. It's impossible to stand in the power of the flesh. God's Word has an admonition. *In II Corinthians 10:3-4, the Apostle Paul, writing for the Lord, says:*

> *For though we walk in the flesh, we do not war after the flesh, (For the weapons of our warfare are not carnal, but mighty through God to the pulling down of strongholds;) Casting down imaginations, and every high thing that exalts itself against the knowledge of God, <u>and bringing into captivity every thought to the obedience of Christ.</u>*

- **Know what you believe**. Think through how to effectively present what you know and believe as fact.

- **Recognize the techniques used to "facilitate" or manipulate** a group discussion to bring the group to a consensus.

- **State facts. Avoid saying "I believe" or "I think…:** which can produce the response, "That's just your opinion."

- **Sit back for a time and listen**. If someone states a good fact-based point, join them. If the *facilitator/teacher/ change agent* tries to move on, get recognized, even later, and say, "We need to look again at what so-and-so presented." **It may encourage others who agreed but didn't speak up.**

- **Realize that differences between God's Word and worldly thinking and ways** cannot be resolved. The Lord Jesus warned in Matthew 10:34-36:

Think not that I am come to send peace on earth; I came not to send peace, but a sword, For I am come to set a man at variance against his father, and the daughter against her mother, and the daughter in law against her in law. And a man's foes shall be they of his own household.

- **Study the final chapter in John A. Stormer's book** *None Dare Call It Education* on the ways to respond to the Delphi method for controlling a meeting and what to do when responding to a consensus.

- **Get Dean Gotcher's 50-page booklet:** *DIAPRAX AND THE END OF THE AGE.* Send $6 per copy to Institution for Authority Research, Box 233, Herndon KS 67739

Thank you and God bless you John Stormer for educating the blind.

A Long Over-Due Open Letter *to* the Children, Young Adults, and Past Two Generations of Adults-- This is what has happened to you:
(with comments to the people who are and should have been responsible for your safety and security)
Gabriel Stokes (2005)

After 35+ long years of studying and researching the following data and information, it's off to the woodshed to administer a far-too-long-overdue, *sound verbal whip lashing*

to the following recipients: First and foremost the public school educational system via the National Education Association (NEA) Teachers Union and (AAUP) American Association of University Professors Union, the ACLU (American Civil Liberties Union) and like organizations, TV networks and local stations, newspaper media's biased and lying liberal views, and all secular-become-porno magazines (placed at a child's eye-level in grocery stores), pornographic internet websites, Planned Parenthood Federation of America (PPFA) and other abortion mills, entertainment/music/ theatre and electronic game producers, the large volume of seductive books with cult/witchcraft themes now filling the shelves of our school libraries, the radical subversive feminist movements National Organization of Women (NOW), and sister organizations, greedy-materialistic working parents who MUST be away from their homes because enough is never enough, and Liberal Democratic Lawmakers who keep raising taxes as an instrument of redistribution of income/wealth (Socialism) that is fracturing families while forcing Mothers out of the home in order to supplement family income, and last but not least of all, even my silent-too-long self.**

I, for one, and the countless people I speak for, am sick and tired of watching and hearing about fifty percent *(that's 50% and growing fast)* of our youth being utterly destroyed by the filth and misinformation coming at them daily, hourly, through the above enterprises. And the above cannot wiggle out of their guilt because they, 1) just may happen to provide *some* "good" education, along with all the sordid misinformation they indoctrinate our children with, and 2) the exorbitant materialistic lifestyles of absent parents who comfort themselves as they reason that the *toys and extras* they provide their children and themselves with are *necessities.* (I'm not referring to those parents who both have to work to keep food on the table—though some schedules could be rearranged so that one parent could be at home at all times.) By the time our children are out of high school, (*if* they make it through graduation—the keyword being *if*), so many have suffered through depression or ruined lives and alternative schooling due to immoral lifestyles learned through the above institutions (or) have been so dummied down in the public schools, they are not even prepared to support themselves. I hope and pray they give the following thoughtful review.

We adults have the audacity to look down our noses and blame the kids for their de-moralized lifestyles because of "their choices!" It is sickening to hear adults say that a 15 year-old child made bad alcohol or drug or sexual encounter choices while at the same time providing them the roadmaps to do so right in school. *Can anyone else out there see the lonely, sad, confused, dejected, angry, depressed, cold, bewildered, dead, dull, HURT, de-moralized, desensitized, cold looks in the eyes and poor body language/dress code and voices of over 75% of our youth, besides me??? It's not hard to connect these dots!*

Most of those kids had God-given good minds that were totally lost and demolished due to all the above-listed influences in their lives. We all should bear our blame and shame for this outrageous neglect of our children—they should not have to bear it the guilt and shame—but they do. Even our so-called good students are inwardly depressed and lost to a certain extent, morally—and why shouldn't they be? We people who were responsible for their well-being are to blame for the loss of their innocence and have taken away all the "sweet mystery of life" from them. They really feel there is nothing left for them— nothing to really live for and plan for—and so they continue to numb their senses. The immoral filthy lifestyles many have adopted were *taught* through the following, just to name a few, and any sane and thinking person should be able to see it:

1) "Sex" education/*"health"?* classes—including pure beastly *instinctual sex* and pornographic immoral lifestyles, classified as "alternative," (bestiality, anal, oral sex, masturbation, homosexuality, lesbianism, bisexuality,

transsexuality—*(some actually recommended as birth control!)*—and never responsible *love after marriage taught*—with no differentiation between sex and love—are taught. Really, adults, just what would you have done if you were educated this way? Plus being told that "It's your choice when you wish to….." Actually, none of this "sex" or health education belongs in elementary, junior high, high schools, or colleges. The NEA usurped the parents' job to do this for their own hidden agendas. You poor children, nor we parents or nation, would have 90% of the sexual problems, STDs, and abortions, if we parents/educators would have kept **sex** education out of the public schools, starting in elementary); as one noted author states: "You can't tell the *sick new morality from the old immorality;"*

2) Unnecessary ***ultra-pornographic—ultra-violent television*** programming, and 30-second filthy commercials advertising deviant promiscuous programs and violence, with every product being sold via sexual innuendos, all that used to be *beyond imagination,* and that one cannot click off quickly enough, that leave ***permanent mental pictures*** on children's and adult's minds;

3) Three-fourths naked people on most magazine covers placed at the little child's/youth's eye-level in supermarkets and stores;

4) No secular decent moral movies or secular television programming with "real" hero/heroine role models, only ones that continuously indoctrinate the children with the aberrant/abhorrent seedy side of life/lifestyles;

5) Horrible rap music, etc., promoting illegal activity and hideous behavior;

6) And to top it all off, you were/they are bombarded with "hate America" speeches in school and all the depressing false science categories.

Okay! Please tell me, thinking person, what else could/can we, they, expect for their lives? We are all so guilty for ***allowing*** this to happen to our children over the past 40 years, so guilty. And, I know, that word "guilty" is taboo now, right? Somebody might be offended—well we should know who has been *very offended.* But healthy guilt should conjure up healthy repentance, perish the thought! Repentance? Our kids are made to feel mighty guilty for our mistakes, aren't they, when you really think about it?

Other areas that are of ***much*** concern are the facts that good classroom time is spent demoralizing/confusing the minds of our students with the use of *negative media reporting, lambasting of our government and nation and elected officials (who happen to have been elected by the majority), plus fuzzy nonsensical ways of teaching academics, and lastly worrying them with unproven theories regarding global warming, and false facts about environmental issues.* The change agent NEA teachers and AAUP professors ***have no right*** to discuss these topics and use liberal newspapers/books/handouts to push their one-sided personal depressing liberal-left lying biased opinions and viewpoints, daily, into/onto our ***captive-audience*** children in the **classrooms,** against the parents' wishes, clearly, *knowingly and purposefully* brainwashing our children away from their parental ideals and influence, ***rightfully*** taught and instilled in them by their parents/churches, who, by the way, are the ***only*** ones who have the **right** to do so. I truly believe some or maybe even most of the teachers are unaware of what they are doing to OUR children. I plead with you to just *imagine* how it ***confuses*** the young minds and hearts terribly, and ***depresses*** them immeasurably. They love their parents and in their hearts and minds, want to go on believing what their parents say is truth to them, *but they are not allowed.* Much of what they are taught and forced to believe goes against their gut-feelings and beliefs. (Parents: "No *love*-making before marriage, children, is the way to a happy fulfilled, safe, life for you and *all* your future children"…..**in direct opposition to**….School: "All kids will investigate *sex*, so be sure to wear a condom, and if pregnancy occurs….well, there's always the "choice" for abortion—and we'll help you without your parent's knowledge—they have no right to know anyway—this is *your* business [Lie].") Don't you realize that these children have to "hide" what they're being taught because so much does not go along with what their parents have taught them? It makes them sick, literally! This tells our children that if their parents don't approve of their lifestyle should they "decide" to have sex, (and that registers as anything: drink alcohol, use drugs—only with clean needles, etc.) just keep it hidden—that's the "hidden" message to them. Do it all safely, responsibly, regardless of the law—Hah! After all, everyone expects and knows you are bound to try these behaviors—subtly encouraged and actually stated to them. *This is highly destructive for them to be put into this most unusual, heavy, mental torment.*

Parents, please, for the sake of all children, past, present and future put yourselves in their places. Why, I don't think we could stand it either. We would become confused, depressed, promiscuous, and druggies, addicts, too. I would like to remind all of us, OUR schools, and variety of media, *have no right to do this—it does not fall within their duties or jurisdiction to* <u>*steal*</u> *our children's minds and hearts and bodies away from their parent's desires for their morals and ideals and politically correct—culturally Marxist-ideas—or to steal them away from their God!*

It is no wonder that fifty percent of our children's great minds were/are lost and lives ruined when they were/are not being taught how to properly read, write, do math, exercise their God-given brains on concrete matter, etc. Intentionally dummying them down along with all the **inaccurately revised** history of our nation curriculum, *conveniently and purposefully distorted or totally eliminated to further the Socialism via the hate America concept*—leaves them with no real solid *connection or attachment* to THEIR nation—*no BELONGINGNESS OR RELATIONSHIP to, or solid foundation on, their past ancestry, and certainly they are guided away from their family relationship which is taken over and usurped by the school and peers.* (OUR children are national citizens of the United States of America—thank you very much!—PART of OUR world—they are NOT global or village or United Nations citizens.) This erosion of their very foundation must be stopped if we and they and our nation are to survive. Add to this what they are demanded or commanded to read, so much of what opposes all ideals instilled by their parents, plus meaningless content, leaves them sadly changed, effected by the "change agents," the teachers, who we have erroneously trusted to be teaching our kids the basic necessities of reading, writing and math, but are subversively undermining the very morals and ethics our country has been founded on and what we as parents have a right to instill in our own children.

The "core curriculum," inserted into all the above classes, is *Multiculturalism* a buzz-word, (along with buzz-words Environmentalism, and Globalism). Every other year it's a new buzz-word to disguise Socialism, Communism, Marxism/Fascism—first it was Tolerance (for all religions except Christianity) and Multi-Culturalism, then Environmentalism and man-made Global Warming/Climate Change, pressured into the students—our children—our future adult citizens (we cannot discuss the pathetic state of our children and nation without discussing globalism—see below). Again, it mattered/matters not a smidgeon what parents' beliefs or ideas were/are on these topics—the public schools superceded/supercedes the parents' rights for their children—constantly undermining and confusing the child and opposing the parents' rights. Again, imagine the child's emotions and mind being manipulated in such a way.

Young people, this is what has happened to you. As a result, you, our children were/are left with no hope for yourselves or in yourselves, individually or collectively—and years later, now, there almost seems no hope for our nation as a result of all of this. These student's minds are being, and have been for so long, utterly confused every day of their lives, all those hours every day! Perhaps the most tragic part is that they have been brainwashed into having very high self-esteem and have been taught to think that it is o.k. not to apply themselves—that being dummied down is o.k.—that promiscuity and drug/alcohol use is "expected" of them in their teen years and that it's o.k., too, and that if they are not partaking of these activities that they are "not normal" teens. They don't even know how they were purposefully led into these lifestyles by the "programmers" in the public schools.

Also, it is simply *not permissible* for teachers to mantra and complain to our kids all the time about being "underpaid, underappreciated, or under respected," and that "schools are not receiving enough money to do a decent job of teaching"—honestly, I think the kids I listen to have learned these verses very well. Much to our chagrin—they recite it, regurgitate it vehemently with passion, like it comes right from a textbook—and, incidentally, none of it is true according to statistics. If they were given a test on the plight of the teachers and education they would receive a A+--that is if they could write a coherent essay on it. My how our children have been cheated—shame on us!

Speaking of textbooks, (which, of course, were/are not used much anymore) they are not allowed in public schools if they are too patriotically pro-American or give a true history of the founding of our nation. Being proud of our nation is taught as being an awful taboo. Ask any kid! A great revealing book for private, charter and home schools would be *Hidden Dangers of the Rainbow* by Constance Cumby, 1983, ISBN 0-910311-03-X. It should be required reading of all public school teachers and future teachers. The author foretells, in 1983, exactly what has happened/is happening today.

QUESTION: Why, the more money we pour into the schools over the years, the worse the outcomes??? (And we are not even given the truth about the actual costs!) Let's face it *truthfully*—we have continued to pour more and more money into the shameful public school educational system, and the product—so much of the product—our children—have miserably failed, with broken lives. It shouldn't be that hard to see and to understand, people. Why, the more money we spend on schools, the more pathetic and disgusting is the programming and curriculum—leading to our students' failure?

Movies, media, magazines, and dress codes, which are offered to our children (and young adults)—why must they be so degrading? Come on, people! We've Been Asleep Too Long— We Must Wake Up!! I pray the young people whose lives were devastated as a result of their decadent schooling, et al, who may be reading this, will be able to understand what has happened to them.

Parents and Citizens, when will we all wake up and take *all of these areas* to task and **demand and insist** on going back to decent, moral, standards? *QUESTION:* What would be wrong with that? Can you not see what is happening to a great share of our precious commodity—our children/young adults—and to us and our nation as a result? Don't be deceived! Do you NOT CARE? By our inaction, that is what we are telling the producers and our precious children. They're hurting badly and dying inside. I truly believe a lot of our teachers are too, and they don't know why! They truly don't and not just the secular teachers who see the failure but even the Christian teachers in the schools do not understand what has happened.

You just cannot *send your impressionable, darling children to cesspools every day, or permit your children to see, hear, smell, taste, and touch, trash every day, hours at a time, while at home alone, at school, at the supermarket, in the news media and programming, internet, books and entertainment, and not EXPECT them to come out without the slime and bacteria all over them, and expect them to stay well, and if they don't, well...."it was their decision"---baloney—they're children! Can you understand we have a real moral problem? We've killed their moral immune system—left them with incurable illnesses. Can we rescue them? Yes—but we must wake up first! And we must wake them up and de-program them from their brainwashing performed in school and help them understand what has happened to them and give them a reason to live decent lives again.* We just can't expect them to have the adult decision-making powers to say "no" to all of this when they are indoctrinated with it day and night at such young ages. I'm so sick of hearing, from supposedly adult thinkers, the "It's their decision," phrase. And then, of course this leads to, "It's so easy to blame them" type of thinking that gets us off the uncomfortable hook of accountability to them. *Wake up and be responsible for your children's lives, and help the young adults understand what happened to them, adult people*—if you really care. Become aware of what is going on. That means before they leave high school or get into trouble in elementary school. Because once they are adults away from home, they are responsible and accountable for their own lives and actions and will reap the rewards or difficulties of them—and we have not prepared them for this. If we had done our jobs in the first place, way back then, we could have alleviated so much of theirs and our own suffering. We all are now affected by all this trash because we didn't. Much praise to those who home school and send their kids to charter schools and private schools—they just may blessed and be saved from dummied-down negativism, depression, scarred immoral lifestyles, ill health (STDs and abortion, young teen pregnancies and single parenthood, etc.,) and perhaps they will be called on as leaders to really help save our nation in the future--*if* we have one to save. (But don't you be mistaken—you can't hide from the effects of the masses who have been educated in public schools, either—you must also become active against what's happening. You are making a good statement now, so hang in there and keep on doing what you are doing!) We need <u>Christian and Charter High Schools</u> and more <u>Christian and Charter Colleges</u>, not under the NEA and AAUP influences!

For 40+ years the subversive educational goals pursued by the NEA/AAUP and their hidden political agendas they financed have been strengthened by the Federal Dept. of Education (the rest of the media have been brainwashed by the so-called *sic* "intellectual elite" thereof and have helped the Liberal Left produce the sad state of affairs in our nation): **Dumb down the future generations, demoralize and destroy lifestyles and our culture and make the masses government dependent so the U.S. will succumb and fall like an over-ripened fruit, into the hands of the one world, one government, one economy, one world United Nations Court systems, one "new age" secular humanistic state religion, together equaling Socialism/ Globalism.** *Predicted, I might add, in 1917. It's been planned for a very long time—we should be ashamed it has come so far so fast.* (That word *globalism* is not new—it's been around for a long time, since the '70s, and it's used constantly, only lately. The Liberals planned to filter it in slowly so we would all become accustomed to it and accept it as a mere "word or concept"—just like the other buzz-words mentioned.) It's the ONLY way the U.S. would fall into a dictatorship global society. Here are the buzz words for Socialism/Communism: (*Multi-culturalism/ Liberalism/Collectivism/Gradualism/Incrementalisml/ Progressivism/Environmentalism /Global Warming- ism/Globalism*) and be *forced* (not willingly) to ultimately give up OUR nationhood/ sovereignty of the U.S. of America, and become a ***third-world nation***—a "state" in the global community. It was necessary to explain all of this here because that's what's at stake now and exactly what our children and we have been, and are being, sacrificed for through the educational system. How I wish our last two generations could have this thoroughly explained to them. But, alas, it seems we are trying to lock the barn door after the horse has been stolen.

The Liberal Socialists been patient—worked very hard in the schools and media stealing our children's minds and hearts and bodies and faith, day-by-day, even now as you read this. So you see, young adults and children, why you have been so completely cheated out of your very happiness and freedoms and ultimately your lives and your Christianity. How I wish you would all join together now and take these organizations to task for what they have robbed you of. The NEA/AAUP/ACLU plan, and *know exactly* what they are doing, as well as all the various media outlets, and so many citizens do not want to be bothered with the truth or the knowledge and have no courage to fight back for our beloved country. Perhaps too painful, too scary, we must close our ears and hide our heads! But if we join together we would be a force of unified strength and we would be a formidable force against the enemies of our children and nation.

These enemies of you and our nation know the "hands that rock the cradles" and who "own the schools" (Hitler's Nazi comments) will run the world (get our kids from the time they're born into daycare centers—family life and feelings negotiated out of our children—one nice village). And it's all money oriented for the few dictators that will follow. But the misguided, deceived, teachers of the NEA/AAUP and the ignorant lawyers of the ACLU refuse to know or cannot see or cannot understand the "business" minds of the instigators that use them as "useful idiots," as they "preach," "it's for the common good of all people"—secular humanism/socialism/communism—or multi-culturalism, progressivism, or environmentalism or globalism, or whatever the buzz-word they introduce each year, to the students. It's always the *same hidden* socialist/communist agenda. It has NEVER worked in any country and NEVER will work *"for the good of all people." It's the same ancient lying message of the Socialist Party and the Liberals have bought it and proceed to forcefully feed it down our throats.* The outcome is just the opposite. It always leads to a high-class and poverty-class society—two classes. Evidence the third-world countries under the dictatorship of Socialism/ Communism. Well, LOOK at US—SEE and KNOW—we are 85% there now, and the general population still doesn't want to know it because they're crazed and stressed for the materialistic lifestyle and *incredibly worried about their children and society but refuse to listen to the cause of the decadence.*

All young adults and children my heart breaks for you and for what we have allowed to happen in our country. Parents are not at home to guide the hearts and minds of their own children— they have willingly given them over—and find every excuse they can for doing it. We all must look courageously into ourselves for the answers and face up to the changes we need to and must make now in order to keep our homeland. We can only say, "Don't bother us with the kids" for so long. When our possessions, monies, babies and freedoms are lost to Globalism/Socialism, we'll hear loud cries from all of us— "HOW, WHEN, WHERE, WHY and WHO??" By now we should all know Why! And How, and When and Where and Who!!

Young adults and children, all the above filth and degradation of our society is "in" and God has been "outlawed," literally, to make way for planned Globalism and the new Spirituality, the one world New Age Religion. I pray you can see this. And it's going to get far worse than all of this! Well, may God help us because only HE can now—we've gone too far, too long—against Him—and I pray for His mercy and that He will withhold His holy wrath from such a disobedient and rebellious people that we have become. He will not wink at this filth forever—nor listen to His hurting children crying forever. Like it or not, believe it or not, His patience will not last forever, as we all now know from the obvious, deep in our hearts. It's really very simple for all of us.....personal repentance and correction of lifestyles is the name of the game now, along with healthy strong patriotism. And let's not be ignorant any longer—let's do it quickly—for all of our sakes, young and old. Nothing else, all the new programs and ideas/concepts in the world that our educators mistakenly come up with, can help us now. Perhaps if we obey and ask God to help us unify and work together He will help us overcome this threat to our nation.

I am not personally condemning or attacking teachers, parents or institutions, or anyone else—however, I am condemning what they do because all of us, especially the children, have to live with, and fear, and pay for their mistakes. I know that there are those who agree with all that I have written and those who partially do, and those who do not. And there are those who are afraid to stand up and be counted. Maybe I have said some of it right and some of it wrong, but I have painted the landscape well enough to get the picture.

To sum up, it's just one big ball of tangled confusion that our young adults and children don't understand and cannot possibly untangle at their young ages. We hand this ball to our children and it demoralizes them because they have **no clue as to how to fix it or what is really wrong**. All this has transpired under our noses so that the U.S. can be forced into Socialism/Globalism. And our kids and nation are paying the price—we hide our heads as they are "sacrificed" for the ultimate goal—only, ironically, we are all being sacrificed too—for globalism at all costs—even our children—their lives and their futures—and ultimately ours, too!!! Again, only GOD can help us now, as always, to untangle the mess we've concocted or allowed to happen. And I wish I could be sure He cares anymore. I pray for His mercy and that He rescues us from our vain imaginings and stops us from our current self-inflicted rotting on the vines. He is a loving God— but He is holy and just, too. His eyes cannot endure all the trash anymore, and we should be deeply concerned for our entire world. We ought to be out picketing and demonstrating every day at every public school, State NEA and State AAUP offices, ACLU, Planned Parenthood Federation Clinics, pornographic websites, magazine publishers, newspapers, television stations, theatres, music houses, grocery stores-magazine shops, etc., who promote such filth and lure our children to it, until the immoral lifestyles, are absolutely, finally, eliminated. They ought to be hearing from us! It is our loving responsibility to our children/grandchildren/great grandchildren of our nation/world to prevent our rotting from the inside out. Look at us—we are rotting!

We need to demand and insist that our public schools, that we own, and media, stop dummying down our kids, and brainwashing them with global, anti-American philosophy, and the liberal/immoral *sex education* ideas that sacrifice their spirits and very souls, and begin once again teaching necessary basics so they can make it in life. Young adults and children and citizens of our nation, we have become morally bankrupt because *all* of us have been blind, or lazy, with uncaring, disgraceful negligence. Not a one of us can point our fingers at anyone else but ourselves, all parents/adults/teachers, NEA-AAUP, public, private, charter, home schools, and churches and pastors, for our outrageous, deafening, silence regarding these matters.

An apology to our young students and young adults:
In closing my letter/article, the desire would be that every child/young adult who has been cheated and sacrificed, (by our institutions and parents/adults/teachers, etc., who were supposed to be in charge of your welfare), could read this article. I want you to see the truth as to why so many of you have "missed the boat at this time and in the past two generations." It's not your fault! However, I hope you can learn from this admission of our guilt and bad example, so you and your children can make a future in our/your/their national homeland, and be more aware and make the much needed changes, and that you can relieve yourselves of the guilt that is ours. Perhaps this would enable you to free yourselves, to make new and fresh moral adult decisions, becoming new people, for the rest of your and your children's lives—unencumbered by the miserable influences we

have allowed and pushed on you during your critical years of life formation. I pray you learn from our disgraceful, negligent behavior in your upbringing, and that you stop it from continuing to happen to you and your children, and our nation. That's a lot to put on your shoulders now, but it really is possible for you because you are strong in your youth. Since we have not prepared you for a decent lifestyle and many of you have the time (we need to contact all the really intelligent but so-called "dropouts" and enlist them to work on this), perhaps you can be our leaders for this movement. My prayer is that you become angry and aware enough, and use your energies to demand and insist that the Liberal NEA/AAUP educational system be outlawed from OUR schools, so that they cannot get their hands on your children. Oh, we have all cheated/sacrificed you (and ourselves! in doing so)! Who are the "we"? "We" have to look in the mirror. And I, for one, and many others, humbly apologize for this and ask for God's forgiveness AND your forgiveness, as we weep and hang our heads in utter shame because of our refusal to take the necessary time to be aware of the deceit and immorality that was/is hidden and is continually happening in our schools and media.

The obvious results of natural disasters are not hard to recognize. But as supposedly intelligent human beings we fail to recognize, right now, that we are experiencing an unseen but a dramatically felt tsunami, hurricane, earthquake, flood and out of control fire-like results of the inner moral decay of our youth and nation and it is almost incomprehensible for the average human mind to understand the extent to which it has happened—or how, because we have been so subversively deceived *with hidden agendas*.

The above may help in understanding how we got there, along with the book recommended.

(2007: Since writing the above piece, Three Rivers MI school district is excited because a Health and Psychological Testing clinic is in the process of being erected on the Public

School grounds. People are so blind they cannot see "the writing on the wall" as to what this means for our beloved children—perhaps not "beloved" in the true sense of the word, anymore. We seem to have a rather odd idea of the true meaning of love these days. The children have been slowly stolen—taken taken over and "state-owned.) These types of clinics are the final step. These children will be medicated, psychologically tested, subtly instructed further in promiscuity and the girls forced by law to be vaccinated against cervical cancer because of multiple sex (not *love)* partners, and now they will not only be "dummied-down" but in the short future, also "numbed-down." So many of them are already! This is all in the name of "false" health, of course. Perhaps this will be the avenue they use for future embryonic stem cells, too—over stimulating our girl-children's ovaries while paying the students for them. All of the morality that parents try feverishly to instill in their children, will be "taught" out of them—as they accept homosexuality/promiscuity/ abortion even more through these clinics. Once they are brainwashed this way, the mind is almost impenetrable to change and teach them truth because brainwashing/indoctrination is so thorough and deep. Their mind-processing-brains have been taken over. Cross dressing by homosexual/lesbian teachers will be the norm (which research shows that 90% of them are predators on the young) and the NEA is feverishly pushing this lifestyle through so fast (see their June 2006 Convention Agenda). This will allow them use of the same bathrooms as our young boys and girls (dramatic increase of AIDS and psychological illness and suicides, as research shows, will be forthcoming). This should ***set off an alarm*** —to the parents and grandparents regarding these clinics-- which have been planned for 15-20 years and are now actively being built. *But the folks, (the parents and clergy and teachers our children should be able to count on to protect and watch out for them), refuse, or are of the age (30-50) who have been brainwashed by the radical Liberal educators themselves, and are unable or unwilling to connect the dots or learn anything about the plans that have been and are being carried out against the children and our nation. They are ignorantly or* *innocently deceived by the Liberal propaganda, adapting to and adopting the radical Liberal indoctrination and brainwashing of their precious children. These clinics will eventually (very soon) also be used to "treat and test" our day care center infants-to-Kindergarten babies. That is the goal of the NEA and radical Liberal democrats now in control of our government and our government public school system via NEA/AAUP teachers' union and professors' union and the ACLU, People for the American (sic) Way, etc. Unless we Christians, parents, clergy, and teachers, wake up and work together to gradually rid our nation of the atheist Socialists' agendas now perpetuated and in control of our classrooms/clinics and our children, we will indeed wake up--- but it will be too late—and I'm not sure that it isn't already too late!!!---and we'll HATE the nightmare we will have to live out in a third word nation.*   (end)

THE PPFA—NEA—AAUP—ACLU's (plus) JOINT VENTURE: [Part 1]
(Planned Parenthood Federation of America; National Education Association Teacher's Union; American Association of University Professors; American Civil Liberties Union; plus other Liberal Leftist/Socialist Organizations)
Gabriel Stokes (2008)

Best to start with Scripture, for **true knowledge** and **understanding:** II Corinthians 10:3-5, and a prayer for Godly wisdom. Ironically this article is being written on Independence Day, July 4, 2007. I have a dream, too! Dr. Martin Luther King! That one day we will celebrate independence from the NEA, AAUP, ACLU, and PPFA's joint venture of dangerous interference, influence and intrusion into our lives and Nation. They've chipped away the mortar of our foundation in our Nation but we have been awakened, and are starting to replace it with the originally intended mortar of our Founding Fathers. And we will do it to completion! With our obedience and God's help!

We must ask ourselves: How much further down the road of insane corruption will we allow *them* to take our children and us with their decadent teachings and work? If we don't act soon, there will be no route of return to sane morality for us, our Nation and for our posterity. And our sovereignty will be lost! Since the sources I use can convey information regarding these important topics better than I, I will let them do it, while making my comments along the way.

Quoted from: *Opinion Journal: from The Wall Street Journal Editorial Page, Tuesday, June 19, 2007:*

"...*Roe* did substantially increase abortions, more than doubling the rate per live birth in the five years from 1972 to 1977. **But many other changes occurred at the same time:**

A sharp **increase** in *pre-marital sex; (hmm—produced by the sex education?)*
A sharp **rise** in *out-of-wedlock births*; *(hmm—produced by the sex education?)*

A **drop** in the number *of children placed for adoption;* *(Students dropping out of school to become promiscuous parents—children raising children—some on the streets.)*

A **decline in marriages** that occur after the woman *(child)* is pregnant. (The boys feel no responsibility as the *responsible girl is expected to have and will be guided to an abortion. Besides, it was just sex—not love.)* (All ( ) expressions mine)

Continuing:

Some of this might seem contradictory. *Why would both the number of abortions and out-of-wedlock births go up?* If there were more illegitimate births, why were fewer children available for adoption? ......*Part of the answer lies in attitudes to premarital sex.* Many academic studies have shown that legalized abortion, *by encouraging premarital sex*, increased the number of unplanned births, even outweighing the reduction in unplanned births due to abortion." (Emphasis mine)

We'll leave the Wall Street Journal quote now.

The question begging to be *loudly* asked and answered **in the open: *What has been the hidden cause, and continues to cause the increase in pre-marital sex?*** PPFA **and** the NEA classroom indoctrination encouraging pre-marital sex, are hitting our children with a double whammy—*below the belt*—no pun intended—and absolutely true.

Primary Reason: Research reveals *the Public School Sex Education curriculum,* disguised as *health* classes, **SHARPLY** *increases* the immoral sexual behaviors leading to pregnancy of our young teen girls (and boys). It numbs their innocent, vulnerable minds because they are (co-educationally) taught that *"since they would be engaging in sex they should use condoms."* This *powerful* message of *suggestive encouragement* rings LOUD and CLEAR in the ears and minds of our poor unsuspecting young students. It registers in their minds as: *"Since I'll be engaging in sex, I need to be responsible and use condoms."* **They've been sold a "false" responsibility for promiscuous behavior condoned and taught by the subservient teacher change agents of the NEA. Can you imagine the embarrassing atmosphere in the classroom when this subject is first broached for our children? And with each subsequent "class," how they become desensitized to morality?** *Instinctual sexual* intimacy (practiced by evolutionary people who descended from animals) is promoted as a hedonistic ritual instead of a *normal "loving devotion" between two married human beings.* Our children do not want to tell Mom and Dad about this—creating the burden of a ton of guilt for them to carry. The STDs that will be transmitted between our young are not a part of their sex "education," nor are the complications that can occur during an abortion, including possible death, which most pregnant girls will be forced "to choose," with a whole lot of help from the School Counselor/Clinic. Again, of course, if pregnancy occurs, the schools can "counsel" and connect the pregnant teen with a free abortion (free *to them*—however, but not to the taxpayer—us). This can take place unbeknownst to the Parents—though to give the "child" an aspirin would take notification and permission of the Parent.

Likewise, ***Drug Usage "Education" subliminally encourages usage of drugs, e.g., "Best not to use, but IF/WHEN you choose to use, be sure to use sensibly, with clean needles, etc., to the extent that, socialistically, we should have laws to provide free clean needles"*** Any intelligent, reasoning, Parent should be able to see the incompatibility of this rationale. Truly, it is paradoxical teaching in an educational (public school) setting. This presents more *confusion and dilemma* for our students that they must endure.

None of this teaching belongs in any school classroom and when polled, parents do not want it. It is NOT the public schools' business to take over the responsibility of the Parents—though NEA claims parental rights stop at the school door. We need to tell THEM explicitly that it does NOT.

Add to the above, the fact that they consider Atheism as the only option for our children, and it is taught in a hidden way, as in the unproven, unscientific *theory of Evolution, taught as fact!* Atheism rules out any "right or wrong" connection to premarital sex— because human beings in the Atheist's mind basically are evolved animals who live by instinct. This is why Christianity has been outlawed in the public schools by the NEA and ACLU.

They fed the lie to the American citizens/parents that there is a "separation of Church and State" and there is not, simply to remove it from the schools for the end goal of Socialism in America. The gullible American citizens/paretns swallowed the lie and did not research the truth until several decades later. Now it is "catch-up" time and we must work feverishly to change things around again.

The NEA has convinced the Parents into believing we *need* them to control and dictate all curricula! Actually, the parents in most cases are not even aware of who controls the curriculum. **WE DON'T! AND WE DON'T WANT THEM TO ANY LONGER! AND WE MUST *FORCE THEM* TO STOP THIS NEFARIOUS CURRICULUM!** *WE MUST REFUSE TO LET IT CONTINUE! And we can if we all rise to the occasion together, in unity.*

Secondary Reason: *Following suit, and as a result of,* the *primary reason*, which demoralized, desensitized, depressed and promoted promiscuous behavior in our students for the past 35 years, (now become adults), ruining their young AND adult lives with liberal "freedom" ideas regarding sex (not love!), caused their desires for X-rated movies and television—further escapisms from "reality" and excuses their sinking lower and lower into their sad circumstances. These industries cater to their "now need," similarly as does the **Planned Parenthood Federation** business of murder of our future boys and girls. In the Liberal mind, sexual promiscuity, **including Homosexuality (all 30-some different aspects of it now taught K-12)** has been made a legal right and taught to our children as "freedoms." These are blatant immoral degrading nefarious lies! These kinds of behavior lend to the dummying down of the students as they begin to lose all respect for themselves and suffer from a self-defeating attitude toward themselves. *This is in addition* to the academic standards being lowered while the NEA further progresses in their intentional dummying down of the students.

According to a letter from Rev. Lou Sheldon, *Traditional Values Coalition:*

"There is a Father who landed in jail (David Parker, Lexington MA—a hotbed area, ground zero, of the homosexual activists going after our kids big time) because he was unaware of a social (ist—my comment) experiment concocted by GLSEN (Gay Lesbian Straight Education Network) (consorting with the hubristic NEA—mine) to indoctrinate public school children from the day they step into ***Kindergarten!***

Continuing:

"They must be taught that homosexuality is fine and homosexual families are just wonderful. *David was locked up in jail and banned from stepping foot onto school property—even to vote!"* (Right here in America!) "David simply wanted to exercise his *legal right to remove his son Jacob from the class when homosexual issues were discussed.* After indicating the school district would obey State law, the Superintendent had local police arrest David for trespassing—even though the principal invited him to come! He wasn't even allowed to call an attorney and in court the next day *he was informed he could never step foot on school property without first getting permission—which he knew they'd never give him.* As a result, 5-year-old Jacob was grabbed by a crowd of students during recess, dragged behind the building, and beaten. (Obvious blatant intolerance is shown for anything other than the liberal agenda.) The school is still arrogantly refusing to notify Jacob's parents when discussing homosexuality issues with their son. They claim "gay marriage" is legal in MA and they will teach young Jacob about homosexual families and issues <u>whenever they want.</u> This is what they believe every elementary classroom needs to have: 1) Posters on the walls depicting homosexual families; 2) More books exposing children to homosexuality; 3) Teacher initiated discussions to lead children into **ACCEPTING** homosexuality."

According to Rev. Sheldon's letter: "The school got around the *Parental Notification Legal Right* by stating that Parent's can be notified regarding Sex Education, *but that since Homosexuality was not "Sex Education,"* the Parental Right to Notification does not exist!! Rev. Sheldon included a Petition to our MI Representative Fred Upton that we could sign, stating that these classes on homosexual behavior and marriage are being taught before our children can even read, and were also in the Gay Straight Alliance clubs on school campuses—recruiting in more than 2000 schools now— and are nothing but recruitment efforts sucking our kids into the sick and perverted lifestyles. In the petition we are asking that parents be provided the opportunity to opt their own children out of such clubs/classes."

(But don't we HAVE to be concerned and take responsible action for ALL children in this regard? And remove these classes altogether? These are the types of petitions we must start (or) never miss the opportunity to sign!) Please support his efforts: Traditional Values Coalition, P.O. Box 131808, Houston TX 77219-1808.

I just learned the Maryland State Board of Education has informed Parents that they *supercede the Parents' will* in how parents want their children educated, and the *State* will educate the children *the way that they wish to educate them*. This had to do with the incredibly awful, deeply in-depth homosexual and sex education classes dictated by NEA, K-12. Ladies and Gentlemen, they claim that MD will be a leader-State-pattern for the rest of the States! We certainly are in deep trouble.

(I must insert here that at the NEA Annual Convention in June 2006, they *mandated* that our children *MUST* be taught to *ACCEPT*, it is *not* enough to *TOLERATE,* the homosexual agenda(s), which are many (30-some) and very far reaching, beginning with *Kindergarten*, before they can even read! NEA has increasingly demanded we teach "feeling" and "imagination" instead of "thought"—logical, factual, critical thinking—one example is the *Harry Potter's witchcraft series* given *extensive exposure* and *encouragement* in public school libraries)

This does not even take into account the fact that Parents, who trustingly send their choicest possessions to public schools, are unsuspecting of the Atheistic Humanist Socialist Religion indoctrination and propaganda that has been/is being fed daily, subversively, to their precious young, too, until it's too late, and the damage has been done. I have watched for DECADES as fifty percent of our young students (OUR children) in taxpayer funded humanist public schools, (perhaps they should be renamed the Pubic Schools), drop out and never can readjust to normalcy in our society—and have to live with ruined lives unless a proper person comes along and helps them regain their true humanity in a Godly way. This is the result of teaching the false Humanist Religion in their "Sunday" schools, only every day of the week.

[Part 2]

Recently I watched and listened to Lou Dobbs at the National Press Club luncheon and I loved his comment: "I recall mention of an email that was circulating the internet that asks *if* we call illegal aliens "undocumented workers" or "undocumented immigrants," *perhaps* we should call drug dealers "unlicensed pharmacists." Let me take that comparison one step further. Perhaps we should call our *teacher-become-psychological-change-agents* "Socialist Propagandists" or "Atheistic Humanist Religion" teachers since both elements are now core-curriculum in each subject—these titles would be a whole lot more *Honest!*

Sadly, honesty is a word the NEA and PPFA don't seem to know or understand the meaning of. And they're in charge of so much of our children's welfare now.

I mustn't leave out the mantras of *"hate America"* and "environmentalism/global warming alarmism/evolution ***theories as segments of that religion that are force-fed to our children.*** I would certainly be remiss to omit mentioning the lying done with falsely revised History and Geography subjects. The NEA and its Public School Teacher Change Agents, under NEA direct COMMAND, the PPFA, the ACLU, and our "entertainment" industry, and the variety of media, plus other leftist organizations are hitting **all of US** below the belt, and demolishing the foundations of our God-given culture and Nation, while they demolish our children's future lives for the end goals.

To produce Socialism/Communism in a country, the masses must be: 1) dumbed-down; 2) God removed; and 3) amoralized to the extent of losing control of one's self, produced by the capture of the children's minds in school (as e.g., suicide bombers, Nazi-ism, Socialism/Communism **and** having to be taken care of by the State with absolute control of our lives); all of this = Public School education = Socialism. We are *all* then owned by the State, not as *Godly individuals*, but as Socialist Global *Common grouped Citizens*. **What's Hillary's philosophy once again? "It takes a Village/State to raise the children!" NO! It takes PARENTS to raise THEIR child.**

What these pushers of Socialism do not understand is that they are termed "Useful Idiots" by the very people they are serving, and that they will be the first "to go" when Socialist Dictators are in charge. They need to internalize deeply that title they are given by their masters of deceit and the fate that will befall them. As any ex-Socialist/Communist.

There is no doubt, folks, that the National Education Association Teachers' Union and the American Association of University

Professors and the Public School Teachers/Professors have become **guilty of malfeasance** (impropriety of a public servant). The colloquialism "Catch them if you can" is appropriate and is something we citizens, if we truly desire to save our Nation, must act to perform this, ourselves. Right Now! They must know they have been caught at their antics—and punished—**by removing our children from their grasp AND INSISTING ON SCHOOL CHOICE (with choice for parents and NO government entanglement)**! The Schools are sick and rotting from within and our children have been indoctrinated with their **toxic venom**. Most assuredly we, as a collective people acting as individuals, **acting quickly,** as we did in stalling the Comprehensive Immigration Bill (the Liberals say they'll bring it back after 2008—they are relentless in their pursuit of Socialism for our country!!) we must **decisively storm** our elected representatives phones and emails and faxes, and **DEMAND SCHOOL CHOICE. THE FUTURES OF OUR INDIVIDUAL CHILDREN AND OUR NATION DEPEND ON AND DEMAND WE CARRY OUT THIS ACTION!**

Further, we really should be examining what gives **them**, the enemy within, the right to re-program our children away from their Godly moral values taught at home, into the liberal atheist socialist ideologies as stated above. We also must examine our own consciences and ask ourselves, "Why aren't we stopping them?" And "Why haven't we stopped them?" *A couple of decades ago I used to think: That's o.k., they'll abort their own (though sad) and their abortion mentality will then fade out. FOLKS, OUR CHILDREN HAVE BEEN STOLEN! THEY CAN CONTINUE TO PUSH THE ABORTION IDEOLOGY AND ABORT THEIR OWN—BECAUSE THEY JUST SIMPLY STEAL OURS IN THE CLASSROOMS ACROSS AMERICA.* Surprisingly, I am asked over and over, "What has happened to my child—he is now a Liberal and votes as such—and we never raised him/her that way?" These parents truly are confused and disappointed AND ignorant of this "planned" outcome by the *Curriculum Dictator: The National Education*

Association with the dedicated help of their legal co-conspirator the ACLU. Intellectual honesty no longer exists. These teachers' and professors' union's primary goals are to:

1) **Eliminate God from the classroom and the Nation** (done! In the classrooms—and are doing! In the Nation)—(but now the war has begun regarding the *myth/lie* of the "separation of church and state" having been uncovered by dedicated servants, they now have a battle on their hands because Parents have become aware and very angry about this deception—and much to the NEA and ACLU and PPFA chagrin, we're winning court cases brought by brave, dedicated, generous and highly moral Parents and dedicated legal organizations.);

2) **Subversively insert intense brainwashing of Socialism**: the teaching of the *theory* of Evolution *(disguised Atheism)* along with the *Religions of Environmentalism and Humanism and Global Warming, and Liberalism/Progressivism*, plus *Universal Healthcare*, as core curriculum in every subject and the outlawing of the true meaning of Christian holidays *(Socialism disguised in these lying titles, produced by Gradualism/ Incrementalism/Progressivism—their methods of indoctrination and brainwashing slowly—their slogan being: "Move forward with haste--slowly— gradually"—you have to give them credit here—they are very patient and focused on their goal)*;

3) **Dumb-down the God-given intelligence in the child,** concentrating on the middle-to-low-income families to the "drop-out" stage, ensuring their dependence on the State's Welfare rolls, (and) convincing the young minds of the rest of our children with all the "garbage" of the above;

4) **Demoralize and Desensitize and Depress as many children as possible** into immoral lifestyles via the "Sex Health Classes" and "Drug" Education Classes— You know, the "How-To" classes. And now we have the many Homosexual Agenda(s) which the *majority* of the American people find not only *sinful, unnatural and degrading,* but incredibly *physically and psychologically unhealthy*--perverted lifestyles forced on our children—and as a result, on us. Folks, remember, let this sink in! I have an incredibly long list of all the agendas associated under the "homosexual" lifestyle that reads as a pornography list. Is it also taught in the public government schools/colleges that most child molesters and predators are homosexuals? This perverted lifestyle is *mandated* by NEA to be taught to *K*-12 public school students who are OUR children! It bothers me intensely that we have not put a stop to it. As more children are "led" into the unhealthy homosexual lifestyle, which they will be, are they also taught that research shows they will die 20 years earlier than their heterosexual peers—from very painful diseases? Research also shows that this lifestyle produces many, many psychological illnesses. Do we want this for our children?

I know that it is hard for some to believe that all of the above has happened over the past 35+ years of pubic school education— oops!—public school indoctrination—which no longer can be legitimately called an "educational" system—but it has happened! **It can no longer be permitted to continue**. Education by this **public** institution **(financed by US)** has become dangerously, meaninglessly worthless, since taken over by the NEA, as far as preparing a massive number of children to live in an adult world. Have you ever tried to reason with a graduate of the public school system to explain what has happened to them? They cannot even think that what you say is true. That shows the depth of indoctrination that has taken place in their minds. This is known as *Socialist Gradualism and Brainwashing /Indoctrination—it is how all Third World Nations have been founded in Socialism, resulting in their extremely poor Third World sub-standard living conditions—by **taking over the education of the children**—and here* **WE are now.** *All of the above steps were incrementally, slowly, deceitfully implemented in our Public Schools' curriculum by the NEA/AAUP and backed by the ACLU, plus.* If anyone argues this point, simply refer them to the deplorable condition of so many of our drop-out-from-school-and-life, homeless or jailed or drugged or psychologically or physically sick, State-dependent citizens. It is absolutely unspeakable—no words can define—the "subjective meaningless condition" of the state of the "lost" souls' minds—and this in America—due to what we have allowed the Public School Classrooms to become. We neglected to be watchful for the past **four decades** and that is a real *SHAME ON US!* Someone must speak out for those that are lost and try to rescue as many as we can. We have a responsibility to prevent the continuing of this force-fed, farce-of-an-educational-system, because the future of our posterity and also our future depends on us to do it. **We either care—or we don't. We're long overdue for action!**

With all the above garbage being pushed at our children daily, 6.5 hours each and every day, when is there time in the school hours to teach the basic necessities of a successful life—e.g., Reading, Writing/English (and all that it pertains to), and Arithmetic (all levels of Math)?—**which Parents mistakenly thought the Public Schools were doing**—until the research showed that Internationally we are among the very lowest scored students in the world. By this time, generations were lost to us—but gained to *back* the Liberal Socialists Party as brainwashed *voters* in our country. We spend the most money per child than any other Nation on earth.—and tenured teachers/professors are among the highest paid employees in the Nation. And what do we American citizens get for it? Traitorous acts against our children and nation. Previously, *before NEA started*

DICTATING the curriculum, when per student costs were lower and there were more students per class, we had the highest scoring students in the world. Children become utterly confused when "meaningless-to-them-at-their-age-levels" ambiguous confusing non-content classes of indoctrination are relentlessly forced on them. They have no desire and are incapable of learning this nonsense at their age, except by memorization of repeated mantras, and they become numb to learning, leaving them very discouraged and depressed. Believe it or not, this is what the Socialists want—it HAS to happen—*a necessary component and main goal of theirs.* The other goal is to cause dissatisfaction with every aspect of decency in the nation—enter in the *Hate America philosophy which they also "teach" the children..*

 Little concrete knowledge of value is taught our children. They focus out and concentrate on the "sex and drug" education (educated in supposedly "safe" sex and "safe" drug behaviors) that make sense to them and demand their full attention--hence so much experimentation at younger and younger ages. Of course, the Evolution-from-animals *theory* condones and excuses the "base instincts" of their desires, plus the false Evolution and Environmental Religion (Godless) indoctrination depresses them—because in their hearts they KNOW they are not animals. *Most* children have been taught at home that they were created by God. Can you even imagine the confusing pressure they are under trying to maintain what their Parents have taught them while trying to assimilate with the Evolution *Theory (not fact!) of coming from monkeys?* But they'd better learn Evolution well—because they'll be tested on it. If the child states that they don't agree with it, they are humiliated in front of their peers! More stress for them. Of course, they are allowed to question, belittle or berate any conservative idea. I think to myself, if I was forced to learn all the above as an *adult,* having all my ideals berated, I do believe I would become promiscuous and drug-addicted, too, or at the least be forced to drop out, to escape the emotional pain. We certainly expect our children to face incredible odds of turning out decently, and continue believing as we've taught them to believe, while making them attend these Public Schools, that have become very toxic. Just imagine for one moment what it must be like for our children every single day at their public school as they try to assimilate two world views—the Godless Socialist and the Christian worldviews—two directly opposing belief systems. What mental anguish!

I like puzzles! Now let's put some puzzle pieces together. People who are dependent on the State to care for them (includes single teen parents and their children, drop-outs, drug-addicted, promiscuous, people, some having very bad diseases because of their lifestyles, and unemployable) AND people who have been **liberally socialistically** programmed/brainwashed, who have attended public K-12, and public Universities to boot, ***usually vote--how?*** Remember, they have been manipulated into a mind-set that tells them they ***need*** the State/Federal governments to take care of their every need. The mantra we hear lately as reported by the liberal media is: ***The Liberals didn't win the 2006 elections—the Conservatives lost it!* Don't you believe it for one minute! Our children, products of the public school system, are now VOTERS—PROGRAMMED and BRAINWASHED VOTERS! HONEST-TO-GOODNESS FRUITS OF NEA teacher-change agents' LABOR!** *That's precisely how we lost it. And we have the most critical elections coming up in 2008! What do YOU think will happen? The writing is on the wall—and we're not King Nebuchadnezzar—and we don't need Daniel to interpret this bad dream!*

[Part3]

Let's rehearse who NEA, AAUP, ACLU and PPFA are:
(Planned Parenthood Federation of America; National Education Association Teacher's Union; American Association of University Professors; American Civil Liberties Union; plus other Leftist Organizations)

**BECAUSE little concrete valuable basic education—
READING, WRITING/ENGLISH/LANGUAGE and MATH
and TRUE SCIENCE—and yes! Thank you! plenty of
FALSELY REVISED HISTORY** (lying about how America
was founded and about the Christian Founding Fathers of our
Christian Nation, and how it became the great country it was and
still is) **AND GEOGRAPHY AND CIVICS, has been taught**,
**research shows all National scores reflect the DUMBING
DOWN (and) PROMISCUITY of our Nation's children—this
CANNOT BE ARGUED. Simply look at the decadent
condition of our Nation and so many wasted lives, directly
caused by the NEA and their "friends." This to me is utterly
despicable and sadly deplorable! Is it any wonder that
Planned Parenthood Federation of America is screaming for
more federal funds to meet the higher demand to murder
more of our future boys and girls—in the coming year?**

Referring to the CNSNews.com release titled: *Planned
Parenthood Reports Record Abortions, High Profits*, by Randy
Hall, June 15, 2007:

> "Planned Parenthood Federation of America (PPFA),
> despite a drop in donations and the first fall in income
> from clinics in its history, the nation's biggest abortion
> provider made a *high profit* last year, *thanks to the
> American taxpayer. Pro-lifers want this to stop.*" As
> stated, PPFA performed a record **264,943 abortions
> (murders)**, attaining a high profit of $55.8 million, and
> *received record taxpayer funding (you and me) of
> $305.3 million.*

> Let's fast forward through the article to: "Jim Sedlak,
> Executive Director of Stop Planned Parenthood
> (STOPP) International, told Cybercast News Service on
> Thursday that the flow of *taxpayer dollars* to the
> abortion provider *"has to be stopped. Since our elected*

officials won't do their job, it's up to us. Clearly it was a good overall year for Planned Parenthood," he said. "Total income went up 2.4 percent, passing $900 million for the first time." "...The final category of PPFA revenue sources is you and me—The American Taxpayer." He noted that the amount of taxpayer funding reported by PPFA exceeded that of the previous year by $32.6 million, or 12 percent!!! *"The bottom line is the PPFA is losing donations, its clinic income is down, and you and I are being FORCED to pay more so the organization can kill our children through abortion (and) spread its perverted ideology throughout the land,"* Sedlak said. **(PPFA is now requesting an "increase" in funding from the government—us—this year.)**

Further in this article: Douglas Scott, Jr., President of Life Decisions International (LDI), stated: "This *'not-for-profit' entity ends every fiscal year with tens of millions of dollars in 'excess revenue over expenses,' which is known to regular people as 'profit.'* ....On June 30, 2006, PPFA had net assets valued at $839.8 million, of which ..... *This is essentially a savings account," he said. "The money is sitting in a bank and drawing interest that will further advance Planned Parenthood's deadly agenda." (emphasis mine)*

Can we see the **Joint Venture** that has evolved between the NEA Socialist Public Schools' Progressive/Gradual curriculum and the Humanist Religion (no right, no wrong, no God), and the Planned Parenthood business with the help of the ACLU and their "sister" organizations, as co-dependently existing and totally related? THAT'S ALSO KNOWN AS A "JOINT BUSINESS/ SOCIALIST VENTURE." If not in direct concert contractually with each other, certainly needing and benefiting from each other, and without each one, the outcomes and survival of the others, would be in jeopardy.

If you don't believe by now that these organizations function together, read PPFA's own future projection of teens who will need abortions this coming year, as follows, and be sickened by their knowledgeable projections. After all, they should know! These "children" will also become *our children* drop-outs and on public assistance, no doubt, with future pregnancies, poor darlings, and wasted, ruined lives, unless, by some Godly miracle, we can save them. *WE CAN—AND WE MUST! We cannot allow ourselves to wiggle out of this responsibility to them.*

Let's proceed in quoting from the above-mentioned article:

> "In a recent statement, PPFA President Cecile Richards argued that more funding was needed for its work, stating: "Currently, more than *17 million women in the U.S. need "publicly-funded family planning (abortions) and there is not enough funding to meet the need," she said. "NEARLY 750,000 TEENAGERS IN THE U.S. WILL BECOME PREGNANT THIS YEAR!!"*

(That quote shows just how sure the PPFA is in regard to their future "business" outlook. They are counting on our young children to need their services and that this will be forthcoming under the current practices being furthered in the public school classrooms. This literally screams at us "to Get the Sex Education Out of the Schools Now!" When we did not have it, a few unfortunate girls ended up pregnant in HIGH School—compare this to the figures now!)

Can you even fathom or imagine that the President of PPFA, Cecile Richards, the organization that murders our future boys and girls, has the audacity to tell us that SHE has the answers: What the *"medically accurate health information* and *EDUCATION"* should be for our Children? Absolutely ludicrous! It would be **much more of the same!** Or that **her information** would actually "reduce teen pregnancy and build strong families?" Smells like rotten phony baloney to me! **That would be suicide for their organization!** But guess what? We've let them peddle their phony answers to our children long enough! PPFA, along with their co-conspirators, in my estimation, the NEA, and ACLU, plus, are the very organizations responsible for intentionally *increasing the promiscuity* of our young *children* that result in teen pregnancy, and therefore, increases the great financial wealth of the PPFA.

The Socialist NEA/AAUP Humanist Religion agends taught in the public schools created the problems in the schools, and families, intentionally, (they are **masters at creating conflict and deceit and dissatisfaction**) to further Socialism in our Nation, **and they, together with PPFA and ACLU, plus, now will pretend to correct the huge problem *they created*,** with innocent sounding deceiving rhetoric proclaiming they have the answers, as above, with "education," but ultimately by abortion and other solutions that will disintegrate American families to cause the final slide into the end goal of Socialism. **The TRUTH is "twisted" by them** to sound noble and believable, and the unsuspecting, gullible Parents/Citizens are thereby deceived. We have been sold a horrible bag of so-called politically correct tricks that are ruining our children's lives and our Nation as a whole, not to speak of the trashing of the families broken by the way our children have been mutilated by their public school "education." All to set the stage for a massive population that eventually will be dumbed-down, demoralized and dysfunctional, and will need the government/State to take care of them. **But folks, that's socialism.** And in the end—the big lie is that Socialism *does not take care of anybody except the dictator and the top echelon of it.* **That's almost us right now.** These organizations are funded by US! **We have a responsibility to STOP funding them now and we must be LOUDLY HEARD, SHOW OUR DISGUST AT BEING TAKEN ADVANTAGE OF, by our NEA schools and their ELECTED OFFICIALS.**

Dr.Gregory Thompson

Back to the article: Family Research Council's Mr. Perkins agreed:

> "With assets totaling more than $839 million, Planned Parenthood hardly needs a government handout. (As they have requested!)

In conclusion, do you know what? **We need to demand the right to educate our children the way we want to educate them—and NOT as we are TOLD WITH FORCE to educate them by the NEA and the AAUP and the ACLU. We need to stop funding PPFA and remove it entirely from the school curriculum! and the subversive organization known as NEA** *Teachers Union and their dictatorship* **of** *our* **curriculum, too, with OUR tax dollars. We need to expose the Democratic Liberal Left Socialist politicians (and provide a list of them) whose campaigns are heavily funded by the teachers' dues through the NEA/AAUP. We need to start praying fervently for this outcome.** *We can do this IF we loudly proclaim and demand parental choice education vouchers in order to school our children in a productive, successful, emotionally and physically healthy manner—or, we can withhold taxes if it must come to that. And we should be willing to do that considering the welfare of our precious lives of our nation's children are at stake.* **We need to take back control of the classroom from the National Education Association. Civil disobedience may be the only way we can accomplish this at this late date—so much damage has been done thus far. The NEA and the AAUP are** *Teachers' and Professors' Unions—* **that** *gradually* **became** *DICTATORS o***f the curriculum taught our children, and through that, have mind-controlled them. Their** *sole* **purpose is supposed to be to "protect the Teachers'/Professors' benefits" ONLY. NEA is one of the most powerful and generous contributors of the Teachers Union Dues monies to Political Campaigns to gain favors to further their Socialist goals AND obtain more and more**

money from the elected officials they support. They do their despicable work in concert with each other—feeding off of OUR CHILDREN AND OUR NATION'S CITIZENS like parasites. Approximately 93% of the many millions of dollars go to Liberal Left Democrats while 3% are donated to Conservative Republican campaigns. WHAT DOES THIS TELL US? THEY ARE DEFINITELY A "POLITICAL LIBERAL LEFT MACHINE OF SOCIALIST FORCE AND PROPAGANDA—and MUST BE DEALT WITH BECAUSE THEY HIDE BEHIND A ONCE SAFE AND SACRED SCHOOL/CLASSROOM BANNER. A great number of dedicated good public school teachers are very opposed to this funding of political campaigns and the Socialist Humanist curriculum. Perhaps they will soon realize they do have an "out." They can visit the Web Site: for the *Fellowship & Association of Christian Teachers Union*. There are also other Teachers' Unions that are out there that offer benefits for teachers.

Close consideration reveals that unless we become as passionately devoted to our goals, to return our Nation back to the intent of the founding fathers, more devoted than these organizations are in furthering their goal of Atheistic Socialism for our Nation, we *cannot* win this silent civil war we are engaged in. If you can support financially any pro-life legal organization *fighting to end abortion*, OR *fighting to obtain our right to Parental Choice School Vouchers*, please do so. We must originate and/or sign every petition, AND make phone, email and fax contacts with our elected officials and *demand we be given parental choice of schools via vouchers*. We must realize that these so-called voucher monies are NOT the Federal Government's monies—but our parents' own money that has been confiscated from them unfairly by the Government so the Government could control the schooling of our children. We are simply asking for OUR OWN MONIES back and we have a legitimate right to them. It's our money we'll be saving as private schools educate far better and far more cheaply than the abusive Government Public School System. And **all** of our children deserve and will hopefully once again be given a legitimate *equal* chance to excel and succeed in life.

Are we to continue to stand by as we suffer violence to our own children, and allow them to suffer so? We must not fear. We must not close it out. We must, when situations seem hopeless, realize that is when God loves to show His power, while using His people—this is something we can count on. While suffering the persecution we know will follow our works, if we truly believe, we'll stand firmly on the Word of God and let Him lead, protecting us as we move boldly forward. We are here for such a time as this—we must have courage to risk *everything* for God, His children, and our Nation. We ARE in a real cultural civil war against factions that are out to destroy our *freedom loving Godly Nation* as we know it. The ungodly organizations have started it—with God's leading, we will finish it. How shall we escape if we neglect His leading at this time? We must make the choice to fight back. **This is the noble "choice for life" for our pre-born and existing children—it is the right thing to do**. They are not only aborting our pre-born boys and girls at PPFA, NEA is providing PPFA their product, AND *causing the abortion of 50% of our existing children's future lives and their inalienable right to happiness,* via the NEA's (no longer ours) Public Schools. They are also, with their Atheist Humanist core curriculum *gradually* removing God from Our children's minds and hearts.

How I wish we could un-ring the school bells for the past 40 years—and bring back the wasted lives of nearly half of our public school children and see what the aborted children would have become. Dear ones, this is a real cultural civil war—evil vs. good—with the winner controlling *all* of our lives. Choose thee this day who you will serve: The State or God? Together, we must choose God—march forward in this war! Too many battles have been lost—but we don't have to lose the war, unless we choose to do nothing.

I must close, but this article hasn't even touched on the "Clinics" that are scheduled to be erected and staffed by Medical and Psychological "experts" right on the public school grounds— Three Rivers MI, a small community, have all but broken the ground for one. I hate to leave you with the parting knowledge that children raised in Christian homes are now considered "mentally ill" when registering for kindergarten. The book: *FedEd* by Allen Quist is an insightful "must-read" for any concerned true Parent that wants the best for their children. (All emphasis, throughout this article and referenced articles, is mine—Gabriel Stokes)   (end)

Eliminate Hurtful Classes— Get God Back into Schools
Gabriel Stokes (2006)

Evolution is a *hypothesized theory,* an unexplainable, farfetched *idea.* The supposed outcome of it, man, was never observed being formed—nor can it be repeated—so it cannot legitimately be taught as fact—which has been done for decades—without so much as a hint of objection from the Christian community. To expect a *thinking* person to accept it as factual science is nonsensical. Evolution is a false religion, maneuvered into our captive-audience children's minds in the governmental public schools, against most of the people's wishes.

Religion is the act of having faith in something. Our children are being duped into having faith in—unscientific evolution, under the guise of proven science via the Religion of Humanism. I, for one, want it removed from the schools. I am appalled, stunned, and cannot understand, that supposedly *thinking* people, "the intellectual elites(?) *(they call themselves),* have even bitten on this bait. It flaws their supposed intelligence. Some don't realize this is simply a handy tool used to subject our children to the

atheistic idea of no God, taught under the dictate of the NEA—
thus the current frantic fight carried on by them and the ACLU
to keep *Intelligent Design (ID)* out of the public schools. ID does
not *have to be* taught in the schools but Evolution *should not be*
taught because it is not a proven fact. We would not teach our
children that 2+2=5. That's absurd—and so is the ***theory of
evolution flawed because the facts don't add up either.*** The
children are being lied to.

A growing number of science professors and teachers, having
taught this *concept* to children, tearfully admit *they* were duped,
and anguish over the fact they led so many astray. They are
trying desperately to correct the error they taught, to the extent of
writing books about it. Bravo! for their courage and humility.
We need more like them. The majority of people in this nation
know evolution to be an unproven, unscientific *idea*, taught as
truth/fact, to a captive audience, with our tax dollars. A child,
age 7 through college age, subjected to ***repetitious*** statements that
a cat is a dog will—guess what!—grow up believing that a cat is
a dog, if no one tells him/her the truth. That is precisely how the
religious *concept* of evolution has caught on, as being taught in
the public school system for the past 40+ years. Children to
adulthood—have quite simply been *indoctrinated/brainwashed*
about a *false theory/idea from youth onward.* Put yourself in the
child's place. What vulnerable child, who had been taught that a
loving God created them, could possibly refute this *theory* while
under the dominating teacher's influence? If that child is taught
differently at home, the confusion and stress it causes the child is
excruciating for him/her to bear, and undermines the rights of the
parents to teach their child as they wish. The only avenue to take
is to eliminate teaching *unscientific evolution* in the schools. It is
terribly flawed and should not be taught at all. *If* unknowing
parents wish to teach their children *unscientific* evolution, let
them do so at home!

Children lose heart when they grow up thinking falsely they are
nothing but evolved animals. Actually, they are intricately

woven created human beings. The *theory* that the evolving man gets better and smarter at each level is an ideal climate for the idea of racism to blossom—one level better than the other. However, the creation of human beings, of man/woman, by God, allows no racism. All are created equal—no mention of race or color is made since all are brother and sisters, descended from the original human beings. (Acts 17:26—NKJV) I would love to take this further with the AABBaabb dominance area of biological science, but space does not allow. Being *created* certainly elevates one's opinion of one's self, doesn't it? Imagine that—children would realize they are human beings, with human ancestry, not animal ancestry! Our children could immensely benefit from this information—talk about producing a humble self-esteem—this would increase theirs immeasurably!

Further, we people who make up our nation desperately need our schools to return to using classroom time for teaching basics so our children will be employable after finishing high school—if we can help them to actually graduate. It certainly can be that way *again.* Leave out the *religion of evolution, health/sex classes and all hidden agendas pushed at our kids through these courses.*

Research now shows that sex and drug education encourages promiscuous behavior rather than discourages it, as certainly evidenced by the downturn of our national teen culture. Including these courses in the governmental schools, has led us to be the sickest nation of teens/young adults in the world. And that sickens the heart and soul of so many parents and childen. Promiscuity, minds dominated by sex *(not love)*, young teen single parenthood, abortions, fatherless children, malnourishment, addictions, STD's resulting in sterility, depression, suicide, murders in school, homosexuality, ad nausea, are exhibited damaging effects realized in their ***pre-adult*** lives and carried into their adult lives. Before the above nonsense courses were force-fed daily to our captive children, and God and prayer forced out, our nation led the world in teen academics and teen morality, and teens were healthy. Consequently, that led to a vibrantly blessed nation. Observe what we have allowed to shamefully happen to a great percentage of our precious suffering-teens-now-turned-young adults—who are paying the price for our neglect—and the sick status of our nation. There is no excuse for us! Again, the *so-called intellectual elites* would have us believe that the solution is a complex, complicated one, that only they could devise and implement. Actually they are who got us into the sad state of affairs we now face. The majority of thinking people know complexity is not the case but a simple fact—get the hurtful courses out and get God back in. Period. A terrific Educator, Ken Ham, Biology Professor, has devised the following chart that provides a significant visual picture comparing ***Evolution Theory*** to ***Creation.***

Evolution	*Creation*
Humanism	Christianity
Abortion/Euthanasia	Meaning of Life
Pornography (e.g.)	Standards
Homosexuality	Marriage
Racism	One Race
Man's ideas	God's Word

We've discouraged and deprived and dehumanized/degraded and demoralized a highly significant percentage of two-plus generations of children who have ended up damaged by Evolution/Health/Sex courses being force-fed to them—with logical "garbage in—garbage out" results. It doesn't take a lot of brains to connect the dots for a *thinking* people. The money spent on just these two courses could be used to add productive, decent, courses to educate and turn our children's minds *optimistically* on their future (and ours!) and get their minds back on decent tracks. And guess what! Their behavior would improve too. ***AND THEY WOULD BE SO MUCH HAPPIER!***

Let's fight to remove these classes from the schools now and give back to children the "sweet mystery of life" to discover for themselves at the proper adult times of their lives, in marriages, and help equip our children with a healthy, and high academic, future. While we're at it, we could add back in the accurate account of our nation's history—not rewritten false and negative history. Let's get on a *restoration* track for, and then ultimately by, our healthy children. Even though it seems like an impossible task, *if* we get started now, we may still be able to produce a turnaround for the well-being of all of us. If not, we all know where we are headed—further downward. "There can be no substitute for victory" over this decline. Sadly, the public schools have written their own fatal fate, and also for those for whom they have been given charge over. Let's turn it around! WE CAN!! *If* WE CARE!!

On the Subject of Global Earth Warming as Planned by Him

A word to Al Gore and his disciples: All it requires is a little humility to understand this—you can judge yourself as to whether or not you have that virtue. It's pretty obvious you don't. Virtues are different than values. Values are subjective and there is no right or wrong. Virtues, however, are hard-and-fast-held truths. The only One who can destroy our earth is the One who created it. Man cannot do it! The only reason the Creator would do so is if His created ones go on disobediently, rebelliously, ignoring His laws and blaspheming Him and His Word, which is what you are doing and encouraging our children to do by forcing them to learn the false science of Global Warming/Climate Change. You people dubbed it "Manmade Global Warming"—God's science is cyclical and will go on forever, warming and cooling. And for that I say: "Thanks, God, the PERFECT balance is all in *Your* Hands." And those that are intelligent enough, and have no other **hidden subversive agendas**, can understand this. Simple, factual truth!—that's what THOUSANDS (not Al Gore's one-hundred liberal socialists) learned scientists attest to, write about and teach. Yet our NEA-run schools REFUSE to hear, or teach, what the THOUSANDS of scientists teach—to our beloved children. They HAVE to lie about it! along with their evolution *theory. It's all part of their Socialist agenda to financially and economically bankrupt our nation—which has to happen for the Socialist Dictatorship to be realized here.*   (end)

(Author's note: Gabriel Stokes (not the author's real name), is a Christian who is fighting the moral decay, as a vessel of Christ, listening to His Word, and researching to teach and educate others of the evils we must stand against. *I thank you for your dedication to Jesus and your love for the children.)*

Run as fast as you can from the government schools!!!

Because of the research and efforts of three warriors, John Stormer, Gabriel Stokes, and Dr. Robert Dreyfus, who have been in the battle for over 30 years, you have now heard of some manipulative tools used to lull Christians into a new mindset and to start compromising the word of God with man's ways. As this is done, with man thinking that he does not need a foundation, a higher power to rely on, because he is smarter than God, it is no wonder that kids are killing kids in our schools. For love of the children, two great warriors for Christ will speak to this in the next chapter.

"Trust in the LORD with all your heart and lean not unto your own understanding. In all your ways acknowledge Him, and He shall direct your paths. Be not wise in your own eyes; fear the LORD, and depart from evil." Proverbs 3:5-7

Hopefully, all of the previous and following additional background information, with the indwelling of the Holy Spirit, will fall on wonderfully fertile minds and hearts of the Christian Pastors, lay people and parents, and will produce a lively fruitful response to a leadership call on their lives on behalf of all children in our nation, and on the whole nation itself.

Chapter 10

WHY KIDS ARE KILLING KIDS

"When you spread out your hands in prayer, I will hide my eyes from you; even if you offer many prayers, I will not listen. Your hands are full of blood..." Isaiah 1:15,16

Rev. Flip Benham, National Director of *Operation Save America/Operation Rescue* and Pastor Rusty Thomas, are two front line Generals putting Minutemen into the battles to protect life and bring others to Jesus so that they may live eternally. These two men lead with authority, no fear, and no compromise, because of obedience to God and His Word.

By Rev. Phillip "Flip" Benham
April 25, 2007
NewsWithViews.com

Part 1 (below) was written the day after the massacre at Columbine High School on April 20, 1999. Nothing has changed! There is no repentance of our war against Almighty God. We have learned nothing from that horrible day eight years ago. Bloodshed continues coursing down the corridors of our schools, workplaces, and streets with ever increasing ferocity. Now it has come to one of our colleges—this time it's Virginia Tech! (Author's note: Since this writing, also to Northern IL University in DeKalb, IL)

The media is busying itself trying to point its long crooked finger of blame on police, college administration, city, state, federal officials and, of course, George Bush! Yet there is absolutely no solution any of these can offer to prevent the violence that is savaging our kids. Our problem is with God Himself!

He has a controversy with us. It is delineated in six simple verses found in Hosea 4:1-6. We have cast God behind our backs, expelled Him from school, and banished Him from the school yard. As we have done this, an enemy has crept in to rob, kill, and destroy our children. Yes Virginia, there is a devil!

We have shed blood in the womb (over fifty million children slaughtered) and we have been reaping an ever increasing harvest of bloodshed in our streets (Hosea 4:2). We are not getting away with it.

That is why we mourn today for those who have been so needlessly slaughtered (Hosea 4:3). We throw up our hands toward heaven and ask, "WHY!?"

It is my responsibility today to tell why: *"My people are destroyed from lack of knowledge. Because you have rejected knowledge, I also have rejected you as my priests; because you have ignored the law of your God, I also will ignore your children."* (Hosea 4:6) What happened at Virginia Tech on the morning of April 16, 2007, is a sign and judgment from God that we have turned our back upon Him.

America, "Unless the Lord watches over the city, the watchmen stand guard in vain." (Psalm 127)

Part 1: During a week of bringing the Gospel of Christ to local high schools and confronting the abortion industry with its savaging of our children in Buffalo, New York, *Operation Save America* Director, Rev. Flip Benham made the following Statement:

Blood is coursing down the corridors of a high school in Littleton, Colorado and the blood shed in those hallways is on our hands. We have no one to blame but ourselves. In **high schools** across this country, (Edinboro, Pennsylvania; Pearl, Mississippi; West Peducah, Kentucky; Jonesboro, Arkansas; Eugene, Oregon), it has become increasingly obvious that our schools have become the very gates of hell. Violence of every sort is overwhelming our public schools in spite of the vehement protestations of school officials and the Department of Education. These people have refused to face reality for years.

Why has the public school become, apart from the local abortion mill, the most dangerous place for a young person to be? Why are our kids, who have been given everything money can buy, killing their friends in school? Why have our schools become veritable jungles where "survival of the fittest" has become a reality? The answer is simple. Violence was done in the hearts of our children long before it murderously manifested itself in the hallways of our schools.

God was violently expelled from school by a Supreme Court decision in 1962 (Engle vs. Vitale). He was banished from the schoolyard and His Commandments removed from the school walls in two other Supreme Court decisions (Abbington vs. Schemp, 1963, and Stone vs. Graham, 1977). He has been replaced with police guards, metal detectors, drugs, condoms, (author: abortion and legally drugged children) gangs, assault, rape, murder and violence of unprecedented order.

We have violently robbed our children of purpose and destiny by allowing God to be removed from their education. Genesis 6:11-13 tells us that violence filled the earth because the people God created chose to remove Him from their minds and hearts. When God is removed, violence always fills the void.

We fathers have violently removed God from our children by abdicating our responsibility to live Godly lives before them. Mothers have violently removed God from our children by denying them divine maternal love and dropping them off at day care centers. We have all done violence to our children by allowing the smallest and weakest to be slaughtered at abortion mills. Government schools have done violence to our children by removing the knowledge of God from them.

(Author's note: We have driven our very young children to sexual promiscuity and illegal drug usage via public schooling.)

"Do not be deceived America! God cannot be mocked. A man reaps what he sows." That's what the Bible says! We in America have sown violence into the hearts of our kids, and we are reaping a whirlwind of violence in our schools. We have removed every vestige of the knowledge of God from our children and should not be surprised at the manifestations of senseless brutality and violence that replaced Him.

We are today raising a nation of predators! We have kids who don't give a rip about God, their neighbor, or themselves. They will rob, kill and destroy simply to get what they want when they want it. We are raising kids without a conscience who kill at a whim. Then we look at each other with awkward amazement and wonder what in the world happened. We have purposely removed God from the hearts and minds of our children and are suffering the horrible consequences of our foolish arrogance.

To restore peace in the classroom, we must first corporately and publicly repent of our sin—the removal of God from the lives of our kids. We must acknowledge the fact that we are not smarter than He is, and invite Him back—Ten Commandments and all! We must bring God back to school! He promises to return if we will humble ourselves and pray (2 Chronicles 7:14).

What will it be, America? Another godless million-dollar program that will never touch the cancer of violence destroying our kids? Or, will we have the courage to call on the Great Physician Himself, and ask Him to perform the surgery that will completely remove the cancer forever? (end)

We do need to decide the answer to the questions Flip has raised. Thank you Flip

Christians Listen!!! Let's think about this yet again!
Are you giving aid and comfort to the enemies of God, family, and country? Do you send your children to the altar of Be-li-al, the government education system? Do you pay for this system to lie to your children and put them at risk of Hell for eternity? Listen to one of the greatest men of Law that the country has ever known who was also a Christian, Daniel Webster. He gave this great truth to posterity:

> *"If religious books are not widely circulated among the masses in this country, I do not know what is going to become of us as a nation. If truth is not diffused, error will be. If God and His Word are not known and received, the Devil and his works will gain the ascendancy."*

Welcome to Satan's "Sacred Cow," the government schools of America! God is eliminated along with the influence of parents, and in comes the influence of Satan and his dupes, the atheistic

Communists and Humanists, (most of the Democrats, the NEA, ACLU, Planned Parenthood, Republicans-in-name-only (RINOs), Sodomites, ACLU, and others). The vacuum of the absence of God is replaced with evil that overflows as it consumes our innocent children with ugliness.

"Finally, my brethren, be strong in the Lord, and in the power of his might. Put on the whole armor of God that ye may be able to stand against the wiles of the devil. For we wrestle not against flesh and blood, but against principalities, against powers, against the rulers of the darkness of this world, against spiritual wickedness in high places. Wherefore take unto you the whole armor of God, (so) that ye may be able to withstand in the evil day, and having done all, to stand." (Ephesians 6:10-13)

Chapter 11

AMERICA'S SCHOOLS TODAY—
GATES TO HELL

KILL**STEAL**DESTROY:
WHAT CAN PARENTS DO?

"And whoso shall receive one such little one in My name receives Me. But whoso shall offend one of these little ones which believe in me, it were better for him that a millstone were hanged about his neck, and that he were drowned in the depth of the sea. Woe unto the world because of offenses! For it must needs be that offenses come; but woe to that man by whom the offense comes!" (Matthew 18:5-7)

Joseph Califano, when head of the Department of Health, Education and Welfare in the 1970's, stated:

> *"The worst place that a teenager can be today is in the public school system."*

A 1983 report issued by the National Commission on Excellence in Education said:

> *"If a foreign power were responsible for the state of education in America we would have considered it an act of war."*

In the last decade a book by John Stormer, a former school superintendent, researcher and author, had another nationally known researcher and author, Cal Thomas, indicate that:

"If parents knew what was happening to their children in the public schools, there would be a revolution."

Since these men in their reports have spoken, the devastation to the children in spirit, mind, and body, by the government school system has gotten worse.

Government schools have indoctrinated generations of children to believe in situational ethics, multiculturalism, socialism, sexual promiscuity, homosexuality, radical feminism, and evolution, social justice which is a form of liberation theology. They teach children that God has no say in these things, because it's just their opinion that He even exists. They shame and coerce the child into giving up their belief in Christianity's God.

The government schools teach that God is irrelevant in addition to lowering academic standards. Homosexual organizations indoctrinate children as young as five years old into acceptance of homosexuality as a normal and acceptable lifestyle, and studies show that ten (10) percent of students are sexually abused by teachers or school employees. They failed to report and halted one study after finding that the abuse of children in schools was over one hundred times greater than the pedophile pastor scandal. Sexually transmitted diseases, drug use and violence is rampant among youth. Sex education classes have culpability in the ugliness of over 8,000 of our children 12 to 25 years old, coming down with a sexually transmitted disease (STD) every day—Yes! Every day! Young people believe there is not absolute truth and 88% of the 48.4 million children who attend government schools leave the Church after their atheistic indoctrination. We must remember, too, that Atheism is a Religion of Faith being taught in the public schools. Over 40% of high school graduates are functionally illiterate and American children have the lowest academic achievement of nearly all industrial nations. The teacher unions cry out for bigger government and more money continually, as they have miserably failed, while spending more money per student than any country in the world.

The social engineering that is taking place in our government schools is intentional and purposeful, so the decay of our system mentioned above is no accident. The past and present indoctrination of the government schools, done subversively and deceitfully, incrementally and with pretty rhetoric, has made us a sad nation. Our academic status has become a laughing stock to the rest of the world and quite frankly it is downright embarrassing and humiliating to those of us who remain patriotic to our beloved nation and who desire and fight to maintain her sovereignty.

Elementary schools provide a foundation on which further learning takes place, and studies show that by the time children reach the age of 13, they have developed their worldview (the way they see the world) which they will maintain throughout their lives! Parents need to provide an education which is academically sound and that preserves moral values either by Christian Home Schooling, or enrolling them in a truly Christian School that receives no funding, books, curriculum, testing, or indoctrination from the unions or government.

In spite of all the evidence to the contrary, most parents believe that the government school their children attend is the exception and is a "good school". They don't realize that government schools are a big factor in devastating their children spiritually, morally, and intellectually on a daily basis. They are ignorant of the daily brainwashing their children are receiving that truly leaves the child amoralized and poorly behaved. NEA/AAUP thought they could remove Christian morality, virtues, and values from the child and replace them with their atheistic system and ideas of goodness. They have been sorely mistaken for *they will never correct the negative behaviors they have produced in the children* with their false ideas of promiscuous freedoms they have instilled in the children. A return to Godly virtues taught to the children once again, and the elimination of the NEA/AAUP and Federal Department of

Education dictatorship of curriculum is the only answer to the problems the unions and Federal government have caused our nation and families. Society has become increasingly dysfunctional because we've been treating symptoms rather than *the cause of the problems, "government schools."* which have become a cancer eating at the soul of America. Parents need to reclaim absolute control of the education of their children.

God's Word says, "**Knowing** the truth will set you free." *and without God being a part of education, the children will never know the truth, and that ignorance will cause a loss of freedom, virtue, and an increase in moral decay. Without Christianity there will be no freedoms because Christianity is the basis of all freedoms.*

Thomas Jefferson said, *"If a nation thinks it can be ignorant and free, it thinks something that never was or never will be."* The government education system in America has been culpable in keeping the people ignorant over several decades. The results have followed in our county as predicted by Noah Webster, 'School Master to America', who stated, *"The moral principles and precepts contained in the Scriptures ought to form the basis of all our civil constitutions and laws...All the miseries and evils which men suffer from vice, crime, ambition, injustice, oppression, slavery, and war, proceed from their despising or neglecting the precepts contained in the Bible."*

"Lifting JESUS back up as the foundation of this nation is the most important issue facing our families and our nation." Mark Kiser, Minutemen United, Jericho Rider, and President of America Asleep kNOw More.

The education you choose for the children can determine the type of person they will become and whether they will spend eternity in heaven or hell and it is a reflection of who you are as a Parent. You the parents are responsible and you can choose the beauty of

God's ways which leads to knowledge, wisdom and life, or the continuing failure of man's evil ways, which leads to foolishness and death of spirit, mind, and soul. It is also the responsibility of the Pastors to guide and teach the parents how to make the decisions as to how their children will be educated, and it is a sad reflection on the Pastors if they are negligent in this area of instruction.

May the Holy Spirit open the eyes and ears of His children to see and hear the Truth. Pray and ask Him to show you why the schools are damaging the children in Spirit, mind, and body, and why they must be stopped. With an open heart and mind to Him, He will not disappoint you by keeping the answers hidden from you.

Absolute: In God's Word, parents are responsible to see that God is the center of their children's education.

Know that there will be attempts with rhetoric coming from those that seem to know what they are talking about to tell you not to listen to the Truth, but look at the fruit of the government education system, and the lies that are being told to your children. When anyone challenges any of this, read Jeremiah 17:5-10 and remember that Jesus said, *"Take heed that no man deceive you."*

Many Christian parents out of ignorance, lies they have been led to believe, or personal convenience, have sent their children into a government education system that is against everything Godly. Your child cannot survive emotionally, spiritually or academically under its influence and curriculum.

Truth: The children belong to God and not to the nanny State, and Christian parents are paying the government education to teach the children to kneel to the state or global government and the global religion and not to the One True God. As a result, approx. 88% of children raised in Christian homes are leaving their faith by 21 years old. If we willingly send our children into such a system and pay for it, is this giving "aide and comfort" to those against God, family, and country? The answer is unequivocally, *"Yes!"*

Truth: The government education system in America is atheistic and pagan with a humanistic worldview. As a result, Christian parents and grandparents are sacrificing their children to Be-li-al.

Just some of the LIES that Atheistic Humanism teaches:

- Government is god;
- There is no individualism—it's the group think and government will take care of you (nanny State);
- Buhdism, Hinduism, Witchcraft, Islam, Satanism, Humanism, Socialism and Christianity are all equal;
- Man evolved from apes, and green algae pond scum (Atheistic Darwinism/Evolution);
- Sodomy is normal and children are taught to accept that as fact and even experiment with the variety of lifestyles that fall under it (30+); California has passed the law that homosexuals/ lesbians may marry;
- Abortion, the murder of children, is a right and it is good;
- Truth is relative; Situation ethics;
- Everything is about "me," misguided self-esteem as "proud to be ignorant and dummied down" with false self-confidence; and this selfishness is reinforced;
- The children are animals so teach them that all *instinctual sex* is good for them and at anytime, with no mention of the act of *love and devotion* after marriage only.

Some of the TRUTH that God's Word teaches:

- There is One true God;
  - Jesus said, "I am the way, the truth, and the life, no one comes to the Father except through Me;"

- God created all things;
- Sodomy is a sin, it should never be accepted, and it should never be taught;
- Abortion is the murder of a baby—God knew us before we were in our mother's womb;
- Truth is absolute, there is a right and wrong way, and man's opinions are foolish when in conflict with God's Word;
- Everything in life is about loving God and loving your neighbor;
- The children belong to God and should abstain from *making love* until after marriage.

Truth: A Christian parent is never to allow their children to be taught in an ungodly environment. Education is a tool, either directing toward God or toward the devil. This must be understood.

Truth: Many people think that they are smarter than God, or they rationalize so that they can design God to be what they want Him to be, rather than who He is, *"The same yesterday, today, and tomorrow."*

Truth: We are to love the soul above all other interests, and a loving parent would never put their children into a system that puts their soul at risk for eternity. The gates of hell will not prevail against the church, and the church with that authority should step up for God, and help the parents educate the children outside of the government education system. Churches should band together and provide Christian schooling for children who cannot be home schooled—free of charge, if necessary. Step out in faith—God will provide and do the rest! He promised!.

Parents, please get on your knees and cry out to God for your children, and pray that your Pastor is strong enough to help you with Christian Home Schooling, or will start a good Christian School that will out-perform the government education system throughout all parts of education. This will then give you the most positive bonus of a Godly education, a development of Godly character with convictions that are good, and training in obedience as opposed to rebellion, and a much greater opportunity for heaven, for your children. It will also ensure you of a Godly Nation for your future posterity.

Truth: Education that either disdains Christianity or supports anti-Christian values, are violations of Biblical principles and thus our principles as a nation, and should not be supported by monies received from Christians in any way.

Truth: Responsibility for the education of the child was given by God to parents, and parents should be free to choose the method, type, and amount of education received by the child. Every State should mandate the "parental choice" system—let the money follow the child wherever his Parents wish to have him educated.

Truth: Attempts to prohibit or remove Christianity or its influences from government schools or any part of society are tantamount to treason.

Truth: Religion and education are individual and are local and state rights, and as such, should not be controlled in any way by federal regulations or federal judicial decisions.

Truth: A free nation derives its just powers from God, and their laws from the consent of the governed. This, today, is being grossly manipulated by the Courts and Judges.

Truth: God gave man the free will to choose whether or not to serve God. Your choice could affect a child's soul going on a track that takes them to Hell. Jesus can see your heart right now. Pray fervently and read on, seeking knowledge, wisdom, and understanding that can only come from God.

We should be ashamed *if* we decide to stay ignorant about what is happening, *if* we decide not to face the evil, or *if* we decide to continue to sleep while our children are harmed.

EVIL: A system that deliberately dummies-down children, indoctrinates children into accepting homosexuality as a normal lifestyle, destroys children's Christian belief, sexually molests children, leads to increased illegal drug use by children, drugs children to make them easier to handle, places children in physical danger, teaches children there are no absolutes, promotes New Age philosophy, indoctrinates children with the philosophy of Socialism and the Religion of Secular Humanism, increases children's promiscuous sexual behavior, and reinforces a 'me' attitude in children to the extent that they are unmanageable and rebellious. Government schools, teaching all of these deviant ways, devastate children morally, spiritually, emotionally and intellectually. Many knowledgeable experts and people in general, consider sending a child to a government school as legalized child abuse.

Your children deserve better than what man offers you. It is past time to turn to God's ways.

Even with all the rhetoric, parents that truly love their children must read the following, and then decide what they must do to keep from giving aid and comfort to the enemy.

Can you handle the mentioned truths? I pray that you can, even though we have a society that lives by the following quote given to me by Flip Benham, National Director of *Operation Save America*:

"Truth is Hate, to those that Hate the Truth."

Decide how much you truly love the children. Then pray that the Holy Spirit opens your eyes to what follows.

Chapter 12

Biblical Principles of Education
Listen to God Speaking

Even if you feel that you already know, ask the Holy Spirit to open your eyes and ears about how you should educate the children. Even some pastors try to help people *feel good*, rather than call them to educate their children in God's ways, and away from the government education system, perhaps causing them a little *consternation* at first. Pastors need to help them through this time. Repent, and ask God to help you to fulfill His words. He really doesn't give us a choice.

In order to raise up generations of Godly men and women, students—preschool to post graduate school—must be educated according to *the Truth found in Scripture*:

1) **God, as Creator and Sustainer of all things, defines reality.** (*Colossians 1:16-17*) *For by Him were all things created, that are in heaven, and that are upon earth, visible and invisible, whether thrones, or dominions, or principalities, or powers: all things were created by Him, **and for** Him: And He is before all things, and by Him all things consist.*

2) **Wisdom, not the mere accumulation of information, is the principal learning objective.** (*Proverbs 4:7*) *Wisdom [is] the principal thing; [therefore] get wisdom: and with all thy getting get understanding.*

3) **The acknowledgment, reverence, and worship of the Lord is the very beginning, the foundation, of wisdom and knowledge.** (*Proverbs 1:7*) *The fear of the LORD [is] the beginning of knowledge: [but] fools despise wisdom and instruction. (Proverbs 9:10) The fear of the*

LORD [is] the beginning of wisdom: and the knowledge of the holy [is] understanding.

4) **The family has been ordained by the Lord as the primary training institution with Home as the center of teaching, and every father being particularly responsible for each child's learning, as follows:**

Deuteronomy) 6:5: And thou shalt love the LORD thy God with all thy heart, and with all thy soul, and with all thy might.

Deuteronomy 6:6: And these words which I command thee this day, shall be in thy heart....

Deuteronomy 6: And thou shalt teach them diligently to thy children, and shalt talk of them when thou sittest in thy house, and when thou walkest by the way, and when thou liest down, and when thou risest up.

Deuteronomy 6:8: And thou shalt bind them for a sign upon thy hand, and they shall be as frontlets between thy eyes

.

Deuteronomy 6:9: And thou shalt write them upon the posts of thy house, and on thy gates.

Psalm 78:1: Maschil of Asaph. Give ear, O my people, [to] my law: incline your ear to the words of my mouth.

Psalm 78:2: I will open my mouth in a parable: I will utter dark sayings of old:

Psalm 78:3: Which we have heard and known, and our fathers have told us.

Psalm 78:4: We will not hide [them] from their children, showing to the generation to come the praises of the LORD, and his strength, and his wonderful works that he hath done.

Psalm 78:5: For he established a testimony in Jacob, and appointed a law in Israel, which he commanded our fathers, that they should make them known to their children:

Psalm 78:6: That the generation to come might know [them], [even] the children [who] should be born; [who] should arise and declare [them] to their children:

Psalm 78:7: That they might set their hope in God, and not forget the works of God, but keep his commandments:

Psalm 78:8: And might not be as their fathers, a stubborn and rebellious generation; a generation [that] set not their heart aright, and whose spirit was not steadfast with God.

Psalm 78:9: The children of Ephraim, [being] armed, [and] carrying bows, turned back in the day of battle.

Psalm 78:10: They kept not the covenant of God, and refused to walk in his law;

Psalm 78:11: And forgot his works, and his wonders that he had shown them.

Proverbs 1:8: My son, hear the instruction of thy father, and forsake not the law of thy mother:

Proverbs 4:1: Hear, ye children, the instruction of a father, and attend to know understanding.

Ephesians 6:14: Stand therefore, having your loins girt about with truth, and having on the breast-plate of righteousness;

5) **Parents may delegate some of their God-granted authority to others who seek to support the father and mother in educating their children. Those who receive this delegation of teaching authority are then judged by the strict standard, since students can be very much influenced by their instructors.**

Galatians 4:2: But is under tutors and governors until the time appointed by the father.

James 3:1: My brethren, be not many teachers, knowing that we shall receive the greater condemnation.

2 Timothy 2:2: And the things that thou hast heard from me among many witnesses, the same commit thou to faithful men, who shall be able to teach others also.

2 Timothy 2:15: Study to show thyself approved to God, a workman that needeth not to be ashamed, rightly dividing the word of truth.

2 Timothy 3:14: But continue thou in the things which thou hast learned and hast been assured of, knowing from whom thou hast learned [them];

2 Timothy 3:15: And that from a child thou hast known the sacred scriptures, which are able to make thee wise to salvation through faith which is in Christ Jesus.

2 Timothy 3:16 All scripture [is] given by inspiration of God, and [is] profitable for doctrine, for reproof, for correction, for instruction in righteousness:

2 Timothy 3:17: That the man of God may be perfect, thoroughly furnished to all good works.

Luke 6:40: The disciple is not above his master: but every one that is perfect, shall be as his master.

6)   **Parents, however, can never abdicate their own accountability before the Lord, since children are His express gifts to the family. Thus, any schooling endeavor outside the Home, to be valid must minister as an extension of the home.**

Psalm 127:3: Lo, children [are] a heritage of the LORD: [and] the fruit of the womb [is his] reward.

Psalm 127:4: As arrows [are] in the hand of a mighty man: so [are] children of the youth.

Psalm 127:5: Happy [is] the man that hath his quiver full of them: they shall not be ashamed, but they shall speak with the enemies in the gate.

1 Corinthians 4:2: Moreover, it is required in stewards that a man be found faithful.

Luke 12:48: But he that knew not, and committed things worthy of stripes, shall be beaten with few [stripes]. For to whomsoever much is given, of him shall much be required: and to whom men have committed much, from him they will ask the more.

7)   **Children are uniquely created in God's image and are to be rendered unto Him. Therefore, their education is to please and glorify Him. Consequently, the Lord (not the state) has the vested and compelling interest in children's schooling.**

Genesis 1:26: And God said, Let us make man in our image, after our likeness: and let them have dominion over the fish of the sea, and over the fowl of the air, and over the cattle, and over all the earth, and over every creeping animal that creepeth upon the earth.

Genesis 1:27: So God created man in his [own] image, in the image of God created he him; male and female created he them.

Genesis 1:28: And God blessed them, and God said to them, Be fruitful, and multiply, and replenish the earth, and subdue it: and have dominion over the fish of the sea, and over the fowl of the air, and over every living animal that moveth upon the earth.

Proverbs 22:6: Train up a child in the way he should go: and when he is old, he will not depart from it.

1 Corinthians 10:31: Whether therefore ye eat or drink, or whatever ye do, do all to the glory of God.

Colossians 3:23: And whatever ye do, do [it] heartily, as to the Lord, and not to men;

Coossians 3:24: Knowing that from the Lord ye will receive the reward of the inheritance: for ye serve the Lord Christ.

Matthew 22:20: And he saith to them, Whose [is] this image, and superscription?

Matthew 22:21: They say to him, Cesar's. Then saith he to them, Render therefore to Cesar, the things which are Cesar's; and to God, the things that are God's.

Matthew 22:22: When they had heard [these words], they marveled, and left him, and departed.

8) **Because a child is God's individual handiwork, it is unwise to compare any child intellectually or academically to another. God created individual people—not groups.**

Psalm 139:13: For thou hast possessed my reins: thou hast covered me in my mother's womb.

Psalm 139:14: I will praise thee: for I am fearfully [and] wonderfully made: wonderful [are] thy works; and [that] my soul well knoweth.

2 Corinthians 10:12: For we dare not make ourselves of the number, or compare ourselves with some that commend themselves: but they measuring themselves by themselves, and comparing themselves among themselves, are not wise.

9) **A child's self-worth cannot be enhanced or undermined by either his intellectual prowess or academic attainment. It is determined by two God-established facts: 1) The wonderful act of creation and 2) the merciful gift of redemption to all whom, by His amazing grace, would receive salvation.**

Genesis 2:7: And the LORD God formed man [of] the dust of the ground, and breathed into his nostrils the breath of life; and man became a living soul.

Romans 10:9: That if thou shalt confess with thy mouth the Lord Jesus, and shalt believe in thy heart that God hath raised him from the dead, thou shalt be saved.

Romans 10:10: For with the heart man believeth to righteousness; and with the mouth confession is made to salvation.

Romans 10:11: For the scripture saith, whoever believeth on him shall not be ashamed.

Romans 10:12: For there is no difference between the Jew and the Greek: for the same Lord over all, is rich to all that call upon him,

Romans 10:13: For whoever shall call upon the name of the Lord shall be saved.

10) **Due to every child's value in the eyes of God, their educational process is to be protected and nurtured. This process must work diligently to keep the child *wise concerning righteousness* and *ignorant regarding evil*. True education, education for the real world, must be Christ-centered education. It is what has kept our children safe, has been the foundation of our nation, and must be followed to re-establish our nation as a Godly one protecting Christianity as a whole.**

Romans 12:1: I beseech you therefore, brethren, by the mercies of God, that ye present your bodies a living sacrifice, holy, acceptable to God, [which is] your reasonable service.

Romans 12:2: And be not conformed to this world: but be ye transformed by the renewing of your mind, that ye may prove what [is] that good and acceptable, and perfect will of God.

Romans 16:19: For your obedience is come abroad to all [men]. I am glad therefore on your behalf: but yet I would have you wise to that which is good, and simple concerning evil.

Ephesians 5:1: Be ye therefore followers of God, as dear children;

Ephesians 5:2: And walk in love, as Christ also hath loved us, and hath given himself for us an offering and a sacrifice to God for a sweet-smelling savor.

Ephesians 5:3: But lewdness and all uncleanness or covetousness, let it not be once named among you, as becometh saints;

Ephesians 5:4: Neither filthiness, nor foolish talking, nor jesting, which are not convenient: but rather giving of thanks.

Ephesians 5:5: For this ye know, that no lewd, nor unclean person, nor covetous man, who is an idolater, hath any inheritance in the kingdom of Christ and of God.

Ephesians 5:6: Let no man deceive you with vain words: for because of these things cometh the wrath of God upon the children of disobedience.

Ephesians 5:7: Be ye not therefore partakers with them.

Ephesians 5:8: For ye were sometime darkness, but now [are ye] light in the Lord: walk as children of light;

Ephesians 5:9: (For the fruit of the Spirit [is] in all goodness, and righteousness, and truth;)

Ephesians 5:10: Proving what is acceptable to the Lord.

Ephesians 5:11: And have no fellowship with the unfruitful works of darkness, but rather reprove [them].

Ephesians 5:12: For it is a shame even to speak of those things which are done by them in secret.

Ephesians 5:13: But all things that are reproved, are made manifest by the light: for whatever doth make manifest is light.

Ephesians 5:14: Wherefore he saith, Awake, thou that sleepest, and arise from the dead, and Christ will give thee light.

Ephesians 5:15: See then that ye walk circumspectly, not as fools, but as wise,

Ephesians 5:16: Redeeming the time, because the days are evil.

Ephesians 5:17: Wherefore be ye not unwise, but understanding what the will of the Lord [is].

Ephesians 5:18: And be not drunk with wine, in which is excess; but be filled with the Spirit;

Ephesians 5:19: Speaking to yourselves in psalms, and hymns, and spiritual songs, singing and making melody in your heart to the Lord,

Ephesians 5:20: Giving thanks always for all things to God and the Father, in the name of our Lord Jesus Christ;

Ephesians 5:21: Submitting yourselves one to another in the fear of God.

Colossians 2:6: As ye have therefore received Christ Jesus the Lord, [so] walk ye in him:

Colossians 2:7: Rooted and built up in him, and established in the faith, as ye have been taught, abounding in it with thanksgiving.

Colossians 2:8: Beware lest any man make a prey of you through philosophy and vain deceit, after the tradition of men, after the rudiments of the world, and not after Christ.

Colossians 2:9: For in him dwelleth all the fullness of the Godhead bodily.

Colossians 2:10: And ye are complete in him, who is the head of all principality and power:

Philippians 1 2:1: If [there is] therefore any consolation in Christ, if any comfort of love, if any fellowship of the Spirit, if any bowels and mercies,

Philippians 2:2: Fulfill ye my joy, that ye be like-minded, having the same love, [being] of one accord, of one mind.

Philippians 2:3: [Let] nothing [be done] through strife or vain glory; but in lowliness of mind let each esteem other better than themselves.

Philippians 2:4: Look not every man on his own things, but every man also on the things of others.

Philippians 2:5: Let this mind be in you, which was also in Christ Jesus:

Philippians 2:6: Who, being in the form of God, thought it not robbery to be equal with God:

Philippians 2:7: But made himself of no reputation, and took upon him the form of a servant, and was made in the likeness of men:

Philippians 2:8: And being found in fashion as a man, he humbled himself, and became obedient to death, even the death of the cross.

Philippians 2:9: Wherefore God also hath highly exalted him, and given him a name which is above every name:

Philippians 2:10: That at the name of Jesus every knee should bow, of [things] in heaven, and [things] on earth, and [things] under the earth;

Philippians 2:11: And [that] every tongue should confess that Jesus Christ [is] Lord, to the glory of God the Father.

11) **Educate the children on who the enemy is, and what armor they should have on, and why each part is important, and teach this to all the children in all schools.**

Ephesians 6:10: Finally, my brethren, be strong in the Lord, and in the power of his might.

Ephesians 6:11: Put on the whole armor of God, that ye may be able to stand against the wiles of the devil.

Ephesians 6:12: For we wrestle not against flesh and blood, but against principalities, against powers, against the rulers of the darkness of this world, against spiritual wickedness in high [places].

Ephesians 6:13: Wherefore take to you the whole armor of God, that ye may be able to withstand in the evil day, and having done all, to stand.

Ephesians 6:14: Stand therefore, having your loins girt about with truth, and having on the breast-plate of righteousness;

Ephesians 6:15: And your feet shod with the preparation of the gospel of peace;

Ephesians 6:16: Above all, taking the shield of faith, with which ye will be able to extinguish all the fiery darts of the wicked.

Ephesians 6:17: And take the helmet of salvation, and the sword of the Spirit, which is the word of God:

12) **Parents, understand the times we live in and that the local control is vanishing, so that evil men can continue a failing system to indoctrinate the children in things against God, Family and our Nation.**

2 Timothy 3:13: But evil men and seducers will become worse and worse, deceiving, and being deceived.

2 Timothy 3:14: But continue thou in the things which thou hast learned and hast been assured of, knowing from whom thou hast learned [them];

2 Timothy 3:15: And that from a child thou hast known the sacred scriptures, which are able to make thee wise to salvation through faith which is in Christ Jesus.

2 Timothy 3:16: All scripture [is] given by inspiration of God, and [is] profitable for doctrine, for reproof, for correction, for instruction in righteousness:

2 Timothy 3:17: That the man of God may be perfect, thoroughly furnished to all good works.

2 Timothy 4:1: I charge [thee] therefore before God, and the Lord Jesus Christ, who will judge the living and the dead at his appearing and his kingdom;

2 Timothy 4:2: Preach the word; be instant in season, out of season; reprove, rebuke, exhort with all long-suffering and doctrine.

2 Timothy6 4:3: For the time will come, when they will not endure sound doctrine; but after their own lusts will they multiply to themselves teachers, having itching ears;

2 Timothy 4:4: And they will turn away [their] ears from the truth, and will be turned to fables.

13) **Rationalize and your child will suffer in an increasingly moral decay, and be at risk for eternity, as will those that stay ignorant to God's truth.**

Matthew 7:13: Enter ye in at the strait gate; for wide [is] the gate, and broad [is] the way, that leads to destruction, and many there are who go in by it.

Matthew 7:14: Because strait [is] the gate, and narrow [is] the way, which leads to life, and few there are that find it.

Matthew 7:15: Beware of false prophets, who come to you in sheep's clothing, but inwardly they are ravening wolves.

Matthew 7:16: Ye shall know them by their fruits: Do men gather grapes from thorns, or figs from thistles:

Matthew 7:17: Even so every good tree brings forth good fruit; but a corrupt tree brings forth evil fruit.

Matthew 7:18: A good tree cannot bring forth evil fruit neither [can] a corrupt tree bring forth good fruit.

Matthew 7:19: Every tree that brings not forth good fruit is hewn down, and cast into the fire.

Matthew 7:20: Wherefore by their fruits ye shall know them,

Matthew 7:21: Not every one that says to me, Lord, Lord, shall enter into the kingdom of heaven; but he that doeth the will of my Father who is in heaven.

Matthew 7:22: Many will say to me in that day, Lord, Lord, have we not prophesied in thy name? and in thy name have cast out demons? and in thy name done many wonderful works?

Matthew 7:23: And then will I profess to them, I never knew you: depart from me, ye that work iniquity.

Matthew 7:24: Therefore whoever hears these sayings of mine, and doeth them, I will liken him to a wise man, who built his house upon a rock:

Matthew 7:25: And the rain descended, and the floods came, and the winds blew, and beat upon that house; and it fell not: for it was founded upon a rock.

Matthew 7:26: And every one that hears these sayings of mine, and doeth them not, shall be likened to a foolish man, who built his house upon the sand:

Matthew 7:27: And the rain descended, and the floods came, and the winds blew, and beat upon that house; and it fell, and great was the fall of it.

14) **Will this apply to your children or your neighbors children because you are willing to say, "not my school."**

Hosea 4:6: My people are destroyed for lack of knowledge: because thou hast rejected knowledge, I will also reject thee, that thou shalt be no priest to me: seeing thou hast forgotten the law of thy God, I will also forget thy children.

15) <u>**No person in education, a political party, media, and any other entity is telling the truth if it goes against the Word of God.**</u>

Jeremiah 17:5: Thus saith the LORD; Cursed [be] the man that trusteth in man, and maketh flesh his arm, and whose heart departeth from the LORD.

Jeremiah 17:6: For he shall be like the heath in the desert, and shall not see when good cometh; but shall inhabit the parched places in the wilderness, [in] a salt land and not inhabited.

Jeremiah 17:7: Blessed [is] the man that trusteth in the LORD, and whose hope the LORD is.

Jeremiah 17:8: For he shall be as a tree planted by the waters, and [that] spreadeth out her roots by the river, and shall not see when heat cometh, but her leaf shall be green; and shall not be anxious in the year of drouth, neither shall cease from yielding fruit.

Jeremiah 17:9: The heart [is] deceitful above all [things], and desperately wicked: who can know it?

Jeremiah 17:10: I the LORD search the heart, [I] try the reins, even to give every man according to his ways, [and] according to the fruit of his doings.

Luke 11:23: He that is not with me is against me: and he that gathereth not with me scattereth.

Acts 5:29: Then Peter and the [other] apostles answered and said, We ought to obey God rather than men.

Proverbs 3:1: My son, forget not my law; but let thy heart keep my commandments;

Proverbs 3:2: For length of days, and long life, and peace, shall they add to thee.

Proverbs 3:3: Let not mercy and truth forsake thee: bind them about thy neck; write them upon the table of thy heart:

Proverbs 3:4: So shalt thou find favor and good understanding in the sight of God and man.

Proverbs 3:5: Trust in the LORD with all thy heart; and lean not to thy own understanding.

Proverbs 3:6: In all thy ways acknowledge him, and he will direct thy paths.

Proverbs 3:7: Be not wise in thy own eyes: fear the LORD, and depart from evil.

Proverbs 3:8: It shall be health to thy navel, and marrow to thy bones.

Proverbs 3:9: Honor the LORD with thy substance, and with the first-fruits of all thy increase:

Proverbs 3:10: So shall thy barns be filled with plenty, and thy presses shall burst out with new wine.

Proverbs 3:11: My son, despise not the chastening of the LORD; neither be weary of his correction:

Proverbs 3:12: For whom the LORD loveth he correcteth; even as a father the son [in whom] he delighteth.

Proverbs 3:13: Happy [is] the man [that] findeth wisdom, and the man [that] getteth understanding.

Psalms 71:1: In thee, O LORD, do I put my trust: let me never be put to confusion.

Psalm 71:2: Deliver me in thy righteousness, and cause me to escape: incline thy ear to me, and save me.

Psalm 71:3: Be thou my strong habitation, to which I may continually resort: thou hast given commandment to save me; for thou [art] my rock and my fortress.

Psalm 71:4: Deliver me, O my God, from the hand of the wicked, from the hand of the unrighteous and cruel man.

Psalm 71:5: For thou [art] my hope, O LORD God: [thou art] my trust from my youth.

Psalm 71:6: By thee have I been sustained from my birth: thou art he that brought me into life: my praise [shall be] continually of thee.

Psalm 71:7: I am as a wonder to many; but thou [art] my strong refuge.

Psalm 71:8: Let my mouth be filled [with] thy praise [and with] thy honor all the day.

Psalm 71:9: Cast me not off in the time of old age; forsake me not when my strength faileth.

Psalm 71:10: For my enemies speak against me; and they that lay wait for my soul take counsel together,

Psalm 71:11: Saying, God hath forsaken him: persecute and take him; for [there is] none to deliver [him].

Psalm 71:12: O God, be not far from me: O my God, make haste for my help.

Psalm 71:13: Let them be confounded [and] consumed who are adversaries to my soul; let them be covered [with] reproach and dishonor that seek my hurt.

Psalm 71:14: But I will hope continually, and will yet praise thee more and more.

Psalm 71:15: My mouth shall show forth thy righteousness [and] thy salvation all the day; for I know not the numbers [thereof].

Psalm 71:16: I will go in the strength of the Lord GOD: I will make mention of thy righteousness, [even] of thine only.

Psalm 71:17: O God, thou hast taught me from my youth: and hitherto have I declared thy wondrous works.

Psalm 71:18: Now also when I am old and gray-headed, O God, forsake me not; until I have shown thy strength to [this] generation, [and] thy power to every one [that] is to come.

Psalm 71:19: Thy righteousness also, O God, [is] very high, who hast done great things: O God, who [is] like to thee!

Nehemiah 9:5: Then the Levites, Jeshua, and Kadmiel, Bani, Hashabniah, Sherebiah, Hodijah, Shebaniah, [and] Pethahiah, said, Stand up [and] bless the LORD your God for ever and ever: and blessed be thy glorious name, which is exalted above all blessing and praise.

Nehemiah 9:6: Thou, [even] thou, [art] LORD alone; thou hast made heaven, the heaven of heavens, with all their host, the earth, and all [things] that [are] in it, the seas, and all that [is] in them, and thou preservest them all; and the host of heaven worshipeth thee.

*John 14:6: **Jesus saith to him, I am the way, and the truth, and the life: no man cometh to the Father, but by me.***

Matthew 5:3: Blessed [are] the poor in spirit: for theirs is the kingdom of heaven.

Matthew 5:4: Blessed [are] they that mourn: for they shall be comforted.

Matthew 5:5: Blessed [are] the meek: for they shall inherit the earth.

Matthew 5:6: Blessed [are] they who hunger and thirst for righteousness: for they shall be filled.

Matthew 5:7: Blessed [are] the merciful: for they shall obtain mercy.

Matthew 5:8: Blessed [are] the pure in heart: for they shall see God.

Matthew 5:9: Blessed [are] the peace-makers: for they shall be called children of God.

Matthew 5:10: Blessed [are] they who are persecuted for righteousness' sake: for theirs is the kingdom of heaven.

Matthew 5:11: Blessed are ye when men shall revile you, and persecute [you], and shall say all manner of evil against you falsely, for my sake.

Matthew 5:12: Rejoice, and be exceeding glad: for great [is] your reward in heaven: for so they persecuted the prophets who were before you.

Matthew 5:13: Ye are the salt of the earth: but if the salt hath lost its savor, with what shall it be salted? it is thenceforth good for nothing, but to be cast out, and to be trodden under foot by men.

Matthew 5:20: For I say to you, That except your righteousness shall exceed [the righteousness] of the scribes and Pharisees, ye shall in no case enter into the kingdom of heaven.

And now let us hear from Rev. Rusty Thomas:

The Indestructible Book
Rev. Rusty Thomas

"Sanctify them through Thy truth: Thy word is truth." –Jesus

In our modern age, it has become quite vogue to accept the philosophy of relativism. Relativism is a belief system that pervades most of our culture, government, and schools. Its premise is based on the fallacy that all ideas, philosophies, and religions are of equal value, and that there is no absolute right or wrong. Situational ethics is part of this philosophy: What may be wrong for one person (stealing an apple) may be alright for another (if he lacks the money to purchase one). According to relativism, there is nothing that is superior in knowledge, wisdom, and understanding and nothing inferior. All ideas are equal and all cultures have merit regardless of what they profess or how they live. So, if some cultures teach "love thy neighbor as thyself," and other cultures practice eating their neighbors, or who are justified in killing persons who, by their religious beliefs are unbelievers of their religion, who are we to judge the values and practices of others? *After all, every road (no matter how perverse, deceptive, and false) leads to God and heaven, right? Under deceptive Relativism— right! But this is not true.*

WRONG! Dead wrong! My friend, in this life, it is self-evident that not all belief systems are of equal value. Obviously, people who love their neighbors and people who eat their neighbors should never be considered equal. One is superior and one is most definitely inferior. In fact, if all belief systems were equal then nothing would be of any value to man. To help clarify this point, the example of precious metals may help. The concept is "rarity determines value." In other words, if gold, silver, and precious jewels were accessible and available as rocks, they would lose their worth. It is the scarceness of these precious metals that adds to their luster. This proposition is also true when it comes to the Bible, the Word of God.

Many religions and so-called enlightened philosophies either claim divine inspiration or conventional wisdom in an attempt to answer man's eternal questions; questions, such as, "Why am I here?" *"Where did I come from?" "What am I to do with my life?"* And the most plaguing question of all: *"What happens to me when I die?"* Most religions and philosophies of men were established to try an answer these daunting questions that torment men's minds. Each believes its writings to be sacred, true, or one that provides reliable answers to solve man's quest for meaning in this vain, fleeting life. c **But are their claims true? The answer is a resounding NO!**

It is self-evident that there are concepts in the human experience, such as, truth and lies, honesty and deception, time-honored principles and falsehoods. The burning issue and question is where in this crazy, mixed up world can we find a reliable guide to distinguish between these conflicting traits that run rampant in the human condition?

The world considers Christianity a faith or just one of the world's major religions. Biblical Christianity, however, claims to be the Truth with a capital T. Not just a truth out of the many truths that run to-and-fro throughout the earth; no, it claims to be the only Truth. Thus, any idea, philosophy, or teaching that does not originate and proceed from the Bible, it condemns as lies, idolatry, and deceptions that will surely destroy the souls of men.

(Author's note: This is the Christianity on which our founding fathers founded our Nation, The United States of America.)

Jesus declared, *"He that is not with me is against me; and he that gathereth not with me scattereth abroad"* (Matthew 12:30). With that statement and many others besides, Jesus smashes all neutrality, relativism, (humanism) and the idol of tolerance which America worships today. Is it any wonder why we crucified Him? (Isaiah 53) Is it any wonder why our nation increasingly seeks to censor the Gospel of the Kingdom and remove the knowledge of God from the public life of our nation? Is it any wonder why our Supreme Court banished prayer, Bible reading, and the Ten Commandments from our schools? Is it any wonder why everything, no matter how perverse is tolerated, except One, who is Jesus, the Christ of God and His Holy Word?

A good friend of mine, Flip Benham, National Director of *Operation Save America*, penned these words: ***"The truth of what one believes is far more important than how much he believes it."*** This is an important statement. Our beliefs, no matter how sincere, do not determine truth. The Truth must determine man's belief. Those who boarded the Titanic sincerely believed it wouldn't sink. History records they were sincerely wrong.

The nineteen Muslims who crashed airplanes into our buildings and brought America to its knees, sincerely believed they were serving their god, Allah. Their belief brought many innocent people to an untimely death. If these murderers could come back from the dead, they would reveal a horror much worse than the Twin Towers collapsing. Rather than joining 72 virgins as promised by the religion of Islam, they would scream of the torments of hell. Instead of entering a paradise, they found themselves in a place of eternal damnation that they cannot escape. They can't even commit suicide again to be released and no belief in the Koran will deliver them from the severe consequence of the lies they believed.

In John 14:6, the Word of God states: *"Jesus saith unto him, I am the way, the truth, and the life: no man cometh unto the Father, but by me."* Jesus declared that He, as a Person, was the Truth. He declared that God's Word was the Truth (John 17:17) and that the Holy Spirit was the Spirit of Truth (John 16:13). Truth is paramount, because Truth liberates (John 8:32).

(Author's note: This alone proves that the Humanism, Relativism, Atheistic Socialism/Communism, and Darwinism are deceptively taught in the public schools as "liberating" the person. They falsely liberate them and encourage them by their teachings to live unholy sinful lives. None teach anything about the Absolute Truth, Who is Jesus Christ—in fact, they call Him and His teachings, lies, subversively, because they teach unnatural "freedoms" as rights! Christianity's Truth, Jesus, does *totally liberate*—these other false "religion" do not—they subjugate the unsuspecting student/individual to slavery—not liberation—and Liberation Theology's Social Justice is a mere smokescreen to liberation—it is a slavery to the State! Let's go back to Rusty now.)

> Real Truth breaks the chains of sin and bondage within man that are reinforced by the lies, vain philosophies, and false religions that enslave man from without.

> The Bible teaches that all Scripture is inspired or God-breathed. In other words, when God exhaled, His word went forth and it is alive and full of power to transform the souls of men.

(Author's note: Because Scripture is "alive" does not mean that it "changes," as some would have you believe. By the Word/Truth being "alive" it is meant that it "changes" the living life of a human being.)

> God's Wisdom and the time-honored Truths contained in the 66 books of the Bible are more valuable than silver, gold, and treasures of every sort. The God Who created you and the Savior Who died for you chose to record His Word, Will, and Way in one Book. Out of all the books in the world, there is only one where Truth, God's revelation can safely be discovered. Rarity does indeed determine its value.

> The Bible is a self-authenticating Book as well. It declares that God's Word came by holy men of old as they were moved by the Holy Ghost (2 Peter 1:20,21). God, therefore, does not need man's opinions or approval to validate His Word. The creature can never stand as judge over the Creator or His holy, inspired Word.

> Unfortunately, today, we believe we can. We are taught that what we think, our opinions, cultural trends, our many experiences, science, and reason trumps the

authority of God's Word. Man is thus left to construct his own brand of truth apart from the revelation of God's objective Truth contained in the Bible. As a result, God's Word must be bent, denied, or changed if it doesn't conform to our modern day culture and practice.

As a result of this folly of becoming a law and god unto ourselves, we are hurling ourselves against the unchanging, immutable, and inerrant Word of God. The hard lesson, however, is we can't break God's Word and His moral law, it eventually breaks us. This accounts for much of America's woes, such as, divorce, unruly children, abortion, homosexuality, and false religions that are flourishing and defiling our beloved but broken nation.

A Roman political leader, Pontius Pilate, once asked the question of the ages: *"What is truth* (John 18:38)?" He asked it of a Man who claimed to be Truth Incarnate, our Lord Jesus Christ. He asked it of the very One whom the Bible describes as the *Word of God become flesh* (John 1:1-14). He asked it of *Immanuel,* which is interpreted *God with us* (Matthew 1:23)!

The truth is, apart from Jesus and His Word, sin, Satan, and this illegitimate world system that is in rebellion to God's loving rule, will offer you many answers and choices to determine truth for yourself. Every single one of them, if embraced and believed, will rob your God-ordained destiny here on earth and damn your eternal soul. Jesus declared: *"Search the scriptures; for in them ye think ye have eternal life: and they are they which testify of me."* Jesus describes two kinds of men, one wise and the other foolish. How can we distinguish the one from the other? *The wise hears and applies the Word of God to his life, the foolish hear, but refuses to apply the Truth to his life* (Matthew 7:24-27). The wise will stand and the foolish will fall. I encourage you to read, study, believe, and apply the *Word of God* to your life. It is alive and full of promise and power to transform you from the inside out. It will save your soul! (end)

Thank you, Rev. Rusty Lee Thomas, for this inspiring article.

Chapter 13

Is There Hope?

REPENT: *for the* KINGDOM *of* HEAVEN *is at hand!*

In the coming days, as many have faced in the past, it will be very important that you know and understand the importance of repentance and turning your life to Jesus. This is no game and because of the urgency of the times, knowing that you, a loved one, or someone that you touch in life may be dead by morning, listen to what God says:

> *Repent*, *in theology*, to sorrow or be pained for sin, as a violation of God's holy law, a dishonor to his character and government, and the foulest ingratitude to a Being of infinite benevolence.

> *Except ye repent, ye shall all likewise perish.* *(Luke 13 and Acts 3)*

> *Matthew 3:1: In those days came John the Baptist, preaching in the wilderness of Judea,*

> *Matthew 3:2: And saying, **Repent ye: for the kingdom of heaven is at hand.***

> *Matthew 3:3: For this is he that was spoken of by the prophet Esaias, saying, The voice of one crying in the wilderness, Prepare ye the way of the Lord, make his paths straight.*

If you want your prayers to reach the throne of Jesus, then listen to what follows.

> *Matthew 4:17: From that time Jesus began to preach, and to say,* **Repent: for the kingdom of heaven is at hand.**

> *Matthew 6:11: And whosoever shall not receive you, nor hear you, when ye depart thence, shake off the dust under your feet for a testimony against them. Verily I say unto you, It shall be more tolerable for Sodom and Gomorrah in the day of judgment, than for that city.*

> *Mark 6:12:* **And they went out, and preached that men should repent.**

> *Revelation 3:19:* **As many as I love, I rebuke and chasten: be zealous therefore, and repent.**

Our nation suffers because as a nation we have not repented, and it will become more corrupted daily as it is now, until we repent and turn back to God. God says it is of the utmost importance and who are we to argue with Him? We are led by those that think that they are smarter than God and having passions for themselves above all others. We have allowed the *Word of God*, prayer, and the Ten Commandments to be taken from the children. So how do the children have faith if they are not hearing the Word of God? We have robbed them of their most important **right: the right to liberation both on earth and eternally.**

> *Romans 10:17: "So then, faith [cometh] by hearing, and hearing by the word of God."*

When Jesus is not our foundation, we are no longer a *nation under God*, and we put our children at risk for eternity. When the Christians in the pulpits and the pews go to sleep, and become ashamed of the gospel by literally "hiding out" in the pew in the building—it cannot be called the church as the church is to be alive—you have read what will happen to present and future generations. I am fifty-six years old, and my parents' generation started to nap, and then my generation went all the way to sleep. We were comfortable, did not want to make waves, and anxious and willing to show how smart we were, and then not willing to be scorned, or mocked, we became ashamed of the gospel of Jesus, allowing others to put our children at risk now, and into eternity. The following is what our two generations set up to happen to the two youngest generations living today (all the younger people within them and the public schools now), and we need to repent to God and tell you that we are so sorry, and then ask God to use all of our days left, in His service to return our nation back to the gospel, under the Lordship of Jesus Christ.

Read carefully to know why the moral decay in this country has gotten so bad.

We have allowed the encouragement of abortion through teaching of *young girls* (and boys) to choose to murder their babies as taught them from the Planned Parenthood Federation of America's sex manual *It's Perfectly Normal* which depicts grossly pornographic, immoral pictures, that is used in the public schools for children as young as ten years of age (that's 10—co-educationally taught—boys and girls together). Most of this outrageous graphic textbook is paid for with our Christian tax dollars—will we continue to be silent?

We have allowed the sin of homosexuality to be introduced to our young kindergarten children, not only is it taught as acceptable but as a normal lifestyle, as dictated by the National Education Association Teachers Union, which will, and is, leading our children into dangerous life-threatening diseases, and psychological illnesses such as depression and suicide, along with the increased illegal drug usage practiced by those in that lifestyle.

We have allowed radical religions like Islam, which is a lie, to be indoctrinated in our children's minds via a slanted message in their textbooks. Nothing is mentioned about the jihadist mentality that permeates the Koran and encourages attacks against all unbelievers who do not accept Islam as the religion of choice.

We have allowed the mantra of *"hate America"* and the false *revised* history and geography which sews negative opinions and liberal mindsets that are brainwashed into our children's minds. They grow up to be Liberal Socialist voters because of this indoctrination chanting all the reasons why America should be hated. They are taught dissatisfaction and false information about our country and end up in our public colleges and universities causing riots and protests. These are all Socialist behaviors learned well in our public schools K-16.

We have allowed the R*eligion* of the *Atheistic Theory of Evolution* to be brainwashed into our children's minds without even so much as acting to contest it. Shame on us! This fact alone allows the door to be open to all of the above teachings.

So what did God forewarn us would happen if we were ashamed of the gospel—which is what is demonstrated by our silence? Listen to *HIS Word,* as our people are responding to what we have started and allowed in their education and in society. We have turned our backs on the Gospel. So what will happen?

> *Romans 1:16: For I am not ashamed of the gospel of Christ: for it is the power of God to salvation to every one that believeth; to the Jew first, and also to the Greek.*

> *Romans 1:17: For in this is the righteousness of God revealed from faith to faith: as it is written, The just shall live by faith.*

Romans 1:18: **For the wrath of God is revealed from heaven against all ungodliness, and unrighteousness of men, who hold the truth in unrighteousness.**

Romans 1:19: Because that which may be known of God, is manifest in them; for God hath shown [it] to them.

Romans 1:20: **For the invisible things of him from the creation of the world are clearly seen, being understood by the things that are made, [even] his eternal power and Godhead; so that they are without excuse:**

Romans 1:21: Because that when they knew God, they glorified [him] not as God, neither were thankful, but became vain in their imaginations, and their foolish heart was darkened.

Romans 1:22: **Professing themselves to be wise, they became fools:**

Romans 1:23: And changed the glory of the incorruptible God into an image made like to corruptible man, and to birds, and four-footed beasts, and creeping animals.

Romans 1:24: **Wherefore God also gave them up to uncleanness, through the lusts of their own hearts, to dishonor their own bodies between themselves:**

Romans 1:25: **Who changed the truth of God into a lie,** *and worshiped and served the creature more than the Creator, who is blessed for ever. Amen.*

Romans 1:26: **For this cause God gave them up to vile affections. For even their women did change the natural use into that which is against nature:**

Romans 1:27: **And likewise also the men, leaving the natural use of the woman, burned in their lust one towards another; men with men working that which is unseemly, and receiving in themselves that recompense of their error which was meet.**

Romans 1:28: **And even as they did not like to retain God in [their] knowledge, God gave them over to a reprobate mind, to do those things which are not convenient;**

Romans 1:29: **Being filled with all unrighteousness, fornication, wickedness, covetousness, maliciousness; full of envy, murder, debate, deceit, malignity; whisperers,**

Romans 1:30: **Backbiters, haters of God, despiteful, proud, boasters, inventers of evil things, disobedient to parents,**

Romans 1:31: **Without understanding, covenant-breakers, without natural affection, implacable, unmerciful:**

Romans 1:32: **Who, knowing the judgment of God, that they who commit such things are worthy of death; not only do the same, but have pleasure in them that do them.**

Is there any reason, after reading the gospel regarding what will happen to us if you and I are ashamed of the gospel, that we should wonder why the people of the United States have sunken into such moral decay? Listen to God's Word, as he goes past hate, to abomination, which is extreme hate for those that are involved in the following. Those that murder babies through abortion, those that promote the sin of homosexuality and force it into the lives of the children, those that follow the lie of Islam and other pagan gods, those that follow the delusion of evolution, those that follow the rebellion of radical feminism, those that follow the false religion of liberalism, progressivism, communism, et al, those that follow the pretend salt of conservatism, listen well to the following.

Proverbs 6:16: These six [things] doth the LORD hate: yes, seven [are] an abomination to him:

Proverbs 6:17: **A proud look, a lying tongue, <u>and hands that shed innocent blood</u>.**

Proverbs 6:18: **A heart that devises wicked imaginations, feet that are swift in running to mischief,**

Proverbs 6:19: **A false witness [that] speaks lies, and him that sows discord among brethren.**

Psalm 5:2: Hearken to the voice of my cry, my King, and my God: for to thee will I pray.

Psalm 5:3: My voice shall you hear in the morning, O LORD; in the morning will I direct [my prayer] to thee, and will look up.

Psalm 5:4: **For thou [art] not a God that hath pleasure in wickedness: neither shall evil dwell with thee.**

Psalm 5:5: The foolish shall not stand in thy sight: **thou hatest all workers of iniquity.**

Psalm5:6: **Thou shall destroy them that speak falsehood: the LORD will abhor the bloody and deceitful man.**

Matthew 23:33: **Ye serpents, ye generation of vipers, how can ye escape the damnation of hell? Repent, humble yourselves and seek the face of God or you will surely die.**

Mark 9:47: *And if thine eye offend thee, pluck it out: it is better for thee to enter into the kingdom of God with one eye, than having two eyes to be* **cast into hell fire:**

Mark 9:48: **Where their worm dieth not, and the fire is not quenched.**

Mark 9:49: *For every one shall be salted with fire, and every sacrifice shall be salted with salt.*

Mark 9:50: *Salt is good: but if the salt have lost his saltness, wherewith will ye season it?* **Have salt in yourselves, and have peace one with another.**

Revelation 3:20: **Behold, I stand at the door, and knock: if any man hear my voice, and open the door, I will come in to him, and will sup with him, and he with me.**

Matthew 10:27: **What I tell you in darkness, that speak ye in light: and what ye hear in the ear, that preach ye upon the housetops.**

Matthew 10:28: *And fear not them which kill the body, but are not able to kill the soul:* **but rather fear him which is able to destroy both soul and body in hell.**

You have heard and seen God's Word. Have you repented for your neglect to become involved and refusing to become active to defend His Word and save His children? Are you ashamed of the Gospel or are you operating under fear of combating a controversial battleground? If you have not repented, and if you are ashamed of the Gospel of Jesus or are fearful, then understand that you are helping Satan to kill, steal, and destroy children and our Christian nation, and that Isaiah 1:15-16 applies to your pleas and prayers to God:

> *"When you spread out your hands in prayer, I will hide my eyes from you; even if you offer many prayers, I will not listen. Your hands are full of blood..."*

And understand the next passage if you are willing to stay ignorant Hosea 4:6:

> *"My people perish for lack of knowledge, because they have turned away from my commands, I will forget their children."*

Do you need to reread the reasons for what is happening today? Do you need to reread to see why children are killing children, immorality abounds, and the blood of the innocent cries out?

Repent: For the Kingdom of Heaven is at hand!!!

Love and prayers in Christ Jesus to your family,

Is there not a cause?

What about your eternity, the eternity of those around you, and the eternity of our posterity, and the world we leave them and their families to survive in? Do you have knowledge, wisdom, and understanding from God's Word to know that our only hope for ourselves and our children is to do it God's ways? Or are we too proud, too self sufficient, too contented with the atrocities happening, and too deceitful in our hearts that we believe that God's words were for someone else or for another time? Do we feel we can mock Him and do as we please, or do we think we are smarter than God and that there will be no consequences for our actions.

No matter how many times you have heard the following words before, ask the Holy Spirit to give you understanding of the importance as to how all of this applies to our lives and the lives of our posterity now, and our eternity, for God has spoken so clearly of the way we can be healed, and then tells us what will happen if we do not follow His commands.

> *"If my people, which are called by my name, shall humble themselves, and pray, and seek my face, and turn from their wicked ways; then will I hear from heaven, and will forgive their sin, and will heal their land.* (II Chronicles 7:14)

God is still talking—**we must turn** *and* **actively help turn this nation back to a Godly moral nation.**

> *"But if you turn away, and forsake my statutes and my commandments, which I have set before you, and shall go and serve other gods, and worship them; Then will I pluck them up by the roots out of my land which I have given them; and this house, which I have sanctified for my name, will I cast out of my sight, and will make it to be a proverb and a byword among all nations."* (II Chronicles 7:19-20)

A great American Statesman, Patrick Henry, stated:

"Our brethren are already in the field, why stand we here idle, what is it that gentlemen wish, what would you have, is life so dear and peace so sweet as to be purchased at the price of chains and slavery? Forbid it Almighty God, as for me, give me liberty, or give me death."

Because knowing the *absolute* Truth must be our objective if we are to follow God's ways, and be able to turn back evil, listen to the wisdom in John Paul II words:

"Only God, the Supreme Good, constitutes the unshakable foundation and essential condition of morality, and thus the commandments, particularly those negative commandments which always and in every case prohibit behavior and actions incompatible with the personal dignity of every man. The Supreme Good and the moral good meet in Truth: The Truth of God, the Creator and Redeemer, and the truth of man (that leads to HIS Truth), created and redeemed by Him. Only upon this Truth is it possible to construct a renewed society and to solve the complex and weighty problems affecting it, above all the problem of overcoming the various forms of totalitarianism, so as to make way for the authentic freedom of the person. Totalitarianism arises out of a denial of Truth in the objective sense. If there is no transcendent Truth, in obedience to which man achieves his full identity, then there is no sure principle for guaranteeing just relations between people. Their self-interest as a class, group or nation would inevitably set them in opposition to one another. If one does not acknowledge transcendent Truth, then the force of power takes over, and each person tends to make full use of the means at his disposal in order to impose his own interests or his own opinion, with no regard for the rights of others..."

I am sorry for the repetition of this request, but I must I ask you to stop and pray again, because it is evidenced that we as a nation have refused to acknowledge transcendent Truth, and as a result we are seeing the force of liberal dictatorial power ever-increasing over the lives of individual Americans.

The Liberal Leftist Socialist Democrat politicians, RINOs and the NEA Teachers and AAUP Professors Unions are herding us together as a massive group while at the same time causing dissatisfaction on every front whether it be racism (which they refuse to let die) or working unions, motherhood/fatherhood and healthcare, ad nausea—refusing to allow people/students to realize their individuality and forcing "consensus opinions" upon students and citizens that each child/adult does not agree with—performing this atrocity within the classrooms of our public schools and courts in our nation, with "group" activities too numerous to even mention and that people are entirely unaware of what is happening.

Group thinks exist in almost every curriculum from Math, Writing, "Social(ist) Science, Science, Reading and so on—pushing our children-become-adults into giving up their own moral opinions and individuality—preparing us for the eventual life of living under a *no-individual-opinion-dictatorship* right here in the USA. Truth is NOT how each person "perceives" it (humanistic relativism)—it is Absolute Transcendent Truth.

When a CA court can rule against the vast majority of the people's previous votes and grant the right to marriage to homosexuals, then this is a perfect example of a *dictatorship through the courts.* These supremacist judges say: The majority does not matter anymore—this is not a *government of the people and by the people and for the people* anymore—it's a country under dictatorship because the people are too ignorant to know what is good or right for themselves—the courts and the government must tell them what they will or will not do, or have or not have. or live or not live under. Well, let me tell you, the majority of our people do know what is best for our nation. This is a *huge danger to our liberty and freedoms as we have known and experienced them in the past. Christians must awaken, seek God's Truth, and God's ways, or the enemy within the gates will increase his objective to kill, steal, and destroy, present and future generations, like nothing we have ever seen in our lifetime.*

Come to God with a pure heart, then seek, ask, knock on God's door. God loves each of you personally and wants to be intimately involved in your life. It is your choice. You can continue to stay in ignorance and rationalize away the evil you allow, continue to believe it can't happen here, continue to stay asleep and do nothing, or you can STAND UP, SPEAK UP, and TAKE ACTION. Truly we need each and every one of you and you do have the command of Jesus, "Go ye...and do."

Do everything with the love and forgiveness of Jesus, as you stand firm in His Word, for God, family, and country. None of us should be TRAITORS by accident or ignorance, and we can stop the traitorous enemies within the gates that have an agenda to be masters, who do not serve God, and impact the children's souls for eternity in a negative way every single day for many hours a day.

When we die—what then—as we stand before the throne of God?

> *Jesus Christ, "the true Light, which lights every man that comes into the world.." (John 1:9)*

> *"Seeing you have purified your souls in obeying the truth through the Spirit unto unfeigned love of the brethren, see that you love one another with a pure heart fervently: Being born again, not of corruptible seed, but of incorruptible, by the word of God, which lives and abides for ever." (1 Peter 1:22-23)*

I pray that the Holy Spirit will use this book to bring souls to heaven for eternity, that it will help to awaken people to become involved for our nation's sake, and that my witness of God's Truth, made possible because of God's Word, will be a thorn in the side of Satan, because of bringing others closer to Jesus.

Mark Cahill makes a statement for you to think about regarding witnessing, which is used to bring souls to Christ but is also used to keep people on the straight way:

> **Witnessing:** God loves it; Satan hates it. So do you think you should be doing it?

I feel led to finish with a wonderful testimony of one who was witnessed to and is now on fire witnessing to others, so that they can experience our Lord, and not be at risk of losing their souls for eternity. His name is Kevin Thompson, although not any blood kin as the world may say, he is a true brother in Christ, who has spoken what the hearts of many have realized who have come into a relationship with Jesus. Listen to his words and hear the Lord say: *"Thank you my wise son for sharing the Gospel and introducing souls to Me—the Great I AM."*

Listen as Mr. Kevin Thompson Speaks

> Prior to becoming a Christian, I was normally very hostile towards those who wanted to share Christian beliefs with me. Unless, of course, they could show me how those beliefs would give me immediate and personal benefit. I could not understand people who said they had found peace, fulfillment, and (this one always got me) that they had found forgiveness. This forgiveness was supposed to give them eternal life in the presence of a man named Jesus Christ. Their peace came from their knowing without a doubt, that He was their Savior and that He died on the Cross for them.

They claimed a personal relationship, something which I always tried to avoid with anyone other than a few people. The excitement they displayed in sharing the "gospel" would sometimes be so fervent and yes, even irritating, that I would allow my ears to close to the words being shared.

I could not understand why they felt it so important to share this information with me. Though my world had no peace or fulfillment, and was full of conscious sins, I was comfortable in knowing that with the exception of a few good days, life pretty much sucked.

Then one evening, one exciting and glorious evening as I tried to convince myself that I had done fine without Jesus Christ as my friend and Savior, He showed me the Truth. The words that so many had shared with me came back in the form of reality. I felt true peace in my heart and was shown what a personal relationship with the Lord would do for me. I was also shown what I would have if I chose to ignore His knocking on my heart. I do not know how many people prayed for that night, or how many strangers witnessed to me before the seeds finally took root, but it was many. Now, after being forgiven, saved, and having my eyes opened and my ears hearing, I understand the reason why others shared their words with me and prayed for me....because the Bible is the Truth in life, and the Words divinely written by God are the *map for a life of peace, fulfillment, and eternal life with our King, Jesus Christ.*

The Holy Spirit is beyond my comprehension and yet, I am filled with joy in knowing that He now uses my prayers, my voice and my personality to share the news. I am now the one that others do not understand. I am now the person who cannot stop talking about the peace I have found. It seems that once the seed took root, it *exploded* and is growing beyond anything I could have imagined. The bible says we will be new and made whole. *It is true.* The Bible says we shall see and understand the words if we allow the Spirit to work within us. *It is true.* In fact, in the past year, I can honestly say that I have yet to find an untruth in the Bible. The exciting thing is, I have only seen a glimmer of the truths that are written.

I now understand the reason why some people cannot seem to shut-up about Jesus Christ. I can now understand why people are literally willing to die just so that they can share the Gospel of our Savior. What a blessing to be asked to carry the Cross and go forth to share. In fact, in the past year I have now become the person who is called the fanatic and nut. Of course, it's true. (Author's note: Is he calling himself a "peculiar person?") What is interesting is that the Bible said it would happen even before I was born.

How wonderful to have *a map in life* that leads me on the path to eternal salvation and a personal relationship with God, through Jesus Christ and the Holy Spirit. How wonderful to have found peace and fulfillment. What a humbling experience to know that Jesus called me even as He was nailed to the Cross and dying for my sins. *I pray* that He will continue to open my eyes and ears and that He will guide my steps to others so that I can be a witness to His Word and Truths. *I pray* that He will not allow me to hide my salvation but to go forth and shout it from the tops of mountains if that is where He leads me. *I pray* that He will continue to allow me to be fervent and unashamed of what He can and will do if I let Him. *I pray* that He will lead me to others that need to hear the Truth, and though the seed is small, He will grow those seeds and open their eyes and ears to all that He was, is, and will be. I pray that all glory and honor

be given to Him who sits on the throne and is our King.
Amen
Kevin B. Thompson, Jericho Riders. **Storming the gates of Hell.**   (end)

"So then faith cometh by hearing, and hearing by the word of God." (Romans 10:17)

Itt seems to me that Paul was always admonishing God's people to action—faith without works is dead!

We all are faced with looking in the mirror when being admonished by a brother or sister in Christ to mend a way or two in our lives. It takes a lifetime of steps in the right direction in striving for perfection that Jesus said we must do. To repeat the comment, that is true for all of us and that we should not run away from because it may hurt, is this:

The sting in any rebuke equals the truth.

Unless we face up to the stings of rebuke, and without pride or fear truly welcome and look forward to them, there will be no relief from the harm that is being done to our children and our families and nation.

May God find us willing to repent and courageously face and embrace the changes we must make in our lives and schedules, and with His help take the steps necessary to do it.

Experts to Contact, References, Resources

1) Father, Son, & Holy Spirit: Creator of the Universe; Author of *The Holy Bible—Word of God*
2) Baldwin, Dr. Chuck: Presidential Candidate of Constitution Party; Pastor; Research, Writings; Talk Show Host.
3) Beasley, R.L: Pastor; *"The Beacon;"* Researcher, Writings.
4) Benham, Flip: Pastor; National Director *Operation Save America;* Research, Commentaries, Newsletters.
5) Cahill, Mark: Author: Books, Articles; Researcher, Teachings.
6) Carroll, Jim (and) Thompson, Kevin: Founder of *Jericho Riders;* Writings; Testimony and Heart.
7) Chalfant,John: Author: *Abandonment Theology: The Clergy and the Decline of American Christianity.*
8) Curtis, Matthew: College Student of Computer Science Engineering; Writer.
9) Daubenmire, Dr. Dave: Coach; Founder of *Pass the Salt Ministries; OH* Radio Talk Show Host; Participant in National *Shake the Nation* Seminars; Minutemen United; Researcher, Author of Newsletters, Commentaries, Essays.
10) Day, Jim: Newspaper *St. Louis Metro Voice;* Researcher.
11) DeMar, Gary: Author: *Whoever Controls the Schools Rules the World;"* Researcher, Writings.
12) Diamond, John: Pastor; Author, Books; Researcher, Writings, Teachings.
13) Dreyfus, Dr. Robert: State Representative of *Exodus Mandate*; Researcher, Writings.
14) Dunfee, Bill: Pastor; National Director of *Minutemen United;* Researcher; Lectures.

15) Federer, William: Author of *America's God and Country* and other books; Researcher, Lecturer/Speaker; Various Writings/commentaries.

16) Hartline, James: Founder of *James Hartline Report;* Christian News Service; Researcher; Author of Books, Commentaries; Teachings.

17) Holzknecht, Mike: Researcher, Writings.

18) Keyes, Dr. Alan: Former Ambassador under President Ronald Reagan (and) *Independent Party* Presidential Candidate; Author of Books, Commentaries; Researcher; Lecturer, Debater, Writings, Teacher.

19) Kiser, Mark: Pastor; National President of *America Asleep kNOw More;* Minutemen United; Newsletters, Researcher, Commentaries.

20) Larson, Joe: Pastor; Researcher, Author of Articles/Essays/Commentaries.

21) Lively, Dr. Scott: Author of Books and Articles, Newsletters, Teacher, Researcher.

22) McAlvany, Don: *McAlvany Intelligence Advice.*

23) Moore, E. Ray, Colonel; Chaplain; Founder and National Director of *Exodus Mandate; Let My Children Go;* Researcher, Teachings, Writings.

24) Moore, Judge Roy: Founder of *Moral Law;* Author of Books, Lecturer; Researcher, Commentaries, Teachings and Sermons.

25) Noebel, Dr. David: Founder of *Summit Ministries, Biblical Worldview Training Center;* Scholar; Author of Books; Newsletter, Teacher/Speaker/Lecturer; Researcher.

26) Paul, Pope John II, Head of Catholic Church: Scholar, Author of *The Splendor of Truth*; Researcher, Writings/.

27) Sanders, Ernie: Pastor; Researcher Writings, Teacher.

28) Scarborough, Dr. Rick: Pastor; Author of Books and other Writings; Researcher, Teacher.

29) Schlafly, Dr. Phyllis: Founder and President of National *Eagle Forum* with State Chapters; monthly newsletter; Founder of *Education Reporter* monthly newsletter; Author of several Books, Researcher, Commentaries, National Speaker and Debater and Political Activist.

30) Shortt, Dr. Bruce: Author of *The Harsh Truth about Public Schools;* National Board of *Exodus Mandate*; Researcher, Writings, Teachings.

31) Stormer, John A.: Author of *None Dare Call It Education* and four other books which sold over 10 million copies; Researcher, Writer, School Superintendent, Pastor, Korean War Air Force Veteran.

32) Thomas, Rusty: Pastor; Founder of *Elijah Ministries*; Researcher, Newsletter, Writer.

33) Thompson, Kevin: (See Carroll listing.)

34) Voeltzke, Janice Novak-: Researcher, Opinion Writer and Essays; Editor.

35) Wampler, Dr. Dee: Author of Books; Researcher, Writings.

36) Wilkerson, David: Senior Pastor of *Times Square Church NYC*; Founder of *World Challenge* and *Teen Challenge* and *Worldwide Missionary Work*; Founder of *Pulpit Series Newsletter* and *Pillow Prophets;* Researcher; Author of Books.

37) Williams, Bud: Christian School Principal.